Science
and
Faith

Versa

Science
and
Faith

An Evangelical Dialogue

Harry L. Poe and Jimmy H. Davis

BROADMAN
& HOLMAN
PUBLISHERS

Nashville, Tennessee

0–8054–2142–4

Published by Broadman & Holman Publishers, Nashville,
Tennessee

Dewey Decimal Classification: 261
Subject Heading: RELIGION AND SCIENCE

Library of Congress Cataloging-in-Publication Data

Poe, Harry Lee, 1950–
    Science and faith : an evangelical dialogue / Harry L. Poe,
Jimmy H. Davis.
        p.cm.
    Includes bibliographical references.
    ISBN 0–8054–2142–4 (pbk.)
    1. Religion and science. I. Davis, Jimmy H., 1948– II. Title.
BL 240.2 .P573 2000
261.5'5—dc21
                                                                00–029264

2 3 4 5 04 03 02 01 00

For
Christine Menzel and Patrick Davis
beloved wife and son of Jimmy Davis

and

Katie and Billy Poe
the parents who taught Hal Poe
to love creation and the Bible

CONTENTS

ILLUSTRATIONS

PREFACE

THIS BOOK REPRESENTS A DEPARTURE FROM MOST APPROACHES to science and religion. One sort of book by both scientific skeptics and religious people simply attacks the other position. Another approach, primarily by religious people, concedes the playing field to the other position. In writing this book, we have sought to take both science and the Bible seriously. Most books on science and religion are written to make the case for religion to the scientific skeptic, to prove the Bible to people who already believe the Bible, or to disprove the Bible to people who do not believe the Bible. This book is written primarily for Christian college students and their teachers who struggle with how to believe the Bible and accept modern scientific discoveries at the same time.

The book follows a simple format. It examines five major issues for science in the twentieth century and the Christian doctrines that relate to the same issues. Each of the five sections includes a chapter with a scientific perspective, an Evangelical Christian perspective, and a dialogue in which the two perspectives interact. This process leads to the identification of points of dissonance and consonance in the science-and-faith dialogue.

This book has had a long gestation period. We originally talked about writing a book together over lunch at the Subway Sandwich Shop at the corner of Oil Well Road and the 45 bypass in Jackson, Tennessee. Hal Poe had just joined Union University as dean of academic resources and information services. Jimmy Davis had just returned to the campus as director of institutional research after spending ten years as dean of Union's Memphis campus. Like most well-intentioned conversations, nothing came of it.

Some months later we attended a conference on "Revisioning the Evangelical Mind" sponsored by the Coalition for Christian Colleges and Universities at Wheaton College. There we met a representative of the John Templeton Foundation who made a presentation on the foundation's science-and-religion course program. The Templeton program became the catalyst for bringing our thoughts back to our Subway conversation. Davis is professor of chemistry and Poe is professor of Christian studies, both with an interest in the other's field, but because of our heavy administrative loads we only teach one or two courses a semester. We acknowledge our debt and appreciation to Sir John Templeton for providing the stimulus to stir our creative juices.

In January 1998, we attended a workshop sponsored by the Templeton Foundation at St. Anne's College, Oxford. Professor Arthur Peacocke, director of the Ian Ramsey Center in Oxford, led an outstanding week of seminars and discussion groups that led us to rethink our approach. We did not adopt anyone else's approach, but we reconsidered what constituted the critical issues for our students. We received a Templeton Award for the course we taught during fall semester 1998, for which we are most grateful.

During the summer of 1998, Hal Poe happened to be in Oxford again to lead a seminar on apologetics for the centenary celebration of the birth of C. S. Lewis sponsored by the C. S. Lewis Foundation. There he ran into Len Goss, an editor with Broadman & Holman, who expressed interest in a book on science and religion. It was a short step to organize the course material into this book. We deeply appreciate Len's help in guiding us throughout the proposal process and toward the completion of the manuscript.

This book may seem more like a game of tag than a dialogue, because we have taken turns addressing subjects throughout the book. Yet, we could not have written the book apart from the conversation involved. We would never have written this kind of book alone. The conversation took place in class as well, as Poe frequently asked the questions which the students felt would be too dumb to ask. We discovered that our willingness to ask questions freed the students to express themselves in ways we found quite exciting. Because of the student discussion, the book has been enriched, and we wish to acknowledge the debt we owe to our students who taught us: Beth Arbuckle, Jennifer Holt, Kathy Lane, Lance Lee, Jennifer McDearman, Rachel Smothers, Chet Verner, Tiffany Warren, Lantana Wood, Thomas Young.

Of invaluable assistance in helping us clarify our thoughts and deal with difficult issues were two colleagues who audited our course. Kyle Hathcox, professor of physics, and Wayne Wofford, professor of biology, have come to represent for us the model of interdisciplinary dialogue that ought to take place regularly in an institution of higher learning. We also wish to thank those who have read all or parts of our manuscript: Kelvin Moore, David Ward, Christine Menzel, David Dockery, Mary Anne Poe, Wayne Wofford, Kyle Hathcox, and Charlotte Van den Bosch. Others who have discussed this book with us include John Brooke, Mike Smith, Joey Rosas, and Jim Buchholz.

Suzanne Nadaskay has done a splendid job of preparing the manuscript. It would have been impossible to meet our deadline without her usual efficiency and attention to detail. We also thank Jonathan Gilette, who did the illustrations for the book. Finally, we could never have pursued this project without the support and encouragement of our wives and children. The writing of this book has taken time and energy that might have been spent with those we love.

David Dockery, president of Union University, has allowed us the time to attend several conferences as we prepared to submit a course proposal to the Templeton Foundation and to write this book. His commitment to interdisciplinary dialogue and to the integration of faith and learning have created an atmosphere in which this kind of work can prosper.

We have come to the issue of science and religion from different perspectives and life experiences. Poe came late to the issue, having avoided science for fear it might involve touching or smelling something unpleasant. All of that changed in seminary when he took a course on science and religion with Eric Rust, a larger-than-life British theologian and philosopher who came to theology from a career as a physicist at Oxford University. Further study in theology and philosophy with Richard Cunningham, Lewis Drummond, Dale Moody, and John Macquarrie stirred his interest in the nature of the conflict between science and religion. Study of the ancient Hebrew texts with J. J. Owens and Marvin Tate led him to a different understanding of the message of Scripture than is popularly assumed.

Jimmy Davis has been engaged in relating science and faith for as long as he can remember. From the very beginning he has tried to take both science and faith seriously. When he was in the third grade, the space age began with the Soviet Union launching

Sputnik. He remembers playground discussions about whether rockets had really gone into space. Everyone but him thought that they had not since the rockets could not get through a solid sky. He was the only one who had accepted the scientific explanation that the sky was just scattered light. Even at that early age, he was thrilled by the wonders opened to him by science. Being raised in a Christian home, he was also thrilled by discovering a personal God who had created the universe and who has an interest in him as an individual. By the fifth grade, he was beginning to wonder whether the scientific and biblical explanations of the universe were both correct. Would he have to choose between them? He remembers discussing this with his fifth-grade teacher. He cannot remember exactly what she said, but he does remember her saying that he could take both seriously—that science and faith complement each other. From that day forth he has been exploring both science and faith. To use a phrase of C. S. Lewis, he has been "surprised by the joy" each has given him.

We acknowledge our debt to all of those on whose shoulders we stand and we assume responsibility for where we have fallen short.

Harry L. Poe
Jimmy H. Davis

PART I

WHAT CAN WE KNOW AND HOW DO WE KNOW IT?

THE INTRODUCTORY SECTION OF THIS BOOK EXPLORES THE DIFFERENCE between scientific knowledge and religious knowledge. It introduces the particular use of language peculiar to each discipline and explores the methods of each. The role of philosophy in guiding the attitudes and presuppositions of both scientists and theologians will receive attention. This introduction will be designed to expose prejudices and to illustrate the limitations of each way of knowing while laying a foundation for developing an appreciation for the contributions of each.

Scientific texts begin with the assumption that the universe is knowable. One reason that this assumption developed in the West was the Christian concept of a knowable God who created a knowable universe. Since science deals with the physical, a person has to be careful not to assume that the physical universe is all that exists. The relationship between observation, models, theories, and laws will be examined. The philosophical contributions of Aristotle to ways of knowing will be explored.

People all over the world have religious experience that makes them aware of the reality of a spiritual realm they cannot see. More importantly, the tacit dimension of faith makes people aware of the personal nature of this spiritual realm. This section explores the difference between faith and other kinds of knowledge. This section also explores the philosophical contribution of Plato to the Western debate about the nature of reality.

How does our philosophy affect how we interpret our world? In many ways the conflicts of science and religion come not from the methodology of science or the pages of Scripture. Instead, the conflict tends to come from the philosophy of science and the philosophy of religion.

CHAPTER ONE

THE SCIENTIFIC WAY OF KNOWING

WHY SHOULD WE BE INTERESTED IN THE SCIENTIFIC WAY OF KNOWING? We live in a world that is greatly influenced by science. If we consider the world one hundred years ago, we see that science and technology have moderated the effects of disease, have affected how we work and play, have changed the way we travel, have made war much more destructive, and have expanded our views beyond our birth region to the world and beyond. In addition, science has changed how we view our relationship to the animals of our planet. The evolutionary concept of a common ancestor permeates the thinking of our culture. Thus, it is very important for an informed person to understand the philosophical underpinnings for the development of modern science in the West, to identify the limitations of the scientific way of knowing, and to examine what really happens when scientists carry out experiments. This chapter will provide you with the information needed to understand the scientific way of knowing.

Philosophical Basis

Let us consider a couple of recent events to get a feel for the scientific way of knowing. On August 7, 1996, scientists at NASA announced the results of an analysis of a meteorite (ALH84001) discovered in Antarctica. They announced that their analysis revealed that the meteorite was 3.6 billion years old, had structures that looked like fossilized bacteria, and was from Mars. Wait a minute! How come scientists assume that they have tools to deal with very old rocks or rocks from another planet? Science is based on an undergirding concept: that the universe is knowable, is regular, is predictable, and is uniform. It does not matter whether the rock is young or old, terrestrial or Martian; scientists assume that

3

the same physical and chemical processes were and are at work. This undergirding concept is a philosophical concept that provides the framework within which science works. Scientists assume it, but it is a concept that cannot be analyzed by science.

How did this undergirding philosophical concept arise? Or put another way, why did modern science arise in the West during the Reformation and Renaissance? Alfred North Whitehead said it grew out of the biblical worldview that viewed the universe as a product of divine creation. As we consider Whitehead's proposal, let us consider some other worldviews. Ancient Greek culture provided a fertile ground for scientific ideas that resulted in a number of important concepts: Aristotle (observations), Plato (theory), Pythagoras (mathematics), Archimedes (technology), and Ptolemy (astronomy). Yet science as we know it today did not develop in ancient Greece. Why? Because behind every event, there were the gods and goddesses. Whether there was rain or drought depended upon the mood of the god or goddess, not upon observable natural phenomena. Thus, to the Greeks there was no regularity to study.

What about the Chinese? In 1983, at an exhibit at Chicago's Museum of Science and Industry entitled "China: 7000 Years of Discovery," Jimmy Davis observed these discoveries and achievements: compass, gunpowder, rockets, papermaking, printing, silk, accurate astronomy records, and ships much larger than Columbus's ships which had reached the tip of Africa by the 1430s. Yet institutional science did not develop in China. Why? The Chinese were never convinced that humans could understand the divine code that rules nature. To them true reality was behind the appearance of the physical world.

Why did the Christian view of a divine creator lead to institutional science during the Reformation and Renaissance? This concept of a divine creator led to several reasons to study nature. The Christian believes that nature is really there and has value because God created it; this view would be antithetical to other worldviews such as Zen Buddhism. The view that nature is a creation of God and not a god itself removed the fear of studying nature; it would be dangerous, maybe fatal, to probe or dissect a tree if it was divine. The view of God as a moral lawgiver encouraged the Christian scientist to look for natural laws. Also, the Christian view of God as eternal and omnipresent leads to the thought that these natural laws would be uniform through the universe; the same laws should apply on earth as well as in the heavens.

The Christian scientist's belief in a creator God also encouraged the development of experimental science. Their belief that humanity was created in the image of God led to the realization that humanity should have powers of observation and reasoning necessary to gain reliable information about the universe. A further support for experimention was the concept of *creatio ex nihilo,* which is that God created the universe out of nothing. The concept of *creatio ex nihilo* meant that God was not constrained in the creation by preexisting matter. Thus, details of the universe must be found by observation rather than by rational deduction.

The belief in a creator God also encouraged the Christian scientist to develop technology. They believed that the Fall of mankind in the Garden of Eden had a destructive effect upon the human condition. They hoped that applying their scientific discoveries through technology would improve the human condition and somewhat alleviate the destructive effects of the Fall. Thus, science was permeated with religious concerns for the poor and sick.

Finally, the concept of a creator God opened to the Christian scientist another avenue for discovering information about God. Romans 1:20 (NRSV) states, "Ever since the creation of the world his eternal power and divine nature, invisible though they are, have been understood and seen through the things he has made." This led to the concept of the two books: book of revelation (the Bible) and book of creation (nature). Since both were written by God, both books are in harmony and are knowable.

Limitations and Domain of the Scientific Way of Knowing

Does the scientific way of knowing have limitations? Let us consider another recent event: scientific announcements about the Shroud of Turin. The shroud is a linen cloth with a faint image of what appears to be a crucified man that some believe is Christ. From 1978 to 1988, the Roman Catholic Church allowed scientists to examine the shroud. Scientific tests used were photo- and electron-microscopy, X-ray spectroscopy, ultraviolet fluorescence spectroscopy, thermography, chemical analysis, and carbon-14 dating. What kind of information could this scientific analysis provide? It could tell us the type and age of the cloth from which the shroud was made, the chemical nature of the image, whether the shroud had come in direct contact with a body, whether there was blood on the cloth, and whether the image contained brush strokes. Could the scientific analysis tell us whether Jesus was the Son of God? No, that would be outside the realm of the scientific way of knowing. Why? Because science deals with the properties of physical objects, the physical behavior of physical systems, and the formative history of earth and its inhabitants and of the entire universe.[1] Let us examine each category of inquiry in more detail.

- *Properties of Physical Objects.* Questions here might be: What is the surface temperature of the sun? What is the mass of an electron? Or what is the structure of the insulin molecule?
- *Physical Behavior of Physical Systems.* Questions here might be: What process maintains the sun's temperature? What happens when acids and bases combine? Or what occurs in nuclear decay?
- *Formative History.* Questions here might be: What events and processes have contributed to the formation of the Great Lakes? What occurred on Mars to form its craters? What is the history of life forms on the earth? Or what is the life cycle of a star?

Thus, we are saying that science can give us information about the natural or physical world and that the nonphysical is not an object of study for science. The natural sciences in no way deny the existence of other realms of reality; they merely restrict their attention to the physical realm.[2] This restriction largely results from the methods science has of acquiring data. As we will shortly see, modern science uses an *empirical* approach. An empirical approach is based on observation or experience. Thus, to examine something, the scientist must somehow physically interact with the object. Ways of physically interacting range from directly using our senses, such as touching an object, to indirectly using our senses, such as examining how electromagnetic radiation (light) interacts with an object. Anything that cannot be physically interacted with is thus outside the realm of science.

Some scientists have a tendency to go from only studying the physical to assuming that the physical is all there is.[3] A classical example of this is the beginning of Carl Sagan's book *Cosmos:* "The Cosmos is all that is or ever was or ever will be." Another version of this is to assume that only those questions that science can answer are meaningful. These statements are examples of the philosophy of naturalism, which consider nature the whole of reality that can only be understood by scientific investigation.

There are many very important questions that fall outside the physical. What is beauty? What is love? Is there a God? Why am I here? Even with these questions, some scientists will attempt to explain the nonphysical in physical terms. In regard to beauty and love, a scientist might propose an explanation that reduces the totality of beauty and love to the reaction of chemicals in one's brain. In our scientific age, this *reductionism* is everywhere. (Reductionism refers to the attempt to explain all biological processes by the same physical processes that chemists and physicists use to interpret inanimate matter.) While chemical reactions are involved in our response to beauty and love, the scientist has no scientific basis to restrict the discussion to the empirical or deny the existence of the *metaphysical*. (Metaphysical refers to a reality beyond what is perceptible to the senses.)

In regard to God and purpose, again the scientist may say neither exists because he or she restricts his or her analysis to the physical realm and claims not to see any purpose in nature. When the scientist states that only empirical explanations are valid, the scientist has left science and moved to philosophy. This philosophy is called *naturalism*.

The Scientific Method

Now that we have examined the domains and limitations of the scientific way of knowing, let's examine how scientists explore the physical universe. The general procedure is the scientific method.

Traditional View

The traditional view that we will discuss in this section was the dominant view of science from the seventeenth century to the middle of the twentieth century. It is still adhered to in some circles. As long ago as the fourteenth century, it was realized that humans have tendencies that are not always trustworthy.[4] Our emotions, hunches, prejudices, and traditions are not always reasonable guides to understanding the universe. By the sixteenth and seventeenth centuries, thinkers believed that methods could be developed to exclude these human tendencies. Francis Bacon (1561–1626) in 1620 in *Novum Organum* made the most influential early statement of a method of scientific analysis. The method must be:

- *Objective*: Speculation, politics, emotion, bias, preconception, etc. should be removed.
- *Empirical*: Observation was to be purely neutral, purely objective, reproducible, and the same for all observers. Nature would dictate the data.
- *Rational*: Scientific processes must be rigorously logical and mathematical.

No conclusions were to be accepted unless they were logically implied, rigorously confirmed, and empirically proven. How did one do this? Bacon proposed *induction*. In logic, induction is reasoning from a few members to the whole, from the particular to the general. Bacon proposed that one began by assembling a substantial collection of empirical data from observations and from experimentation. The collected data was to be organized and classified to lay bare the basic, simple principles of nature. An example is to collect data on the pressure and volume of a gas. Robert Boyle (1627–91), an early proponent of the scientific method and a founder of modern chemistry, collected such data as shown in Figure 1.1.

Pressure	Volume	1/V
48	29	0.0345
44	32	0.0313
40	35	0.0286
36	39	0.0256
32	44	0.0227
28	50	0.0200
24	59	0.0169
20	71	0.0141
16	88	0.0114
14	100	0.0100

Fig. 1.1. Boyle's Law: Experimental Data.

A common way to organize data like that in Figure 1.1 is to graph (plot) the data to determine if there is a *linear relationship* between the *variables*. In this example the pressure and volume are the variables; they may assume any one of a set of values. A linear

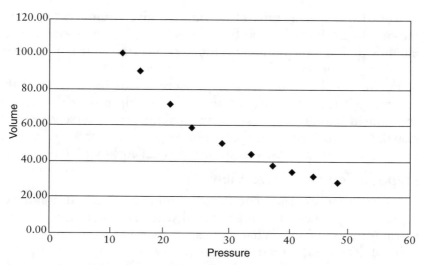

Fig. 1.2. Boyle's Law: Plot of Pressure versus Volume.

relationship results when an increase in one variable results in a corresponding increase in the other variable.

Figure 1.2 gives the plot of pressure versus volume; the result is a curve implying no linear relationship. If this simplest plot failed to give a linear relationship, then the scientist would try some mathematical transformation of one of the variables. The scientist might calculate the *logarithm* (the exponent that indicates the

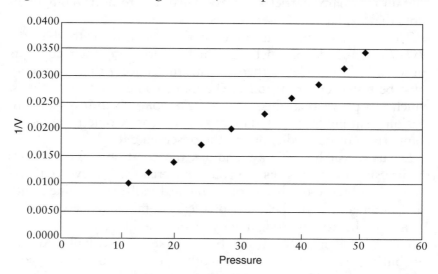

Fig. 1.3. Boyle's Law: Plot of Pressure versus Inverse of Volume.

power to which 10 is raised to produce a given number; for example, the logarithm of 1,000 to the base 10 is 3) or *inverse* (calculated by dividing the numeric value of one variable into the number 1) of one of the variables.

Figure 1.3 shows the plot of pressure versus the inverse of the volume (1/V). In this case a linear relationship results. Thus, one can conclude that the pressure and volume are inversely proportional. Or if one decreases the volume of a gas, the pressure exerted by the gas increases. This relationship is called Boyle's Law.

Hypothetico-Deductive View

It was soon evident that Bacon's inductive method could not cover all of science. It could not deal with the question of what is causing relationships. What causes the pressure to increase as the volume decreases? Creative imagination is needed to develop new concepts, often from *analogies* to everyday experiences.[5] An analogy is a resemblance in some particular property between things otherwise unlike, such as between a behavior of balls in a game of billiards and gas molecules. Bacon's inductive method does not guide the scientist in developing these explanatory concepts. These analogies develop into *models* that lead to generalized *theories.* Models are mental pictures for a system. Models are needed to help us visualize processes or objects that are too far away (planets), are too small (atoms), take too long to observe (coal formation), or contain too many particles (gases). Theories are overarching concepts that explain the observations.

The next step in understanding the scientific method is the *Hypothetico-Deductive* method, which incorporates these concepts (observation to model to theory) with the concept that the theory must be tested experimentally. The name comes from *hypothesis,* which is a provisional theory, and *deduction,* which involves conclusion resulting from stated premises. A theory would be tested by comparison of its predictions to the observed data.

Let us revisit Boyle's Law and ask the question, "What causes the pressure to increase as the volume decreases?" In everyday life we might observe the behavior of billiard balls; they collide with each other and with the walls of their container (edge of table). Mentally, the scientist might move from the game of billiards to proposing that invisible atoms behave like billiard balls. Atoms, like billiard balls, collide with each other and the walls of their container without sticking together; they collide and move on. This is the billiard-ball model of the atom. From this model of the atom came the Kinetic Theory of Gases which relates the *macroscopic* (visible) to the *microscopic* (invisible).

The macroscopic volume represents the amount of space within which the microscopic gas particles can move. The macroscopic pressure results from the average change in momentum experienced by the microscopic gas particles as they collide with and rebound from the walls of the container. (In the case of Boyle's Law, reducing the volume by half doubles the number of collisions and thus doubles the pressure. Daniel Bernoulli first explained this in 1738.) The macroscopic temperature is proportional to the average *kinetic energy* (energy associated with motion) of the microscopic particles. These relationships between macroscopic and microscopic events were used to determine all the empirical gas laws as well as the *thermal conductivity* (how fast an object increases in temperature), *diffusion* (how fast particles scatter), and *viscosity* (the property of resistance to flow in a fluid) of gases. This corroboration between the predictions of the theory and empirical data led to an acceptance of the Kinetic Theory of Gases.

Gradually, it came to be realized that empirical data can never prove a theory since there may be other theories that could agree with the data. Also, there is always the possibility that one more experiment could be run that might not turn out as expected. How then does a scientist assess a theory? The following discussion follows the arguments advanced by Ian Barbour.[6]

One criterion is still *agreement with data*. Agreement with data is the first criterion. If the theory does not agree with the data, then why continue to use it? A second criterion is *coherence* with other accepted theories. Interconnection of a proposed theory with other accepted theories increases the confidence of the scientific community. A third criterion is *elegance and simplicity*. These concepts go back to the ancient Greeks, who viewed nature as simple and elegant. Another label for this is *Occam's Razor,* formulated by the English scholastic William of Occam (1285–1349). Occum's Razor states that the simplest of competing theories is preferred to the more complex. Paul Dirac (1902–84), who made significant contributions to the development of quantum mechanics stated in the 1939 Scott Lecture to the Royal Society of Edinburgh that beauty is more important than simplicity. To Dirac, Newtonian mechanics represented simplicity while Einstein's special theory of relativity represented beauty. A fourth criterion is *scope*. How comprehensive is the theory? Does it unify diverse areas? A fifth criterion is *fruitfulness*. How well does it predict the outcomes of further experiments? Can it provide the road map for a research program? During a scientist's career, the scientist will use a combination of these criteria to assess a theory.

Once scientists recognized that empirical data cannot prove a theory, Karl Popper and others proposed that empirical data can only *falsify* a theory. Yet even disagreement of a theory with empirical data does not always lead to its abandonment. This does happen in some cases. A case of theory abandonment is the shift from the Ptolemy earth-centered theory of the universe to the Copernicus sun-centered theory of the universe. In other cases the theory may be modified. An example is Copernicus's sun-centered theory with circular orbits being changed to Kepler's sun-centered theory with elliptical orbits. Another example of this second case involves the Kinetic Theory of Gases. Real gases do not behave as the theory predicts in all cases; real gases become liquids or solids, which is not predicted by the Kinetic Theory and its billiard-ball atoms. The theory was modified by van der Waals to include the concept that gas particles interact with one another with attractive and repulsive forces. In some cases *ad hoc* auxiliary hypotheses are proposed. The Copernican theory should have resulted in a *parallax* (annual change in the apparent position of near stars relative to the stellar background). No parallax was observed in Copernicus's day. So Copernicus added a hypothesis that the stars are so far away that the parallax could not be seen with the instruments of his day. Copernicus had no empirical data on which to base his hypothesis.

Paradigm View

Through the work of Thomas Kuhn and others, we now realize that Bacon's desire for a totally objective science is impossible. We now know that theories influence observation. Theories guide the scientist in the selection of what to observe, the formulation of the type of questions to ask, and selection of the language to use to report the findings. In addition, we also realize that theories are *paradigm* dependent. A paradigm provides a framework or window that defines for a scientific discipline what kinds of questions to ask and the types of explanations to seek. Examples of paradigms are

Newtonian physics of the eighteenth century versus *relativity* and *quantum physics* of the twentieth century. In chemistry, examples would be that combustion is the liberation of *phlogiston* versus the view that the combustion is combination with oxygen.

Let's examine the two views of combustion to see how a paradigm and its theories directed scientific research. When one watches wood burn, one gets the impression that the wood loses something, leaving only an ash. Thus, combustion seems to result in the decomposition of a material with a loss of weight. The residue appears to be less compact than the starting material: wood and ash, iron and rust. In 1702, Johann Becher and Georg Stah of Germany proposed that combustible materials contain the substance phlogiston. Phlogiston escapes when a material burns. Air is necessary for combustion since the air absorbed the phlogiston that was released. The air does not get saturated with phlogiston because the plants remove phlogiston from the air. Thus, plants become saturated with phlogiston and burn when they are dry. Substances like coal must be composed almost entirely of phlogiston since they leave very little ash. Respiration is considered to be the removing of phlogiston from the organism.

The concept of phlogiston explains combustion and agrees with common-sense observations. The phlogiston idea directed the chemistry of its day. Chemists became interested in isolation and study of gases. Henry Cavendish discovered hydrogen (1766). Daniel Rutherford discovered nitrogen in 1772. Joseph Priestley (1733–1804) identified nitrous oxide, nitric oxide, carbon monoxide, sulfur dioxide, hydrogen chloride, ammonia, and oxygen. These discoveries were not expressed by the modern terms that we listed but in terms of phlogiston. Hydrogen was identified as phlogiston since it is light and very flammable. Oxygen was called dephlogisticated air (air without phlogiston) because wood burns stronger in it than air; this implied that it had more capacity to absorb more phlogiston than air.

Looking at combustion through the window (paradigm) of phlogiston did result in many important discoveries. However, the window caused chemists not to pursue certain questions. Questions concerning the relationship between masses of the materials before and after combustion were not pursued. Answers to these types of questions were not needed to understand combustion in the phlogiston paradigm. Once mass measurements were done, *anomalies* arose which ultimately challenged the phlogiston paradigm and led to its replacement by the concept that oxygen is needed for combustion.

The French chemist Antoine Lavoisier (1743–1794) repeated many of the gas experiments of earlier chemists. He collected weight (mass) data on the amounts of *reactants* and *products* involved in combustion. Lavoisier's most famous experiment involved repeating the experiment of Priestley, which had resulted in Priestley's discovery of dephlogisticated air (oxygen). Priestley had found that when he heated mercury calc (mercury oxide), mercury metal and a gas (dephlogisticated air) were produced. Lavoisier redesigned the experiment so he could determine the amounts of mercury calc, mercury, and gas involved in this process. He found that heating the mercury calc results in the production of mercury metal and a gas (which he called oxygen).

Lavoisier observed that the weight (mass) of the mercury calc equaled the weight of the products (mercury metal and oxygen). When the mercury metal produced by the previous reaction was heated with the oxygen, he found that mercury calc was produced. Lavoisier observed that the amount of oxygen required for this reaction equaled the amount of oxygen liberated by the original heating of the mercury calc. He further observed that the weight of the reactants (mercury metal and oxygen) equaled the weight of the product (mercury calc). On the basis of his careful measurements, Lavoisier concluded that combustion occurs by the addition of oxygen, thus increasing the mass. This discovery is today called the *Law of Conservation of Mass* (the mass of the products equals the mass of the reactants).

What allowed Lavoisier to approach this chemistry in a new light? Maybe it was the fact that Lavoisier was a businessman first, then a chemist. Could he have been applying the analogy of the balance sheet to the reaction of chemicals? Because of his work on the conservation of mass, Lavoisier is considered one of the founders of modern chemistry. But for his work as a tax collector he was guillotined by the French Revolution.

Lavoisier's experiments ultimately led to paradigm shifts: combustion is oxidation and chemical reactions involve the conservation of mass. However, many scientists could not make the shift to the new paradigm. Priestley spent the rest of his life fighting for phlogiston and against oxidation. This is an example of where the paradigm is so strong that one cannot see the data in any other way. In the case of Priestley and Lavoisier, they both had the same observations. Yet theories and paradigms colored how they saw these observations and the type of experiments they did to support their points of view. Bacon's hope for unbiased, objective, empirical science will always be constrained by the paradigm of the scientist.

Summary

Science is based on the philosophical concept that the universe is knowable, predictable, and uniform. Science cannot develop in a capricious universe. Historically, the worldview that supported the development of science was Christianity with its concept of a Creator and a knowable, created universe. This worldview also supported the development of technology to reduce the suffering of people. Science is empirical and thus limited to dealing with the physical universe. Scientists have to be careful not to assume that only the physical is important. Scientists also have to be careful not to give metaphysical statements in the guise of science. The modern scientific way of knowing began with a desire to be objective, empirical, and rational as the scientist organizes data using induction. Gradually, scientists realized that imagination, analogies, models, and theories were needed to develop explanatory concepts. A scientist's theories and paradigms influence the selection of what to observe, the type of questions to ask, and the language used to report findings.

CHAPTER TWO

THE RELIGIOUS WAY OF KNOWING

KNOWLEDGE OF ANY KIND REQUIRES THE ACCEPTANCE OF CERTAIN assumptions. Different kinds of knowledge require different kinds of assumptions. Religious knowledge assumes that something beyond the physical world exists. Scientific knowledge assumes that the physical world exists. Some religious people do not believe the physical world really exists. Some scientific people do not believe that anything exists except the physical world. What we can know depends upon what makes up the "real" world.

Culture and Knowledge

The modern age had great confidence in the certainty of knowledge that comes from observing the physical world. The study of nature led to "laws" that describe how nature works. The absolute nature of truth which the modern age enjoyed, however, has begun to fade as the postmodern age dawns. This new age faces uncertainty where the modern age had confidence. This new age embraces relativism where the modern age embraced absolutism.

The modern age, which experienced so many scientific breakthroughs, grew out of a Christian worldview. A person does not have to be a Christian to have a Christian worldview. They need only share the assumptions about the world that come from the Christian faith. Islam and Judaism share some of these assumptions. Hinduism and Buddhism share virtually none of these assumptions.

The postmodern age, on the other hand, rejects many of the basic assumptions of the modern age. While Christianity provided the central intellectual foundation for the modern world, the postmodern world lacks an integrated worldview for its basis. It has

16

grown piecemeal from a variety of sources. In the past, philosophers played the major role in defining a culture's worldview, but as the postmodern world develops, philosophers tend to describe what is happening more than they define what will happen. The forces driving postmodernity have their roots more in popular culture than in the academic institutions, though these forces have begun to alter the academic institutions.

The music of the Beatles, movies like *Star Wars,* TV experiments like *Sesame Street* and MTV, and the success of the counterculture have created an ever-expanding worldview that has an increasing influence on the way people think. Without ever raising the questions about the existence of God or any particular religious doctrine, the postmodern worldview represents the development of a whole set of assumptions about what we can know. Popular music, movies, and books have introduced many of the philosophical assumptions of Eastern religions into Western culture. One of those assumptions is that the physical world is an illusion. The Buddha taught that desire causes suffering. A person achieves bliss when he or she realizes that nothing really exists, because we cannot desire what does not exist.

The scientific way of knowing did not arise in a culture where the physical world was regarded as an illusion. Every culture has its own approach to science and has certain "scientific" discoveries and technological advances, such as the discovery of the medicinal use of herbs. The scientific method and the scientific revolution of the modern age, however, developed in a Christian intellectual environment based on the assumptions of the Christian faith about what can be known. Over the last seven hundred years, modern science has developed some assumptions that limit its sphere of knowledge. In a sense, faith and science divided up the realms of knowledge which the Christian faith assumes. Originally, the scientists were also theologians, and science represented an aspect of theology just as ethics represents an aspect of theology. Though they now deal with different realms of knowledge, however, Christian faith and Western science intersect at certain presuppositions. Because of their subject matter, they may seem to be unrelated until they intersect.

Basic Christian Assumptions

The Christian approach to knowing grows out of several basic assumptions about the nature of reality. These basic assumptions appear in brief form in the Book of Hebrews, where the writer observed:

> Now faith is the substance of things hoped for, the evidence of things not seen. For by it the elders obtained a good report. Through faith we understand that the worlds were framed by the word of God, so that things which are seen were not made of things which do appear . . . But without faith it is impossible to please him: for he that cometh to God must believe that he is, and that he is a rewarder of them that diligently seek him (Heb. 11:1–3, 6 KJV).

The Christian approach to knowledge assumes that faith provides knowledge in the same way that sight or vision supplies knowledge. Faith provides knowledge of a different kind of experience. Faith provides knowledge about the spiritual realm or the *metaphysical* in contrast to the senses which provide knowledge of the *physical*. The Christian approach to knowledge assumes that both realms exist, but knowledge of them comes in different ways. The Christian approach to knowledge also assumes that the physical world has a metaphysical origin. God made it.

Knowledge of the physical and spiritual realms also relates to the Christian assumptions about what kind of God exists. This passage from Hebrews and many others like it scattered through the Bible declare that God intentionally created the physical realm. The idea of intentional creation has a number of built-in assumptions about what kind of God exists. The one who creates is separate from what is created. Thus, the Christian understanding of knowledge assumes a distinction between God and the physical world. Hinduism does not make this distinction. It views everything as a unity, making no distinction between its concept of the divine and all other aspects of reality.

The idea of a creator God who intentionally creates assumes a conscious God who has consciousness of other things. Buddhism and Hinduism do not share this view of the divine. They would regard the divine as unconscious or nonconscious, but they do not regard the physical world as the result of intentional creation by the divine. Intention implies purpose and meaning. Consciousness of the other, however, and intentionality also imply self-consciousness. Christian knowledge assumes a God who has self-awareness in relation to creation. Self-awareness involves character. All of these aspects of the Christian understanding of God culminate in the understanding of the divine which Christianity shares with Judaism and Islam. God is a personal being. God is a person—not a human, but a person.

One of the most important dimensions of personhood involves the ability to communicate. Personhood requires both consciousness and self-consciousness before communication can take place. The Christian understanding of knowledge assumes that personal beings express themselves through communication. As a personal being, God communicates to other personal beings. Christians understand that God communicates in a variety of ways. Knowledge of God ultimately depends upon communication by God, who intentionally takes the initiative as a self-conscious act of expression to other self-conscious persons. The Christian understanding of revelation relates to the Christian assumption of what kind of God exists. God has at the least as much ability to communicate as humans, but faith assumes incomparably greater ability.

Besides revelation, however, a Christian understanding of knowledge assumes that people may know things immediately by a facility for knowledge other than the senses, though the senses may be involved. In cultures the world over, children have a fear of the dark. It is not so much the dark, however, as what the dark allows them to feel. Darkness takes away sensory perception of sight. Part of the fear of darkness, when nothing can be seen, is the frightful idea that "I am not alone; something is there." Imagination supplies all sorts of explanations of what might be there, but a distinction must be made between knowledge of a presence and speculation about what that presence might be.

Rudolf Otto, a German theologian/philosopher of the last century, explored this idea in his book *The Idea of the Holy,* in which he examined the universal human experience of the spiritual realm, or what he called "the Holy." Otto wrote at a time when the German rational approach to religion had embraced a method that attempted to study the Bible and religious experience "scientifically." This scientific approach usually meant reducing religious experience to a rationalistic explanation of natural or physical forces and their social/psychological context. A spiritual or supernatural understanding of religion lost ground. In this context, Otto's book called on an increasingly materialistic world to take spiritual reality seriously.

Otto described three dimensions of the universal experience of spiritual reality. He did not write to make a case for the Christian understanding of God, so much as to demonstrate the validity of spiritual experience and spiritual knowledge. He made the case that humans have a capacity for awareness of the nonphysical. He used three Latin terms to describe the experience of "the Holy." *Mysterium* describes the mysterious or perhaps creepy feeling people have in the darkness when they feel they are not alone, but they do not know what is there. In ancient times people might have such experiences by the water or on the mountaintop. They then might associate the "spirit" with the water or the mountaintop. They might identify experiences in different locations with different "spirits." Polytheism may have arisen in this way. *Tremendum* describes the intensity of feeling a person has in the encounter with the Holy. The experience is tremendous in its memorability but also terrifying in its intensity. The Bible describes numerous encounters between people and the messengers of God in which people fell to the ground full of fear. *Fascinans* describes the irony that the experience fascinates people so much that they feel drawn into the encounter in spite of its terrifying dimension. People are attracted to the Holy. Nonetheless, the Holy remains hidden from Otto's perspective.

If the Holy remains hidden, what can anyone ever possibly know about the Holy other than that someone has had an experience with the Holy? A person can have the *mysterium, tremendum, et fascinans* experience and still know nothing about the source of the experience. Two people can pass in a hallway and be aware of the presence of each other. Unless communication takes place between the two, however, neither can know what the other is like. Are they friend or foe? It is possible to have a certain amount of knowledge about someone by observing their behavior, but until they open up and talk we cannot know them.

Communication is always a difficult matter. Teenagers complain that their parents do not listen to them. Wives complain that their husbands never talk to them anymore. Husbands complain that their wives do not understand them. Talk may occur in all of these situations, but communication does not. It takes practice to communicate well. This situation accounts in part for why so few Christians engage in meaningful prayer on a regular basis. It is difficult to communicate with someone with whom you are not used to talking.

A Christian understanding of knowledge assumes that some things about God can be known simply because people have a spiritual dimension and the capacity for knowledge of spiritual dynamics as well as physical dynamics. Some things about God can be known simply by observing the physical realm in terms of what God has done as a creator. Most things about God, just as with people, cannot be known unless God speaks.

Nonmonotheistic religions like Hinduism, Buddhism, Taoism, and Shintoism do not share the same understanding of revelation which Christians, Jews, and Muslims share because they do not understand God as a personal being. They have sacred writings written by religious leaders who have responded to their experience of Otto's *mysterium, tremendum, et fascinans,* but these books represent the writers' interpretation of the meaning of the encounter.

The interpretation of religious experience, the interpretation of revelation from God, and the interpretation of physical data represent one of the most difficult tasks of understanding the knowledge which people have. Both in the realm of scientific knowledge and spiritual knowledge, people interpret the meaning of the knowledge they have. People use some standard for interpreting their knowledge, and often they do not even realize that they are interpreting and imposing a meaning on the data. People bring unstated assumptions to their physical and spiritual experiences, and they often filter the data to fit the preconceived assumption.

Philosophical Assumptions

Philosophy provides one of the leading filters by which people view data. On the basis of a philosophical view, we may exclude the possibility of some forms of knowledge without ever giving them serious consideration. Cultural norms like racial prejudice provide another kind of filter to some forms of knowledge which people will not consider. In terms of the dialogue between science and faith, however, the philosophical questions tend to be the leading issues. Everyone has a philosophy of life and knowledge, though most people do not realize it. Most people have philosophical views which they have acquired but never thought through critically. Often the philosophical view has come as a cultural norm expressed as "everybody knows . . . " A philosophy of knowledge might be expressed at the popular level as simply as "seeing is believing" (*empiricism*), "the proof is in the pudding" (*pragmatism*), and "if it looks like a duck, walks like a duck, and quacks like a duck, it's a duck" (*rationalism*).

In the science and faith dialogue, Plato and Aristotle have probably exerted the greatest influence on the philosophy of knowledge in the West. In simplistic terms, Plato emphasized the spiritual while Aristotle emphasized the physical.

For Plato, the physical world represents only a shadow of the "real" world. For him the real things reside in the world of the *Ideal*. The Ideal, the Absolute, Perfection, and the Real all belong to the world of ideas. All efforts to translate the Ideal into a physical *Image* result in something less than the ideal. The Image has an imperfect, distorted quality about it in contrast to the Ideal which has perfection (see Fig. 2.1). People experience the physical world as the imperfect Image of the perfect spiritual Ideal.

To explain his view, Plato wrote a parable about a man imprisoned since birth in a cave. He lived his life chained to the wall with

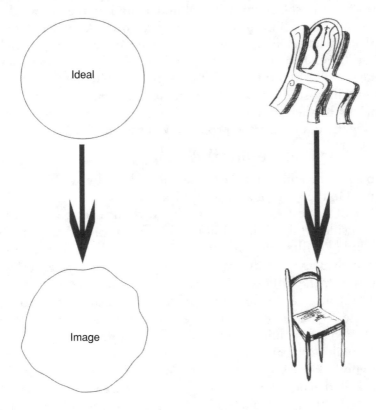

Fig. 2.1. Plato's Worldview. Plato believed that the physical world was composed of imperfect images of the perfect spiritual ideals.

his head clamped in a fixed position so that he could only look straight ahead. In front of him was a wall that stood just above head height but did not reach the roof of the cave. On the other side of the wall a fire was kept burning at all times, and men moved back and forth on a corridor. The flames of the fire cast a shadow of the men on the side of the cave which the prisoner could see above the wall. Because of the echoes within the cave, the sound of the voices had a muffled sound. In this condition, the prisoner would believe that the shadows on the walls were what men looked like (see Fig. 2.2). If the man were released, however, and made his way into the sunlight, he would be startled to discover what men were really like.

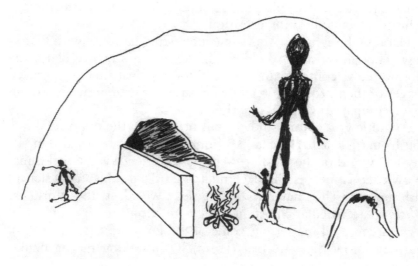

Fig. 2.2. Plato's Parable of the Cave. Plato imagined that the physical world, when compared to the ideal world, is like shadows on the wall of a cave.

Plato applied this story to reality in general. We have grown accustomed to the world of sensory experience so we accept it as the real world. Plato had a low view of sensory experience and equated it with mere opinion. Knowledge of real things came through reason, because reason involves the mind. The mind represents the point of continuity between human experience and the world of ideas. Plato believed that people do not learn about their world so much as they remember what was placed into their minds before they were born. He called this understanding of knowledge *a priori*, which means that people are born with "prior" knowledge. Between reason as the highest form of knowledge and opinion as the lowest form of knowledge lie understanding and faith, which Plato thought of as *conviction*.

Plato's description corresponds somewhat to the experience of Thomas Edison who had in his mind the idea that an electrical current could produce light if it passed through the right medium. The idea worked brilliantly in his mind, but it took more than three thousand attempts at different media before he hit upon a carbonized thread that would produce a dull glow. The physical image of his idea was full of imperfection.

Hebrew thought contains some interesting parallels with Plato's view. Though written over seven hundred years before Plato, the Mosaic Law contains the prohibition against making graven images of the Lord God precisely because of the imperfection of an image compared with the real thing.

Aristotle was Plato's student, but he went in the opposite direction from his teacher in his philosophy. Aristotle believed that the physical world or the world of sensory experience is the real thing. Knowledge comes as the accumulation of particular experiences with matter. The material or physical world is the world of *Substance*. Particular Substance has a relationship to a universal *Form* because all matter has some of the Form in it (see Fig. 2.3). We may know the universal (Form) by observing the particular (Substance). While the Form is perfect, Substance is still a reliable way to know about the Form because it contains the Form. Instead of being born with prior knowledge, Aristotle believed that the human mind is a blank slate. We only know what we learn about the world from our own experience. He called this approach to knowledge *a posteriori*, which means that knowledge comes "post-birth."

Plato and Aristotle represent the two great pillars of Western philosophical thought. Plato represents rationalism which provides knowledge of the world through the reasoning process. Aristotle represents empiricism which provides knowledge of the world through sensory experience. Though neither of these understandings of knowledge has a Christian background nor assumes the existence

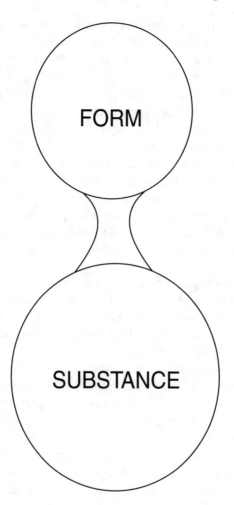

Fig. 2.3. Aristotle's Worldview. Aristotle believed that the eternal form is imbedded in the physical substance, therefore the physical particular can tell us about the spiritual universal.

of a creator God, both have supplied the primary philosophical basis for Christian theologians to develop theology over the last fifteen hundred years.

Augustine of Hippo (d. 430) developed his theological system around a Platonic philosophical understanding. His theological understanding formed the basis for the medieval world for the next thousand years. In his *City of God* which he wrote to discuss the collapsing Roman Empire, he argued that Rome could never be more than a decaying ruin. The truly eternal city is the heavenly city of God. Thomas Aquinas (d. 1274) made a radical move in the thirteenth century when he adopted an Aristotelian philosophical understanding as the basis for his theology. Aquinas laid the foundations for natural theology and modern science which would emerge from the church as the proper work of theologians concerned with understanding the physical world created by God. Aquinas believed that the study of the physical world could tell us about God because the Substance points to the Form behind it. Aquinas became the father of Christian philosophical "proofs" for the existence of God even though others had developed proofs prior to him. He introduced a wedding of philosophy and theology which suited proofs.

Christian theologians tend to accept these and other philosophical understandings of the world as the assumptions upon which they develop their theologies. They may use the Bible to develop the theologies, but they base their interpretations of the Bible upon a worldview which may come from a non-Christian source. Ironically, the Bible affirms both the spiritual reality and the physical reality without building the huge wall between them that Plato and Aristotle constructed. Aspects of Plato and Aristotle have neutral theological positions; however, some of their ideas are based upon religious ideas directly contrary to Christian ideas. Plato's understanding of prior knowledge, for instance, depends upon the preexistence of the soul or a prior existence before birth. Christian faith understands that each person is created by God in the mother's womb. We are created to know and to be known, but we are different from God. Unlike Aristotle, Christian faith teaches that we do not have part of the eternal Form as an aspect of us. More like Plato, we are created in the "image" of God.

If all we can know is what we can learn from our senses, then many things cannot exist from the perspective of some people. Does color not exist because the blind person cannot detect it? Does music not exist because the deaf person cannot hear it? On the surface these questions contain a logical flaw in the conclusion they hope to draw. While the deaf person cannot hear music, some people can. It is not necessary for everyone to have sight in order for color to be accepted as a "real" thing. Of course, faith has been assaulted as a valid way of knowing by those who do not have it. The argument then proceeds that faith involves something that cannot be verified. By analogy, a blind person could argue that vision involves something that cannot be verified. Things known by vision can only be verified by vision. If someone could verify color by tasting, then true verification would have taken place. If someone lacks the facility for receiving knowledge, however, none of the other means of knowing can verify that experience. The blind person could rely on the testimony of someone whom he trusts and believe that color exists, even though he or she may never have the experience of color. This line of thought suggests the validity of relying on *authority* as a valid way of knowing. The Bible would be one such authority, for it contains a collection of experiences with God by many people over many centuries.

The blind person represents an exception to the norm that people can see. Entire forms of life lack the capacity to see. Does this mean that light does not exist? Some forms of life have no sense of taste. Does this mean that flavor does not exist? Some forms of life have no sense of hearing? Does this mean that sound does not exist?

Does a realm of knowledge not exist if no one has the capacity for perceiving it? This question has been captured in the old philosophical question, If a tree falls in the forest and there is no one there to hear it, does it still make a sound? It certainly sets off vibrations in the earth which also travel through the air. Vibrations, however, are not sound. Sound is a perception the brain receives and interprets when vibrations reach the mechanism of the ear. Vibrations do not affect the nose or the eyes in the same way. Sound constitutes a form of communication between certain animals and the rest of creation. It is a feature of the animal, however, rather than the external situation to which it points. It is an internal interpretation of an experience. Faith constitutes another internal capacity for interpreting experience, like taste or touch. Rudolf Otto suggested that people may have an awareness of something which they cannot relate to one of the conventional senses, yet they know it nonetheless. When the apostle Paul said, "We walk by faith, not by sight" (2 Cor. 5:7 KJV), he referred to this way of knowing.

Faith is another way of knowing that involves both revelation from God and an experience in the physical world. The physical world in the Bible is not bad because it is physical instead of spiritual as Plato would argue. In the Bible, the physical world is the context in which people experience God, and God constantly affirms the physical world as valuable beginning with the first judgment: It is good (Gen. 1:4). From the Christian perspective, the ultimate revelation of God came when he took on flesh as a man: Jesus Christ. Thus, the physical world provides a medium for revelation. Using the same terminology as Aristotle, the author of Hebrews declared that "Faith is the *substance* of things hoped for, the evidence of things not seen" (Heb. 11:1 KJV). Faith has a connection with the eternal that it recognizes.

Just as sight and smell deal with different kinds of knowledge, all of empiricism (sensory knowledge) and rationalism (reasoned knowledge) deal with different kinds of knowledge. Even more so does faith deal with a different kind of knowledge than either empiricism or rationalism. Faith is not a good way to determine the temperature. Nor is empiricism a good way to determine the difference between good and evil, or even if good and evil exist. The fact that rival religious views exist does not invalidate faith any more than the existence of rival scientific explanations for the same phenomenon invalidates science. The rival scientific theories do not prove the phenomenon never took place. They only prove that people can look at the same phenomenon and say different things about it.

Rival religious views do not prove that God does not exist and that faith has no objective reference. It only means that people can have an experience with God and give a different interpretation to that experience than someone else would give. Rival scientific views do not mean that all the views are correct any more than rival religious views mean that all religious views are correct. One of the greatest problems of knowledge is the interpretation of the meaning of the knowledge.

The biblical story of Job demonstrates the problem of interpretation as people allow their own prejudices and cultural presuppositions to color how they view the same phenomenon. Job was a wealthy and prominent man who lost his wealth, his children, his health, and his reputation. His friends came to comfort him and considered the question, Why do bad things happen to good people? One could also ask, Why do good things happen to bad people? The questions themselves reflect enormous cultural views that are never discussed or recognized by most people because they operate in the background of "what everybody knows."

Job and his friends ask the "why" question, which is essentially a religious question. It assumes order, meaning, purpose, rationality, justice, goodness, and evil—to name just a few. Rationalism and empiricism cannot address the why question. Rationalism and empiricism ask how and what, when and where. What is it? How does it work? What does it do? When does it happen? Where does it go? Rationalism and empiricism provide the philosophical foundation for science which is concerned with describing things.

Job's friends observed his experience and concluded that God was punishing him for some great sin he had committed. God was angry, and he was getting even. People behave this way, so God must as well. A law of retribution which reflects human character has been introduced into the interpretation of events. By the end of the story, however, after Job's friends have left Job alone on a trash heap, God comes to Job and asks him some questions. The questions revolve around the wonders of creation. God asks Job to consider the marvels of nature from the heavens to the seas. He points out the ironies of some of the creatures from the ostrich to the hippopotamus. God points out how little Job knows about his world.

Three thousand years ago the average person knew very little about nature, stars, animals, seasons, and plants. Priests, soothsayers, shamans, witches, and other religious personnel had made studies of these matters to identify patterns in the heavens and medicinal benefits from plants. Mixed with it all was a desire to seek power over nature. God was not telling Job that it was a bad thing to study nature as King Solomon did. God told Job that he did not understand the world he was most familiar with, so how could he possibly expect to understand God? The Book of Job does not end with a repudiation of knowledge. On the contrary, knowledge and wisdom are extolled as virtues. Job and his friends had the problem of ignorance. They attempted to impose empirical or physical laws on spiritual matters.

The problem of what can be known and how it can be known falls within the scope of *epistemology*. Epistemology refers to the study of knowledge and the theory of knowledge. The philosophies of Plato and Aristotle disagree about epistemology. More often than not, people tend to confuse this disagreement about philosophy with science and religion, particularly science and the

Christian faith. Philosophy provides an organizing principle for approaching both science and faith. One's philosophy can determine how a scientist will interpret data and how a theologian will interpret the Bible. In both cases the philosophical system stands above the scientific method and the Bible as a basic faith assumption. As often as not, however, the philosophical view is never expressed or acknowledged. It falls within the category of what everyone "knows."

When is it appropriate to speak of "knowing" something, and when is it appropriate to speak of "believing" something? In the philosophical debate over epistemology, belief often appears as the poor stepchild which lacks the certainty of knowledge. In modern society people frequently think of belief as a subjective experience without physical evidence or strong rational proof. It constitutes little more than an opinion. Knowledge, on the other hand, deals with facts. The modern world tends to view knowledge as little more than the accumulation of observable, and therefore objective, experiences.

The Apostles' Creed forms one of the oldest Christian statements of faith found outside the New Testament. Though its final form only dates to the early seventh century, its earlier forms date to the second century. The term *creed* comes from the Latin verb *credo,* which means "I believe." The creed begins, "I believe in God the Father Almighty, Creator of heaven and earth." It goes on to present the fundamental assertions of the Christian faith. For the people who first began to speak the creed, belief in God the Father Almighty, Creator of heaven and earth, represented something worth dying for. Belief involves more than simple awareness of data. It involves confidence and even conviction.

In the Bible "knowing" has a personal or intimate dimension to it. The term is used to describe the most intimate of encounters between men and women. Sexuality forms a part of the encounter, but much more is meant by the term. Knowledge involves personal encounter at some level. In his Gospel, John declared that he had been a disciple of Jesus and that his Gospel contained the testimony of what he knew to be true (John 21:24). John had a personal encounter which he knew to be true. One must then decide if John is a credible, or believable, witness. Is John an authority who can be trusted? This personal dimension of knowledge raises the problem of subjectivity. Is religious knowledge just opinion?

Naturalistic philosophers have raised this objection to religious knowledge throughout the modern era as they pointed to science as the only way to real knowledge. At the close of the modern age, however, science finds itself asking the same question about its own observations: Is scientific observation just opinion? We will explore this issue at length in the section of this book on quantum theory.

More than mere opinion, the real culprit of uncertainty related to science and religion is emotion. Freud charged that the concept of God is just a projection of human need on the universe. Rather than dismiss emotion outright, however, perhaps we should realize that emotion actually functions to provide people with information. When I feel afraid, my emotions have supplied me with information that my senses alone do not tell me. My senses provide a certain body of information, but my emotions add something more. Emotions have been dismissed as irrational. In the sense that emotions operate without the need for deliberate thought, they are irrational. More properly, they are nonrational like vision. Sensory experience provides information, but it does not provide knowledge. Knowledge relates to understanding. Neither emotions nor sensory experience provides understanding. They only provide information. Fear provides information about me and my environment, but it does not dictate a course of action. Experience must be interpreted and organized before it becomes knowledge.

A naturalist view of people considers them as physical beings and nothing more. The fundamental distinction between a naturalistic understanding of knowledge and a Christian understanding of knowledge relates to the basic assumption each of these worldviews has concerning the nature of reality and the nature of people. For naturalists like Carl Sagan, the cosmos is all there is. For Christians, the spiritual realm is as real as the physical, and God created both. In terms of what can be known about reality, naturalists regard people as physical objects composed of a variety of chemical compounds which experience life for a time before decomposing into its components. Christians, on the other hand, believe that people have both a physical and a spiritual dimension, though these two dimensions are integrally related.

A study of the human spirit throughout the Bible indicates that the human spirit involves six distinct domains that are interrelated: the intellect, the emotions, the character, the will, the imagination, and vitality itself. Furthermore, the spirit affects the body and the body affects the spirit. The senses of the body send messages to the brain which receives the information. The brain then interprets the data, but the interpretation is more than a mere machine calculating data. Emotions may color the data. The character may filter the data through a set of values. A weakened bodily state may affect the intellect's ability to reason and weigh the complex and competing factors. This spiritual dimension relates to the interpretation of physical or scientific data as much as it relates to the spiritual realm of religion. This complex interrelationship of aspects of what it means to be human only heightens the problem of subjectivity (see Fig. 2.4). It raises the problem of uncertainty for science as much

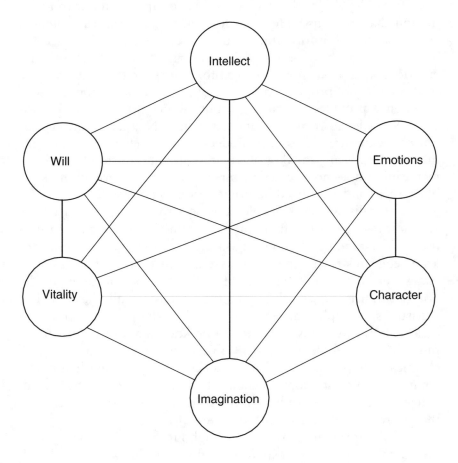

Fig. 2.4. The Human Spirit. The human spirit involves many aspects which affect each other.

as for religion. In this context, belief has a stronger force than mere knowledge. It becomes more clear why Plato relegated sensory experience to the realm of mere opinion.

In the Bible, knowledge is possible because of the kind of God who exists. A Creator God brought order out of chaos. This foundational understanding of reality means that a universe exists which can be known. Because the God who creates is personal and made people in that personal image, a relationship between Creator and creature exists. People have a spiritual dimension which allows for the perception of spiritual reality. General knowledge of God is possible because people are made in the image of God and have spiritual perception. Accurate, specific knowledge of God, however, depends upon God's ability to communicate instead of on human objectivity in its interpretation of spiritual experience. The same aspects of the human spirit which distort the interpretation of sensory experience also distort the interpretation of spiritual experience.

A Christian understanding of knowledge assumes that God has the capacity to communicate in a meaningful way with people. It assumes a real physical world which can be known. It assumes that the Bible represents God's initiative to communicate with people. It assumes a flawed human spirit that stands in need of repair.

CHAPTER THREE

DIALOGUE ON KNOWLEDGE

ARE SCIENCE AND RELIGION MUTUALLY EXCLUSIVE OR DO THEY HAVE a common ground? How should they relate? Some see their relationship as one of *conflict*. They see the story of science almost always contradicting the story of religion. One version of the conflict category sees religion as trying to restrict science. Popular narratives involve the church versus Galileo and the church versus evolution. Two works that popularized this view are J. W. Darper's *History of the Conflict between Religion and Science* (1874) and A. D. White's *A History of the Warfare of Science with Theology in Christendom* (1896).

Another version of the conflict category is *scientism*, an ideology that assumes that science provides all the answers. Scientism, by claiming science has a monopoly on knowledge, relegates religion to myth, to falsehood. The biologist Jacques Monod said, "Objective knowledge is the only authentic source of truth."[1] A variation of this scientific imperialism is not the elimination of religion but the takeover of religion by science. The astronomer Carl Sagan was atheistic but had a scientific religion with answers to the ultimate questions. The ultimate reality was the universe; the ultimate origin was evolution; the origin of sin was our primitive reptilian structure in our brain; and salvation came through knowledge.[2]

Others see no connection between science and religion. They see *independence*. This view states that each exists in its own sphere and that they should keep out of each other's way. This view emphasizes the boundaries of the two methods of knowing. Those in the independence category emphasize that science asks "how?" while religion asks "why?" Steven Jay Gould in *Rocks of Ages:*

Science and Religion in the Fullness of Life (1999) calls this independence *nonoverlapping magisteria* (NOMA). Gould says, "I do not see how science and religion could be unified . . . , but I also do not understand why the two enterprises should experience any conflict. Science tries to document the factual character of the natural world. . . . Religion, on the other hand, operates in the equally important, but utterly different realm of human purposes, meaning, and values."[3] In Gould's analysis, he sees religion violating his NOMA, never scientism violating NOMA.

Still others view the relationship between science and religion as a *dialogue*. Science, in observing and describing nature, raises questions about the origin, rationality, and intelligibility of the universe. Yet, science cannot answer these questions. These types of questions allow for a conversation between science and religion to develop. Finally, some view science and faith as an *integrated* whole. This can take the form of natural theology, theology of nature, or systematic synthesis. Natural theology uses the findings of science to formulate a picture of God.

Proponents of natural theology range from the founders of modern science (Newton and Boyle) to Paley and his watch to the Anthropic Principles of modern cosmology. The theology of nature starts with the tenets of faith which are then rethought in light of scientific findings. A modern proponent of the theology of nature is Arthur Peacocke, an English biochemist and theologian, who says, "Theology needs to be consonant and coherent with, though far from being derived from, scientific perspectives on the world."[4] The proponents of systematic synthesis develop a new metaphysics from the contributions of science and religion. The work of Thomas Aquinas is the classical example of a systematic synthesis. Further discussion of these four ways that science and religion may interact can be found in Ian Barbour's book, *Religion and Science* (1997).[5]

In many cases, when one only sees conflict or independence between science and religion, one is viewing the idealized forms of science and religion. In the idealized form, science is unemotional while religion is emotional; science is rational while religion has leaps of faith. As we saw in chapters 1 and 2, neither science nor religion fit these idealized visions. Science has its faith statements, its love of beauty, and revelatory moments (its "aha" moments) just like religion.

As we saw in chapter 1, the underlying postulate of modern science is that the universe is regular and knowable. A scientist goes about his or her work taking for granted that science will work. For science to work, the universe must be ordered, must be rational, must be lawlike. But these characteristics are not enough; the universe could have all of these characteristics and still be too subtle or complicated for humans to understand. Thus, the scientist must also assume that the universe is intelligible or humans have the mental capabilities to unravel the mysteries of the universe. Taking all of this for granted is an act of faith on the part of the scientist because these postulates cannot be proved by logic.

The Romantic poets were convinced that scientists were cold-hearted and incapable of seeing beauty. As William Blake said,

> Art is the Tree of Life;
> Science is the Tree of Death.[6]

Or William Wordsworth:

> Sweet is the lore which nature brings:
> Our meddling intellect
> Misshapes the beauteous forms of things
> We murder to dissect.[7]

Or Johann Wolfgang von Goethe:

> Unless you feel it, you will never achieve it.
> If it doesn't flow from your soul . . .
> Your listener will not believe it . . .
> Gray and ashen . . . is every science,
> And only the golden tree of life is green.[8]

Yet scientists are awed by the beauty of nature, by the vastness and grandeur of space. The scientist Charles Misner, speaking of Einstein, said: "I do see the design of the universe as essentially a religious question, that is one should have some kind of respect and awe for the whole business. Its very magnificence should not be taken for granted. In fact that is why I think Einstein had so little use for organized religion, although he strikes me basically as a very religious man. Einstein must have looked at what the Christian preachers said about God and felt that they were blaspheming. He had seen much more majesty than they had ever imagined, and they were just not talking about the real thing."[9]

As we saw in chapter 1, the physicist Paul Dirac postulated that a beautiful theory was the correct theory. This agrees with the

Romantic poet John Keats, who wrote, "Beauty is truth, truth beauty."[10]

Two examples of revelatory or "aha" moments come from the work of Archimedes and Fleming who lived about two thousand years apart. Archimedes (287–212 B.C.) was the famous Greek mathematician who spent most of his life in Syracuse, Sicily. He was asked by the king to determine how much gold was in the king's crown without destroying the crown. Or had the goldsmith been honest? Not having all the instruments of a modern laboratory, Archimedes, at first, saw no solution to this request. He retired to his bath to think. As he entered his drawn bath, he noticed that the water level rose as his body sank into the bath. At that instant, he had a revelatory moment, an "aha" moment, an insight. Archimedes realized that the amount of water displaced depends upon the amount of material entering the water. Thus, gold should displace a different amount of water from a mixture of gold and some base metal. He arose from his bath and ran naked through the streets shouting "Eureka" or "I have found it." He quickly confirmed his theory and determined that the goldsmith had been dishonest. Think of all the previous times Archimedes had entered his drawn bath without having this insight, or all the people since who have displaced water in a bathtub without having this insight.

Alexander Fleming (1881–1955) was a British bacteriologist who received his medical degree in 1906. During World War I, Fleming was assigned the task of finding antibacterial substances for the war effort. He was unsuccessful, but did in 1921 discover lysozyme, an ingredient of tears, which had some antibacterial properties but which was not clinically useful. In 1928, Fleming became professor of bacteriology at St. Mary's Hospital at the University of London. He began a research project on *Staphylococcus* bacteria, which cause boils.

In 1928, Fleming prepared a series of *Staphylococcus* slides and then left for a week of vacation. Returning from vacation, Fleming was overwhelmed by what he found. His lab assistant had quit and Fleming now had a lab full of week-old slides to analyze and clean. After examining a slide, Fleming tossed it into a tray of lysol solution to disinfect the slide. The tray was shallow, and soon slides were stacked high enough to be above the lysol solution. One day when a colleague dropped by, Fleming immediately began complaining about all the work he was having to do. To emphasize his plight, he removed a slide from the top of the lysol tray. At that moment, Fleming noticed something on the slide which he had not seen before. The slide had been contaminated by a green mold. During this capricious second look, Fleming noticed that no bacteria was growing around the mold. The inspiration struck him; maybe he had at last found an effective antibacterial agent! The mold was identified as *Penicillium notatum* and Fleming named its active ingredient penicillin.

Fleming was knighted in 1944 and shared the 1948 Nobel Prize in medicine with Ernst Boris Chain and Howard Walter Florey, who were able to mass produce and clinically test penicillin. The *Penicillium* mold is very common, occurring on decaying fruit and ripening cheese. In fact, a very productive strain of *Penicillium* was found on a cantaloupe in Peoria, Illinois. Since *Penicillium* is so common, more than likely many bacteria cultural plates had been contaminated with *Penicillium* before Fleming's time. Yet Fleming had the inspiration while others did not.[11]

Both Archimedes and Fleming responded in a new way to the unexpected. They saw an everyday event in a new light. This response cannot be taught. The best one can hope for is a prepared mind that will be inspired by the unexpected.

We believe that the dialogue and integration categories are the appropriate modes for relating science and religion. This belief comes not only from the similarities between science and religion but also from a belief that there is a wholeness to truth. As Pope John Paul II says, "Truth cannot contradict truth."[12] Ted Peters, professor of systematic theology at Pacific Lutheran Seminary, states this belief as "There is but one reality. So sooner or later we will become dissatisfied with consigning our differences to separate ghettos of knowledge."[13] We further believe that both science and religion have much to gain from interacting with each other. Einstein stated this belief as "Science without religion is lame and religion without science is blind."[14] John Paul II said, "Science can purify religion from error and superstition; religion can purify science from idolatry and false absolutes. Each can draw the other into a wider world, a world in which both can flourish. . . . We need each other to be what we must be, what we are called to be."[15]

What should be the nature of the dialogue and integration relationships between science and religion? For many this relationship would involve proofs like that of natural theology. For example, as we shall see in chapter 4, the current understanding of Big Bang cosmology is formulated in terms of a beginning of the universe. Should this be presented as proof of Genesis? As the followers of Thomas Aquinas found in the seventeenth century, it is risky to prove one's theology with the findings of science. Science is continuously refining its understanding of nature. Sometimes this understanding changes quickly; the Phlogiston Theory was around for only about ninety years. Sometimes this understanding changes slowly; Aristotelian (earth-centered) cosmology had been accepted for two thousand years. If one's theology is being "proved" by a finding of science, what happens to the validity of your theology when this finding of science is modified or discarded? The followers of Thomas Aquinas had this problem with the science of Copernicus and Galileo, which not only replaced their Aristotelian science but seemed to undercut their theology. Thus, proofs of religious concepts are not a productive dialogue mode.

If we do not favor conflict, independence, or dialogue that proves, then what is left for the relationship between science and religion? One possibility involves the concepts of consonance and dissonance. Consonance comes from the work of Ernan McMullin, professor of history and philosophy of science program at the University of Notre Dame.[16] Other theologians have incorporated consonance into their work: Ted Peters, professor of systematic theology at Pacific Lutheran Theological Seminary;[17] Ian Barbour, Bean professor of science, technology, and society at Carleton College;[18] and Willem B. Drees, member of the Interdisciplinary Center for the Study of Science, Society, and Religion of the Free University of Amsterdam.[19] Consonance involves looking for areas of correspondence or connection between the scientific and theological understanding of nature. Robert John Russell, professor of theology and science at Graduate Theological Union and director of the Center for Theology and the Natural Sciences, includes not only consonance but also dissonance in his work. As Russell says, "I first identify a general philosophical theme common to both fields, and see how each field shapes its meaning by its particular context. Through this first step a certain degree of consonance may be reached, though never total univocacy. Indeed, every relationship will contain both supportive and contradictory subclaims that shape the kind of consonance—or dissonance—between the two explicit positions being compared in theology and science. Thus dissonance, too, plays a positive role since it indicates the need for change in at least one of the fields."[20]

As an example of consonance/dissonance, let us consider Big Bang cosmology and creation by God. These themes will be covered in detail in chapters 4 and 5. Current cosmology is consonant with theology, in regard to the past, with the concepts of beginning and contingency of the world. Current cosmology is dissonant with theology, in regard to the future, in that cosmology projects an open universe existing forever, while biblical theology promises a new creation. Russell believes learning occurs by considering how the consonance of one part of a theory is being challenged by the dissonance of another aspect. We will continue the consonance/dissonance theme in future dialogue chapters.

Religion and Models

Religion uses models, just as science does. People use models in theology to talk about God, but God also uses models throughout the Bible to speak of himself. Scripture uses models to help finite human minds have a glimpse of the infinite God. Biblical models use ideas and images with which people have some experience to explain what God is like, how God relates to the physical order, and how God relates to people in particular.

The Bible refers to God as a king, judge, father, husband, shepherd, vine dresser, refiner's fire, shield, and a host of other metaphors. These models might be called *functional models* because they represent how God functions or relates to the world. Because models explain one thing by referring to another thing, the model only hints at an aspect of what is being explained. The thing being explained is never actually the same as the model used for comparison. God is like an ancient king of the Middle East in that he has the power to make and enforce laws, he has the power of life and death over his subjects, and he has no rival authority within his kingdom. Yet God employs the image of King to tell Israel that they will never be happy with a human king. Kings are vain tyrants who fail at justice and abuse the people. God is not like a king (1 Sam. 8:1–22).

In their human or physical form, the models for describing God have flaws. Women who have been abused by wicked fathers recoil from the thought that God is a father. From their experience of fathers, a father is a very bad thing to be. This problem occurs whenever a model is identified as a one-to-one copy of what is being explained. The model in general, when enough examples of the model are considered, provides a suggestion of what is being explained. Any personal experience or observation of a single possible example of the model can distort its meaning. God is like a father of the ancient Middle East in that he provides shelter, food, and protection for his family.

When the Bible uses a human or physical example to serve as a model for God, it does so in a way that corresponds to Plato's distinction between Ideals and Images. God represents the ideal, perfect King, Judge, Father, Husband, Shepherd, or any other model described. God represents the standard by which all the models are judged. Because people are made in the image of God, a king has some shadowy aspect that suggests something of how God governs the universe, but it is a tawdry image. Unfortunately, people usually approach models from the perspective of Aristotle in which the physical example or Substance points to the eternal and perfect Form. The approach of Aristotle suggests that whatever is present in the Substance will be present in even greater number in the Form. If a human father is bad, then God will be very bad.

All models of God break down at the human experience of the shadow. The human king, like pharaoh, is but a shadow of what God is like. When people identify God completely and exhaustively with the model, then the model has broken down and forms of idolatry tend to result. The most familiar expression of idolatry occurs when people deify an aspect of God's creativity or particular manifestation of power, such as the sun, the moon, the oceans, the seasons, or the storms. Particular physical places take on a sacred character because a particular spiritual experience took place there. The human preference for the particular veils the actual experience with God.

Among Christians a curious functional idolatry occurs as a result of a preference for one model of God over another model. The preference will often include the rejection of one or more other models of God. Whereas the ancients built their idolatries around observable phenomena, modern people have tended to build their idolatries around the attributes of God. The attributes represent another kind of model than the functional model. The *attributive model* represents a particular attribute or characteristic of God. Such attributes include holiness, justice, love, righteousness, mercy, patience, jealousy, and wrath (see Fig. 3.1). Some people prefer the

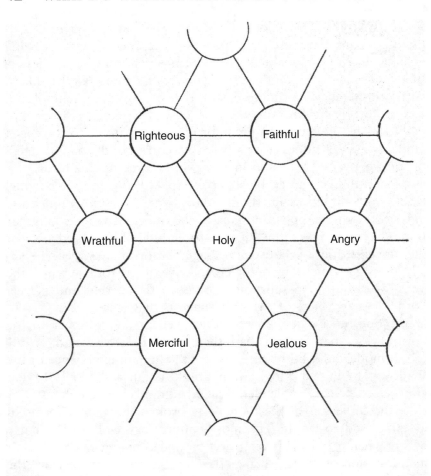

Fig. 3.1. The Attributive Model of God.

attribute of holiness while others prefer the attribute of love. Without due care and attention, people may create God in their own imagination by selecting some attributes and excluding others.

This selectivity has formed a feature of modernity which delights in the fragmentation of knowledge by the specialization of disciplines. The fragmentation loses sight of the relationship between justice and mercy, holiness and jealousy, love and wrath. The attributive models do not merely refer to the functions of people as kings and judges; they refer to the character of people. The functional models contain flaws because of the character of people. Inevitably people confuse the human expression of these character traits with the character of God. This confusion results in a warped picture of God. The picture does not fail because the model is not true as a model, but because of the human distortion of the model.

The Bible builds upon dozens of models of different kinds which work in relationship with one another to give a fuller view of God. Rather than free-standing ideas that work in isolation from one another, the models of God found in the Bible operate in tension with one another. They balance one another and qualify the human distortions brought when a single model receives undue emphasis. The attributive models of God relate to one another like a giant geodesic dome. The giant white geodesic dome at the Epcot Center holds itself up by the pressure and tension of the different geometric shapes pressing and pulling on each other.

This same tension and triangulation appears in the *relational model* of God. The relational or personal model of God involves how God relates personally to people. Within the Christian faith this model is referred to doctrinally as the *Trinity* (see Fig. 3.2). The Trinity refers to the relationship of God to himself and to people as Father, Son, and Holy Spirit. This model tends to break down when people associate the Father only as God while viewing the Son and the Holy Spirit as relatives of God. The model also breaks down when people view the three separately as divine beings. The first breakdown represents unitarianism, while the second breakdown represents polytheism. The Trinity, however, is a single model of God in which all three persons are aspects of the one God.

Finally, the *ontological model* refers to the basic being or nature of God. Every religion will usually have some form of ontological model which describes what kind of God or gods or divine force exists. In Zen Buddhism, the unconscious divine is all that really exists. In some forms of Hinduism, everything is an aspect of the divine which also manifests itself as particular gods. For Jews and Christians, God expressed the ontological model in declaring his name to Moses: I AM THAT I AM (Exod. 3:14 KJV) (see Fig 3.3). God is one and distinct from nature. The basic faith affirmation of Judaism comes from the ontological model: "Hear, O Israel: The LORD our God, the LORD is one" (Deut. 6:4). Islam similarly focuses its faith on this ontological model found among the monotheistic religions: There is one God, and Mohammed is his prophet. Functional polytheism or idolatry occur when one makes an ontological model out of any of the functions, attributes, or persons of God.

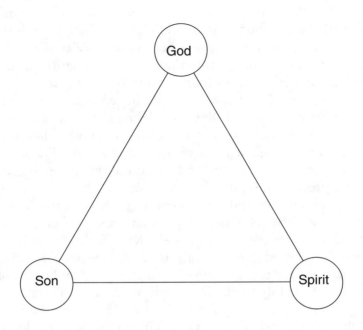

Fig. 3.2. The Relational Model of God—the Trinity.

Something to Prove?

Science and religion do not so much prove each other as they mutually inform or support each other. They provide a consistent picture of an ordered universe when they provide the kind of knowledge each is suited to provide. When science tries to make spiritual judgments and religion attempts to make scientific declaration, however, they have stepped out of their realm of knowledge.

Throughout the modern period religious skeptics demanded some empirical proof for the existence of God. The demand itself has a degree of illogic built into it, since empiricism concerns knowledge from sensory experience of the physical world. As a nonphysical being, God cannot be known through means that observe the physical. The demand assumes that empiricism represents the ultimate determination of truth. Yet empiricism itself is full of problems as religious thinkers pointed out throughout the

Fig. 3.3. The Ontological Model of God.

modern period. The skeptic may ask for a different form of knowledge than revelation to verify the existence of God, yet empiricism does not provide such external verification of many of the major life experiences that people take for granted. Empiricism often relies on correlation between different ways of knowing rather than on actual verification between ways of knowing.

I know I am eating ice cream through the correlation of several empirical experiences. It is cold. It tastes sweet with some flavored nuances. It has a certain soft but thick consistency. I have never noticed a particular sound. It has an aroma, but I am rarely conscious of it unless it gets warm. While these different sensory experiences provide different kinds of information that I process and conclude I am eating ice cream, none of these empirical experiences verifies any of the other. Flavor does not verify temperature. Aroma does not verify sound. The variety of empirical and rational experiences normally provides a correlation of experiences which we interpret, instead of providing a verification of experiences.

The skeptic makes the mistake of assuming that all truth may be verified because some truth can be verified. This assumption veils the radical difference between different kinds of empirical knowledge. Sound reveals something dramatically different from flavor, and the problems of measuring these two forms of knowledge are quite different. The radically different domains of knowledge represented by the senses disappear as the mind draws the correlations together. The spiritual domain makes the connection between isolated and distinct physical experiences. The mind provides people with continuity among all the isolated empirical experiences of life. The spiritual realm brings wholeness and integration to the fragmentary nature of physical existence.

Fragmentation and Specialization

During the modern period the fragmentation and disintegration of human experience have moved forward through the tendency toward specialization. This tendency toward specialization occurs freely in the academic world where people are accused of learning more and more about less and less. The university divides itself into broad divisions such as the humanities, the sciences, the arts, and the vocations. Each of these broad divisions is divided into disciplines. The humanities may be divided into philosophy, literature, history, languages, and religion. Each of these disciplines may be divided into fields. History may be divided into such fields as modern, medieval, and ancient. It might also be divided by continent: Asian, African, South American. It might also be divided by topics, including the history of science, church history, sports history, military history, economic history. Within each field a person may specialize. Within church history, an area of specialization might be the English Puritans.

Each specialization develops its own special vocabulary and special methodology. It becomes increasingly focused on itself and disengaged from other specializations or disciplines. The university and its academic disciplines have fragmented in the modern period as the academy has lost sight of the spiritual basis for the integration of knowledge and the essential interdisciplinary nature of human existence.

Having lost the basis for integration, people have begun to discover that empiricism by itself does not lead to the certainty once imagined by the religious skeptic. This fragmentation of knowledge, however, can occur in any culture. It has occurred in the ancient world in more than one culture. Plato and Aristotle represent a dramatic, mutually exclusive approach to knowledge. Plato's system chooses spiritual knowledge at the expense of physical knowledge. Aristotle's system reverses the priority by choosing physical knowledge over spiritual knowledge. Buddhism denies the physical while Confucianism focuses on the physical.

Pharisees and Sadducees

First-century Judaism was divided along similar lines. The division was represented by two distinct religious parties, the Sadducees and the Pharisees. The Sadducees were identified with the temple; the Pharisees with the synagogue. The Sadducees focused attention on the present and had a concrete worldview. They believed that people received their rewards and punishments in this physical life. Religious observance concentrated on the ceremonial laws associated with the sacrificial system and the priesthood. The Sadducees did not believe in resurrection or life after death. They did not accept the books of the prophets as authoritative Scripture. They only accepted the first five books of the Bible as sent from God. They believed God revealed himself in history through signs and wonders like the plagues of Egypt rather than through the prophets.

The Pharisees, on the other hand, had a strong focus on the spiritual world, including angels and demons. They believed in a future resurrection and judgment. According to the judgment, people would receive either reward or punishment. They believed that God sent the prophets as his messengers and that their messages had been vindicated by the destruction of Israel and Judah. They also believed many prophecies remained to be fulfilled. Religious observance concentrated on the reading of the Law, the Prophets, and the Wisdom books and the application of the law to life. Though their theological understanding was quite different, the Pharisees had an orientation to knowledge similar to Plato, while the Sadducees had an orientation similar to Aristotle. Both groups came into conflict with Jesus, who affirmed both the physical and the spiritual orientations.

How does a person move from the thought processes and biases of one sphere of knowledge to another so that both areas inform and relate to each other in a constructive way? Are two distinct spheres of knowledge mutually exclusive and independent of one another? The academic disciplines represent different spheres of knowledge which are legitimate for what they describe. Intellectual chauvinism regularly occurs in the academy when one discipline perceives itself to be more legitimate than the others. Something of this same dynamic may occur between science and religion from both sides. As has been illustrated from the example of the other disciplines, however, the problem does not lie with either science or religion as realms of knowledge. The problem lies with the philosophical or cultural prejudices of those who set science and religion against each other.

Mind and brain carry on a dialogue in understanding of the everyday as well as the spiritual. The mind apprehends the physical world through the senses and apprehends the spiritual world through faith.

I have amblyopia. What results is crippled vision. I do not have the same capacity for apprehending the world as those who have two good eyes, but I can apprehend the world of vision. It is a slightly distorted world, but the world is still there. Others perceive it better than I do. Some people have a stronger faith and perceive the spiritual realm more clearly than I do. They have a clearer vision of God than I. Some people are blind and cannot see the physical world of light. A subjectivist view of reality would conclude that the world is not there. The correlation of the other senses, however, suggests that it is there. The other senses cannot prove the existence of light, but they give evidence of it.

The Problem of Interpretation

Science and religion share a sticky problem. Both disciplines must interpret the very thing with which they are concerned. Science interprets the physical world, while religion interprets the spiritual world. The interpretation is never the thing itself. The interpretation represents what a person or group of people say about the thing.

The Falls of the Ohio are a vast outcropping of limestone formed of marine fossils. Geologists and paleontologists study the Falls to interpret them. The most current interpretation represents the prevailing theory to account for them. The Falls are the thing itself while the theory is an interpretation of the thing.

The Bible is a vast account of the activity and purpose of God that accumulated over a period of centuries. Hebrew and Greek scholars, preachers, and theologians study the Bible to interpret it. The interpretations given represent theology, or thought about God. The Bible is the thing itself, while theology is an interpretation of the Bible. The Bible is revelation from God, while theology is human thought about God.

Historically in the West, science has spoken dogmatically about the physical world and religion has spoken dogmatically about the spiritual world. Both had an unshakable confidence in their interpretations as the truth. The interpretation became the truth rather than the thing itself being the truth. The problem of this mind-set grows over time as one scientific theory replaces another scientific theory to become the new truth. Among theologians the old theology gives way to the new theology which presents itself as the real truth after all. One may declare that science has a greater claim to truth than religion, but one must then make a case for which science: the science of 1620, 1730, or 1870? One may declare that theology has a greater claim to truth than science, but one must then make a case for which theology: Calvinism, Arminianism, Thomism, or Dispensationalism?

The rock-solid certainty of modernity has given way to the foundationless uncertainty of postmodernity. Scientists have begun to doubt the objective reality of the physical world as they have grown to doubt the validity of their own observations. Theologians have begun to doubt the objective content of faith as the Bible is viewed increasingly as a subjective collection of culturally captive stories. For both science and religion, the absence of certainty has more to do with broad cultural forces than with the objectivity of physical reality or biblical revelation.

The interpretation that claims absolute certainty and the interpretation that dismisses objective truth have more to do with the forces at work within culture than with nature and the Bible. Both approaches have an underlying arrogance about them. The first view claims that I have the truth; therefore, you do not. The second view claims that I do not have the truth; therefore, you do not either! The first claims too much, while the second does not claim enough.

In terms of what can be known, this book affirms the objective existence of a physical world which may be known, though we may misunderstand and misinterpret our observations of our world. This book also affirms the existence of a Creator who is responsible for the physical universe of which people are a part. Because the Creator is personal, God has the capacity to communicate. The Bible represents the communication of God to people, although God has communicated much more than the Bible contains, as the Bible itself affirms.

PART II

WHAT KIND OF UNIVERSE EXISTS?

THIS SECTION EXPLORES THE CURRENT SCIENTIFIC THOUGHT ABOUT cosmology in relation to the Christian doctrines of creation, revelation, and incarnation. The question of worldview emerges as a dominant issue which has a profound impact on broad culture. In this light, alternate worldviews from Islam, Hinduism, Buddhism, Tao, and Shintoism will be introduced to illustrate how a worldview affects both science and religion.

When science shifted from the study of the universe as it is (cosmology) to the origins of the universe (cosmogony), then the biblical accounts of creation came into question. Since the Renaissance, theologians have read the creation accounts as science. Important issues in this discussion include the meaning of "light" and the meaning of "time" in the creation accounts. The creation accounts not only describe what kind of universe exists but also, more importantly, what kind of God exists. The Christian ideas of "revelation" and "incarnation" depend upon the existence of a Creator.

CHAPTER FOUR

ORIGIN AND STRUCTURE OF THE UNIVERSE

PEOPLE HAVE ALWAYS BEEN INTERESTED IN THE STRUCTURE (*cosmology*) and origin (*cosmogony*) of the universe. Most Western models have been *static*—either an earth- or sun-centered machine that repeats its cycle annually and endlessly. These models gave no clue to the universe's origin; the universe they portrayed was the same yesterday, today, and tomorrow. Only in the twentieth century has a *dynamic* view emerged. The Big Bang model involves cosmogony which states that the universe began with a singularity as well as a dynamic cosmology which states that the universe is expanding.

Cosmology at the End of the Nineteenth Century

At the end of the nineteenth century, astronomers would have presented the following model of the universe. The cosmology or structure of the universe consisted of the Milky Way galaxy with the sun at the center of the galaxy.

Static Universe

This is a static system which provides no cosmogonical information about its origin or even if it had an origin. Ideas that went into forming this static view of the universe can be traced all the way back to ancient Greece. From Aristotle (384–322 B.C.) came the idea of a static universe, although his was *geocentric* or earth-centered with circular orbits for the moon, sun, planets, and stars. The final form of this model was developed by Ptolemy (c. 100–c.165 A.D.) (see Fig. 4.1). Aristotle also proposed a universe

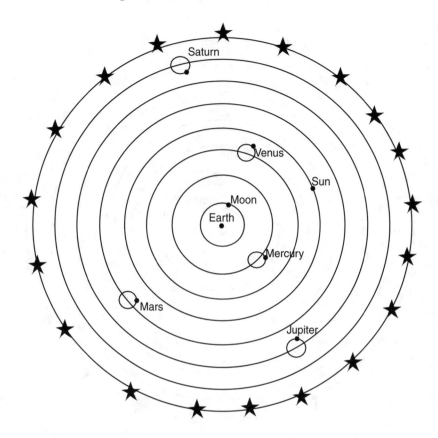

Fig. 4.1. The Ptolemaic or Earth-Centered Model of the Universe.

with no beginning. He also believed that the earth and the heavens were fundamentally different; the earth underwent change, while the heavens were perfect and changeless. When Aristotle's writings were reintroduced into the West in the twelfth and thirteenth centuries, Thomas Aquinas (1225–74) incorporated the Aristotelian model into the prevailing Christian worldview by proposing that God had created the universe *ex nihilio* (out of nothing) and that God was needed to maintain the creation.

The Polish astronomer Nicolaus Copernicus (1473–1543) proposed that the sun was the center of the universe (see Fig. 4.2). The German astronomer Johannes Kepler (1571–1630) discovered that the planets orbit the sun in elliptical orbits (see Fig. 4.3). The English mathematician and physicist Isaac Newton (1642–1727)

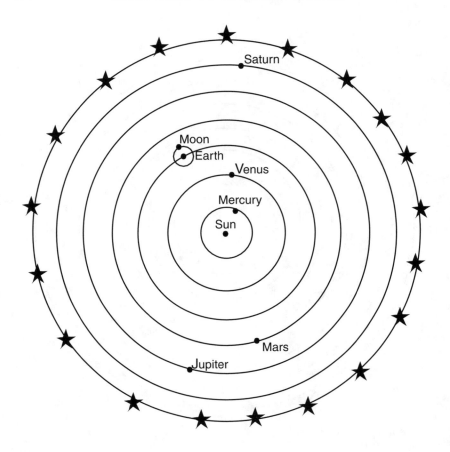

Fig. 4.2. The Copernican or Sun-Centered Model of the Universe.

succeeded in showing that terrestrial and celestial motion could be explained by the same set of laws of motion (Law of Universal Gravitation and the three Laws of Motion). At last, the earth and heavens were united into one universe. The Newtonian laws led to a view of the universe as a great machine whose parts were subject to universal laws that behaved in perfect order and harmony.

Using Newtonian mechanics, the French astronomer and mathematician Pierre Simon Laplace (1749–1827) developed the nebula hypothesis to present a physical explanation for the origin of the solar system. He proposed that a disk of particles orbiting the sun condensed into the planets. The German-English astronomer William Herschel (1738–1822) arrived at the Milky Way galaxy

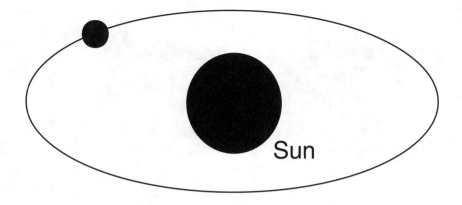

Fig. 4.3. The Elliptical Orbit of a Planet around the Sun.

model of the universe by counting stars in all directions and noting that their distribution defined the galactic plane. An indication of the stellar distances resulted from the observation of the stellar parallax by the German astronomer Friedrich Bessel (1748–1846) in 1838 (see Fig. 4.4). Alpha Centauri was shown to be the nearest star with a distance of 4.3 light years while the brightest star, Sirius, was at 8 light years. (In astronomy, the light year and parsec are used to measure the vast distances to the stars. A *light year* is the distance that light travels in one solar year or 9,461,000,000,000 km [5,880,000,000,000 mi]. The parsec was developed to express distances determined by parallax measurements. One *parsec* is equal to 3.26 light years. A Mpc is one million parsecs or 3.26 million light years.)

We have now returned to where we began this chapter—with a cosmology of a static universe composed of the Milky Way galaxy centered on the earth. The static model gave no information about whether the universe had an origin (cosmogony).

Challenges to the Size of the Universe

From 1914 to 1921, the American astronomer Harlow Shapley (1885–1972) studied *nebulae* or clusters of stars. Nebulae were first catalogued by the French astronomer Charles Messier (1730–1817), a contemporary of Herschel's. Shapley's observations caused two modifications to the Herschel model. Shapley observed that the sun was not at the center of the Milky Way galaxy; the sun

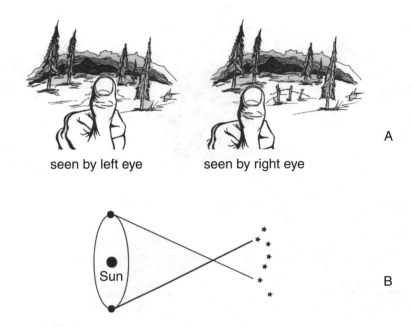

seen by left eye   seen by right eye

A

B

Fig. 4.4. Illustration of the Parallax Phenomenon. A. This demonstrates the parallax, or the apparent change in position of an object (the thumb) due to change in location of the observer (eye). B. The different star pattern as observed from two locations of the earth six months apart.

is about 30,000 light-years from the center in a galaxy 120,000 light-years in diameter and 1,000 light-years thick. Shapley also determined that the Clouds of Magellan, clusters of stars in the southern sky, were outside the Milky Way galaxy: the Large Magellanic Cloud at a distance of 160,000 light-years with the Small Magellanic Cloud at 180,000 light-years. The universe was no longer sun-centered and had just become a lot larger. It was still viewed as static.

Current Cosmology

At the end of the twentieth century, astronomers present a vastly different universe from their colleagues at the end of the nineteenth century. The universe contains billions of galaxies rather than one. The universe is not centered on the earth; there appears to be no preferred point of reference. The universe is vast with objects up to thirteen billion light-years away. In only one hundred years, how did these current cosmological views develop?

In the twentieth century, the scientific view of the universe changed with the development of more sensitive and new observation techniques. Visual observations expanded from the introduction of the one-hundred-inch telescope (1917) at the Mount Wilson Observatory to the launch of the Hubble Space Telescope in 1990. Other information about the composition of the universe became available with the use of radio telescopes (1940), infrared space telescopes (1983), ultraviolet space telescopes (1968), and X-ray telescopes (1949). From their observations, astronomers now state that the universe is very large with matter concentrated into galaxies. The most distant object observed is a galaxy which is thirteen billion light-years from the earth. Let us review four aspects of the current cosmology: stars, planetary systems, galaxies, and the expansion of the universe.

Stars

When one looks at the night sky, the most noticeable objects are the stars. A star is a dense ball of gas whose surface is heated to incandescence by the energy released by nuclear reactions (fusion) within the star. The size and temperature of a star result from the equilibrium between the inward force of gravity and the outward pressure of expansion due to the energy released by nuclear fusion. As gravity compresses the star's gas particles, the star heats and finally reaches the temperature necessary for fusion to occur. Once fusion occurs, the energy released opposes the force of gravitational attraction. The star will expand until the force of gravity is counterbalanced by the force of expansion. The more massive the star, the faster the star will burn its nuclear fuel and the brighter the star shines.

Stars can be classified by comparing their intrinsic brightness and surface temperatures. Such a comparison results in the Hertzsprung-Russell diagram (see Fig. 4.5) which shows that the stars can be classified into five groups. The sun is a *main sequence star* which is an "ordinary" star that steadily uses its nuclear fuel. *Red giants* have surface areas one hundred times that of the sun and are one hundred times more luminous than the sun. *White dwarf* stars are faint, white-hot stars about the size of the earth. The *cepheid variables* are stars whose variation in brightness

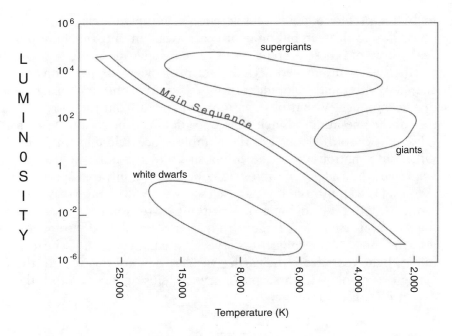

Fig. 4.5. A Hertzsprung-Russell Diagram. The main sequence contains roughly 90 percent of all stars.

changes through a regular pattern. *Novas* are stars that have a violent flare-up with their brightness increasing fifteen times over a short period of time.

One exciting and amazing explanation for all the various types of stars is that stars have a life cycle; they live and die. During the proposed life cycle of a star, the star moves from one classification to another. Stars on the main sequence, such as the sun, with masses between four-tenths and four times the mass of the sun have similar lives. At first these stars fuse hydrogen to produce helium. After about ten billion years, the sun will have used up all the hydrogen fuel in its core, and hydrogen fusion will stop. Gravity, being unopposed, will again contract the gas particles. This will result in a temperature large enough to fuse the hydrogen in the outer shell of the sun. The sun will then expand into a red giant (change of identity). Over a period of millions of years, the sun's core will heat enough to ignite the helium in the core. The sun will then have a radius that would extend out beyond the orbit of the earth. As helium burns, carbon accumulates. The sun is not massive enough to burn carbon.

Once most of the helium has burned, the sun will begin to contract again. Its core will become hot enough to blow off its outer layers, leaving a hot core. The sun will cool and contract into a white dwarf with a radius about the size of the earth. In some cases, one can imagine that a completely cooled white dwarf becomes a "diamond in the sky." The sun is middle-aged (five billion years old) and will continue to burn hydrogen for almost another five billion years.

Stars more massive than four times the mass of the sun will have a different fate after they blow off their outer layers at the end of the helium-burning stage. Such stars are massive enough for gravitational contraction to cause carbon to fuse. Such nuclear reactions occur until iron is produced. Iron cannot be fused by gravitational contraction. Once iron accumulates in the core, fusion stops and gravitational contraction begins again. The temperature of the star reaches such a high temperature that the star explodes as a *supernova*. For days the supernova becomes the brightest object in the sky. The supernova explosion causes nuclear reactions to synthesize all the elements up to uranium. The fate of the more massive star depends upon the mass of the core left after the supernova explosion. If the mass is less than 1.4 solar masses, a white dwarf is produced. If the mass of the core is between 1.4 and 3 solar masses, the core will collapse with such a force that the protons and electrons that make up atoms are crushed together with such force that only neutrons remain.

A *neutron star* is produced with a diameter of ten to twenty km. The rapid rotation of neutron stars produces intense pulses of radio waves. For this reason, neutron stars are also called *pulsars*. The first pulsar was detected in 1968. If the mass of the core is greater than three solar masses, the force of gravity overwhelms the nuclear forces and the star collapses to a *black hole* which has zero radius and is so dense that not even light can escape. (A dimensionless object of infinite density is called a *singularity*.) The Hubble Space Telescope in 1994 presented the first convincing evidence of a black hole. By measuring the acceleration of gases around the center of the M87 galaxy, astronomers found an object with a mass of between 2.5 billion and 3.5 billion solar masses.

Planetary Systems

Another observation one makes in looking at the night sky is that there are objects not associated with any star pattern that wander across the sky. These objects are the *planets*. This name comes from the ancient Greek word that means "to wander." Planets are different from stars in that they do not produce their own light. Rather, they shine by reflecting light from a star. Today we know that these planets form the solar system, a series of nine planets that orbit the sun. The planets range in size from the giant Jupiter (with a radius eleven times that of Earth) to the tiny Pluto (with a radius about two-tenths that of Earth). Until 1995, the solar system was the only known example where planets orbit a star. Since 1995, at least twenty-one planets orbiting stars other than the sun have been discovered. Planets orbiting other stars are detected indirectly by analyzing the variations in the light from the star. Such variations are thought to be caused by the gravitational effect of planets orbiting the star. Currently, only Jupiter-sized planets can be detected by this method.

Until 1998, no planet around another star had been found at an earth-like distance. All were either very close to the star or much farther away from the star than the earth distance. (The Earth-like distance is very important for the possibility of life-supporting conditions on a planet. Life as we know it requires liquid water. If a planet is too close to its star, any water present will be boiled off as a gas. If the planet is too far from its star, any water present will be ice.) In 1998, a Jupiter-sized planet was found with an orbit a little

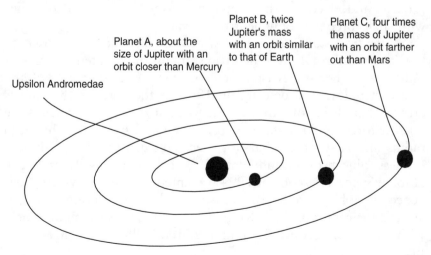

Fig. 4.6. The Proposed Three-Planet-System around Upsilon Andromedae.

wider than the Earth's. It takes this planet 437 Earth days to orbit its star, HD 210277, in the constellation Aquarius about 68 light-years from Earth. Until 1999, the solar system was the only known multiplanet system. Now a three-planet system has been reported around Upsilon Andromedae, 44 light-years away (see Fig. 4.6). The innermost planet is three-quarters the mass of Jupiter and only 6 million miles from the star. By contrast, Mercury is 36 million miles from the sun. The middle planet is about as far away as Venus and has twice the mass of Jupiter. The outermost planet is four times the mass of Jupiter at an orbital distance between that of Mars and Jupiter.

Galaxies

Another observable feature of the night sky is the Milky Way galaxy. At the end of the nineteenth century, the universe was thought to consist of one galaxy, the Milky Way. Today, astronomers estimate that there are 100 billion galaxies, each containing billions of stars. There are three types of galactic shapes: spiral, elliptical, and irregular (see Fig. 4.7). Most galaxies are elliptical. The Milky Way galaxy is a spiral galaxy, while the Magellanic Clouds are irregular galaxies. Galaxies range in size from dwarf

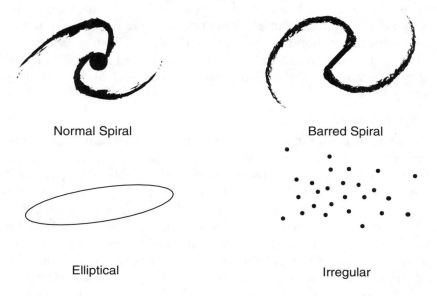

Normal Spiral   Barred Spiral

Elliptical   Irregular

Fig. 4.7. Types of Galaxies.

galaxies, such as GR8 near our galaxy—which are about 5000 light-years in diameter—to giant radio galaxies which extend out more than 3,000,000 light-years. Normal spiral galaxies, such as the Andromeda galaxy, have diameters of 100,000 to 500,000 light-years.

Astronomers have also discovered that most galaxies occur as *clusters* containing from a few to several thousand galaxies. The Milky Way galaxy belongs to a cluster called the Local Group which contains some two dozen galaxies, including the Magellanic Clouds and the Andromeda galaxy. The Andromeda galaxy is a large spiral galaxy comparable in size to the Milky Way galaxy and 2,000,000 light-years away. The Local Group is roughly 6.5 million light-years (2 Mpc) across. Clusters of galaxies can be sorted into poor and rich clusters. Poor clusters contain fewer than one thousand galaxies, with the Local Group as an example. Rich clusters contain a thousand or more galaxies. An example is the Virgo cluster which contains more than 2,500 galaxies. The Virgo cluster is 55 million light-years away and roughly 20 million light-years (6 Mpc) across.

Clusters of galaxies seem to associate together to form *superclusters*. The Local Group is part of the Local Supercluster containing about one hundred clusters of galaxies centered on the Virgo cluster with a diameter of between one hundred million and two hundred million light-years (25–50 Mpc). Clusters and superclusters are not randomly distributed in space but are in a complex structure similar to the distribution of material and voids in a sponge.

Expanding Universe

Challenges to the static model of the universe came from theoretical considerations and astronomical observations. In 1915, the German scientist Albert Einstein (1879–1955) published the *General Theory of Relativity*. Application of this theory to the universe implied an expansion of space and a beginning for the universe. Philosophically, Einstein believed in a static universe and in 1917 he modified his equations (added the cosmological constant) to ensure a static universe. Einstein later said that this was the greatest mistake of his life. Meanwhile, the English astronomer William Huggins (1824–1910) in 1868 discovered that the light from some stars was shifted toward longer wavelengths (the *redshift*). The redshift is an example of the *Doppler effect* which is also observed with sound.

Objects moving away from the observer will have their sound or light waves shifted to longer wavelengths (see Fig. 4.8.).

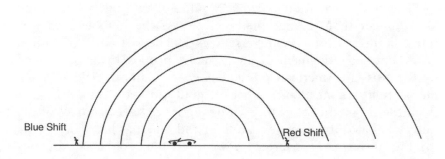

Fig. 4.8. Doppler Effect.

The American astronomer Vesto Slipher (1875–1969) used redshift data to show that most nebulae were moving away from the Milky Way galaxy. The American astronomer Edwin Hubble (1889–1953) in 1929 showed that the more distant an object, the larger was its redshift. How fast are the cosmic objects flying apart? In 1999, astronomers announced that a given galaxy appears to be moving 160,000 miles per hour faster for every 3.3 million light-years it travels away from the earth. The universe was no longer static; it was expanding. What was the cause of this expansion? Did it have cosmogonical implications?

The First Scientific Creation Cosmology (Cosmogony)

The Belgian priest and astronomer Georges Lemaître (1894–1966), after being ordained as a priest in 1922, studied astrophysics at Cambridge University and with Harlow Shapley at Harvard University. After reviewing Einstein's relativistic equations and the galactic redshift data, Lemaître, in 1931, proposed the first scientific creation cosmology or cosmogony. His cosmogony was also influenced by his belief that God's universe is revealed through human investigations. Lemaître's cosmogony was published in *Nature* as an article entitled "The Beginning of the World from the Point of View of Quantum Theory." He proposed that the universe began as a "primeval atom" which exploded to cause an expanding universe. Using the Hubble expansion data, scientists could estimate when the primeval atom exploded.

The first calculations yielded a value of two billion years, an age younger than the age of the earth! As the Hubble data was refined, the age of the universe was extended to fifteen billion years. Further refinement of the Lemaître proposal was performed by the Russian-American physicist George Gamow (1904–1968). He postulated that a cosmic background radiation should remain from the original explosion. At this point we have a model of the universe that is dynamic (expanding) and one that has a beginning for the universe. This latter item caused philosophical problems because of its religious overtones.

Counter Proposal to a Beginning for the Universe: Steady State Theory

In 1948, the Austrian-American astronomers Hermann Bondi (b. 1919) and Thomas Gold (b. 1920) published a paper entitled "The Steady-State Theory of the Expanding Universe." Bondi and Gold thought they had found a way to have an expanding universe without a beginning. They proposed that although the galaxies are moving apart, the universe has always existed in its present state. How can this be? They further stated that as the galaxies move apart, new matter appears between them and forms new galaxies. Thus, they stated that there must be continuous creation of matter rather than an origin for the universe. They have continuous creation *ex nihilio* rather than a one-time "creation" of the universe! The greatest supporter of the Steady-State Theory was the English astronomer Fred Hoyle (b. 1915). Many suspect that Hoyle's atheistic beliefs caused him to continue to defend the Steady-State Theory long after most had abandoned it. Hoyle also coined the term *Big Bang Theory* to distinguish the work of Lemaître and Gamow from the Steady-State Theory.

Before we examine the current cosmogony (the Big Bang Theory), let us review the scientific data that supports the Big Bang. Three major observations include the cosmic background radiation, quasars, and ratio of hydrogen to helium.

Cosmic Background Radiation

As mentioned previously, in the 1930s and 1940s, George Gamow had predicted that a residual cosmic background of radiation should remain from the Big Bang. Although the temperature of the Big Bang radiation would have been billions of degrees hot, this radiation would now have cooled to close to the temperature of space. In 1965, Arno A. Penzias (b. 1933) and Robert W. Wilson (b. 1936) of Bell Laboratories discovered a cosmic background radiation in the microwave part of the spectrum. In 1990, the Cosmic Background Explorer (COBE) satellite measured the temperature of the background to be 2.72 K which is in agreement with the predictions of the Big Bang Theory.

Quasars

Quasar is an acronym for quasi-stellar radio source. Quasars are blue, starlike objects that are strong radio emitters whose whole spectra are strongly redshifted. Hundreds of quasars have been found. Some are smaller than a light-year in diameter. Each emits more radiation than ten thousand galaxies. They are found at great distances as far out as thirteen billion light-years. This distance is where the Big Bang Theory predicts galaxy formation should have occurred. In contrast, the Steady State Theory predicts galaxy formation should be uniformly distributed throughout space.

Ratio of Hydrogen to Helium

The cosmic abundances of these elements are 75 percent hydrogen, 24 percent helium, and 1 percent other. This is the ratio predicted by the Big Bang Theory.

Current Cosmogony: Big Bang Theory

In order to understand the early events in the history of the universe, it is necessary to discuss the particles and forces that make up the universe. There are four fundamental forces (see Fig. 4.9) which control the interactions in the universe.

We are most conscious of gravity (apples fall) and the electromagnetic force (static electricity and compass). However, the strong nuclear force (holds atomic nuclei together) and the weak nuclear force (radioactivity) are also essential to our lives. Current scientific theory says that all matter is composed of quarks, leptons, or bosons (gauge particles) (see Fig. 4.10).

Three quarks combine to form the particles of the atomic nucleus (protons and neutrons), while electrons are a type of lepton. Gauge particles carry or mediate the fundamental forces. For

Type	Relative Strength	Action Distance
Strong Nuclear		Subatomic
Electromagnetic	10^{-2}	Long
Weak Nuclear	10^{-5}	Subatomic
Gravity	10^{-40}	No limit

Fig. 4.9. Four Fundamental Forces.

example, photons carry the electromagnetic force between atoms, while gravitons carry the gravitational force. For each particle there can be an antiparticle. Antiparticles or antimatter are mirror images of the ordinary matter that we know on earth. Antimatter has the same mass as matter, but it has the opposite value in some fundamental property. The antimatter electron is the positron. A positron is identical to an electron except that the positron is positively charged. When a particle and its antiparticle meet, they annihilate each other with the release of energy.

History of the Universe

The following history of the universe, as presented by the Big Bang theory, comes from both experimental and theoretical work. The Big Bang theory assumes that the universe began at a fixed time in the past as a high-temperature, high-density state (a singularity).

Quarks	Leptons	Bosons (Gauge Particles)	
up	electron	Type	Force Mediated
down	neutrino	photon	electromagnetic
strange		gluons	strong nuclear
charm		W and Z particles	weak nuclear
bottom		gravitons	gravity
down			

Fig. 4. 10. Fundamental Particles.

Since that beginning, the universe has been expanding, allowing matter to cool to form stars and galaxies. When one tries to imagine the beginning, it is easy to imagine some process like the expansion of a balloon. However, the expansion of a balloon model is faulty in that a balloon expands into something.

A possibly better model may be raisin bread. In this model of the Big Bang, the raisins represent the galaxies. Before the bread is baked, the raisins are close together. As the bread is baked, the dough expands, making every raisin farther from every other raisin. Similarly, the fabric of space is expanding, taking the galaxies along with it. The distance between the raisins or galaxies is increasing because the dough or space is expanding. Of course, the raisin bread model is not perfect because there is something outside the bread. In contrast, the Big Bang did not occur at some point and expand into something else. The singularity contained all of space. The Big Bang expanded this space into the universe that we observe today. The whole universe has been expanding; the space between galaxies is getting greater rather than one galaxy moving away from the other. This is very hard to visualize because one does not experience in daily life anything that behaves like the expansion of the universe.

The following cosmic history is derived from astronomical and high-energy physics observations and theoretical physics calculations. The closer one gets to the Big Bang, the less certain is the history as theoretical calculations have not yet been confirmed by high-energy physics experiments.

Scientists believe that the universe began about fifteen billion years ago as a singularity of infinite density and temperature (see Fig. 4.11). All of the universe that we observe today was included in that singularity. The singularity began to expand, or the Big Bang occurred. Currently there is no theoretical reason for the Big Bang. Once the universe began to expand, it started to cool. Initially the universe was so hot that the four fundamental forces were united as one force and all existed as high-energy radiation (photons) comparable to gamma rays. At these temperatures, when two photons collided, a particle and antiparticle would be created. They would immediately annihilate each other to produce two more photons. At these temperatures, no particle would be stable. Expansion quickly yielded a temperature cool enough for gravity to separate, followed soon by the separation of the strong nuclear force. The separation of these two forces released enough energy

Time	Temperature	Radius	Event
0	Infinite	zero	Singularity
		10^{-50} cm	Four forces are united and all exist as radiation energy
10^{-43} sec	10^{32} K		Gravity separates from other forces
10^{-35} sec	10^{27} K	Sudden expansion from volume of atom to volume of cherry pit	Strong nuclear separates Inflation
10^{-12} sec	10^{15} K	Volume: a few cubic meters	Weak and electromagnetic forces separate Particle era begins
10^{-4} sec	10^{12} K	150 m	Quarks combine to form protons and neutrons
10 sec	10^{10} K		Radiation era begins
3 min	10^{9} K		Atomic nuclei form
500,000 years	2000 K		Matter era begins Atoms form Universe becomes transparent
1 billion years			Galaxies form
10 billion years			Planets form
10 billion years			Microscopic life
15 billion years	3 K		Today

Fig. 4.11. History of the Universe.

for a sudden inflation in the size of the universe. The volume of the universe increased by a factor of 10^{30}, increasing from the volume of an atom to the volume of a cherry pit. Before the inflationary period, photons had enough energy to make particle-antiparticle pairs. After the inflationary period, the temperature was low enough that the photons no longer had enough energy to make particle-antiparticle pairs.

Since the inflationary period, the universe has gone through three stages: particle stage, radiation stage, and matter stage. The particle stage lasted about ten seconds. The temperature was now low enough for quarks and leptons to be stable. This particle stage raises an interesting question. Why is there any matter in the universe? At first sight, one would expect one particle to be made for one antiparticle and that their annihilation would eliminate all matter from the universe. This would have happened—except quantum mechanical calculations (see chapter 10) indicate that a slight excess of particles (one part in a billion) should be formed over antiparticles. This slight excess of particles survived the particle-antiparticle annihilation to form all the matter we see today.

At first during the particle stage, only free quarks and leptons existed. As the temperature fell, quarks began to combine to form protons and neutrons. Finally, protons and neutrons combined to form the nuclei of hydrogen and helium, which initiated the radiation stage.

The radiation stage lasted about five hundred thousand years. During this stage, the universe was a plasma of nuclei and electrons. A *plasma* is a mixture of positive ions and electrons. Examples of plasmas today are lightning bolts and discharges in neon and fluorescent tubes. During the radiation stage, the universe would have been opaque. The radiation stage ended when the temperature became low enough for electrons to bind to nuclei to form atoms (matter as we know it today).

The matter stage has lasted a little less than fifteen billion years. The atoms formed clumps of matter. Gravity gradually collected this matter into large clouds, which would be the beginning of galaxies. From these large clouds, first-generation stars would form. As discussed above, the first generation stars' life cycles synthesized all the known elements. From the remains of first-generation stars, second-generation stars would form. In the gaseous cloud around the second-generation stars would be the elements needed to form planets. Thus, about ten billion years after the Big Bang, planets began to form. After about another two billion years, life appeared. This is the topic of chapter 7.

Fate of the Universe

The universe's fate depends upon the relationship between the outward expansion due to the Big Bang and the inward contraction due to gravity. If the mass of the universe is great enough (called the *critical density*), then ultimately gravity will stop the expansion of the universe and contract the universe back into a new singularity (the *Big Crunch*), which might then undergo another Big Bang. If the mass is below the critical density value, then the universe would expand forever with the stars burning out and galaxies becoming cold and dark. A complication in determining the amount of matter in the universe and thus the universe's fate has been the realization that at least two types of matter may exist. Ordinary matter interacts with electromagnetic radiation and is visible. Dark matter does not react with electromagnetic radiation and is invisible. Astronomers postulate that dark matter exists because galaxies rotate too fast to be stable without the presence of dark matter. There are three possible categories of dark matter: massive compact halo objects (MACHO) such as dim neutron stars, brown dwarf stars, and black holes; neutrinos, subatomic particles that scientists now propose to have mass; and weakly interacting massive particles (WIMP), theoretical particles that would have mass but would not interact with ordinary matter.

The best estimate among scientists today is that there is not enough matter for gravity to overcome the Big Bang expansion. Thus, the universe should expand forever, becoming darker and colder.

Summary

At the end of the twentieth century, scientists propose that the universe began with a Big Bang about fifteen billion years ago and has been expanding ever since. As the temperature of the universe cooled, fundamental particles combined to form protons and neutrons, which combined to form atoms. This matter collected into galaxies from which the stars began their life cycles. Around second- and third-generation stars, planets formed. On at least one planet (the Earth) life occurred. The universe should continue expanding forever, becoming colder and darker. Finally, it should be emphasized that scientists' view of the universe is dynamic. Considering the changes in the last one hundred years, one can speculate that scientists' model of the universe will continue to change as new discoveries are made.

Chapter Five

THE CREATED UNIVERSE

THE MOST FAMOUS BIBLICAL DESCRIPTION OF CREATION APPEARS AT the very beginning of the Bible. The first chapter of Genesis describes the stages of creation. The account begins with the straightforward declaration by God: "Let there be light." With light comes the first day which is composed of darkness and light, evening and morning. The day begins with darkness and ends with light. Light and time appear together as the beginning of creation.

This opening creation account makes dramatic assertions, but it does not bother with explanations. It does not explain where darkness came from. Does darkness exist in the same way that light exists, or is darkness the absence of anything? This account of creation also raises the issue of the meaning of time. Does time exist? If so, what is it? We tend to define time in terms of events. Time is how long it takes a person to die. Time measures the speed at which the earth rotates. Time measures the speed at which the earth travels around the sun. The earth rotates one time per day. The earth travels around the sun one time per year. My car travels sixty-five miles per hour on the highway. Time is a physical measurement just as a mile is a physical measurement. Science views time as a physical quality just as space is a physical quality. In reading the biblical account of creation, however, one must decide if science should determine the meaning of Scripture or if something else should.

One of the greatest conflicts between science and biblical faith in the modern era involves the understanding of the origin of the *cosmos,* or the universe. The conflict revolves around how long it took for the universe to develop in its present form and how long ago the whole thing began. At one time science concerned itself only with *cosmology,* or the study of the universe as it is. In more recent years, however, physicists have turned to the issue of *cosmogony*, or the study of the beginning of the universe. After taking the lead in the acceptance by the scientific community of the Big Bang theory for the origin of the universe, Stephen Hawking has backed away from the idea of a beginning of the universe because of the tremendous religious implications of the theory. Once the theory has been stated, one still has not answered the cause of the Big Bang or what came before the Big Bang.

The Bible begins by addressing the question of the origin of the universe with the simple statement, "In *the* beginning God created the heavens and the earth" (Gen. 1:1 KJV). This declaration represents the fundamental presupposition of the Bible as well as the faiths of Christianity, Judaism, and Islam. It makes a statement about what kind of God exists as well as what kind of universe exists and the universe's relationship to God. In this translation taken from the King James Version of 1611, the translators have added a word that does not appear in the Hebrew text. Instead of the literal translation "in beginning," the scholars added a word in order to say "in the beginning." What difference does it make? The translators interpreted the Hebrew text according to their worldview or philosophy. They have limited the possible understandings of the Bible by deciding that it means a particular point in time: *the* beginning.

The question of when something happens poses a major issue for science. It represents a major aspect of scientific observation. It represents a critical aspect of measurement. In the Bible, however, when something happens rarely has as much significance as *that* something happens or *why* something happens. Jesus remained vague in his answers to "when" questions. His disciples asked him when the end of the age would come (Matt. 24:3; Mark 13:4; Luke 21:7). He replied with an explanation of what the end would be like for all concerned and an exhortation about how his followers should behave, but he made it quite clear that God had not revealed and would not reveal when the end would come.

One of the greatest problems of faith arises when well-meaning people insert ideas in the text which God has not revealed. Theology tends to speculate in a way that makes the Bible conform to a current cultural understanding of the world. The speculations always proceed with the best of intentions as Eve did in the garden when quizzed by the serpent about eating from the tree of knowledge: good and evil. God had said not to eat it, but Eve added that they were not to eat it *or touch it*. Theology tends to try its best to improve on revelation or make it acceptable.

During the modern era, theologians and scientists have attempted to interpret the creation account of Genesis 1 in terms of the prevailing science. By and large, theologians of both a conservative and liberal stripe accepted the view that science deals with "real" truth; therefore, the Bible must be made to say what science says, or science must be made to say what the Bible says. The conservative Scofield Reference Bible (1909), developed to present the "scientific" study of the Bible, imposes in its notes a major catastrophe in creation between Genesis 1:1 and 1:2 which came as a result of divine judgment. Nineteenth-century liberalism blossomed into a neo-orthodoxy in the twentieth century which regarded the Bible as a collection of stories which bore witness to faith but only as a record of personal religious experiences. This approach avoids the conflict with the prevailing scientific explanations of origins by retreating from the idea of the Bible as revelation.

Preliminary Considerations

From a scientific perspective, the text of Genesis 1 poses some major difficulties. Many of these difficulties, however, arise from imposing a twentieth-century worldview on the text. The order of creation presents one set of problems for someone with a modern mind-set. Genesis 1:1 states that "in the beginning God created the heavens and the earth." The text then goes on to say that heaven was not created until day two and earth was not created until day three. If the earth was not created until day three, how could it be "without form, and void" before day one? If "the Spirit of God moved upon the face of the waters" before day one, then when were the waters created? Did something exist before the beginning? These questions arise in order to put the text in a scientific framework. The modern mind has a need to conform the Bible to a scientific framework, because in the modern era real truth is scientific truth.

Biblical faith assumes that something existed before the physical universe, and that the something which existed is God, who created the physical universe. God is either physical or metaphysical. Some religious approaches and philosophical approaches would identify God with the physical processes of nature. The Bible makes numerous statements about the metaphysical or spiritual nature of God. Jesus declared emphatically that "God is spirit" (John 4:24). The Bible is silent on how the spiritual realm came to be. The spiritual realm is as much a result of creation as the physical realm, but the Bible says virtually nothing about it compared with the elaborations on the creation of the physical world. Part of the problem of understanding the meaning of the creation account of Genesis 1 arises over the difficulty of understanding time from a spiritual perspective.

Not until the twentieth century has science begun to understand time from a biblical perspective. The understanding has begun to come as a result of the work of the Jewish physicist, Albert Einstein. Perhaps it is only a coincidence, but it was a Jew who gave a scientific formulation to a Hebrew view of time. According to Einstein, time belongs to the physical world as much as space does. Time is affected by gravity as much as any other physical thing. At the speed of light, time stretches out to eternity. Time is not a fixed matter but a relative matter.

The ancient Hebrew mind-set had a similar view of time, but without the scientific formulation. This understanding of time related to farming and fishing. When is the right time to plant crops? When conditions are right. It may be May 1 one year and April 15 the next. When is the right time to harvest crops? When the crops are ripe. It may be October 1 one year and September 24 the next. This understanding of time is called *chairos* time. It has to do with appropriateness and quality of time. *Chairos* has to do with "the fullness of time." It cannot be measured. It is not equal. It is not sequential. It is unique.

The ancient Greeks developed a new understanding of time based on the effort to measure and quantify. The most primitive of peoples had observed the seasons and established calendars based on observations of the sun, moon, and stars. The Hebrews kept a calendar and observed such festivals as the Passover accordingly. The Greeks, however, advanced the notion of a mechanical understanding of time measured chronologically in equal measure. This understanding of time is called *chronos* time.

If I say, "I stayed at the party for two hours," I have made a statement about chronos time. If I say, "I had a good time at the party," I have made a statement about chairos time. Any consideration of the meaning of Genesis 1 must determine whether it deals with chronos time or with chairos time, physical time or spiritual time, scientific time or theological time.

Likewise, one must decide if the light and darkness referred to in Genesis 1:2–5 are physical or metaphysical. In the sequence of creation given in Genesis 1, light comes first. Light sources, however, do not come into creation until day four. Do day one and day four refer to the same kind of light? Throughout the Bible, "light" refers to a spiritual situation as well as to a physical situation. Proverbs 8:22–30 suggests that God first created wisdom. Is wisdom alive, or does the Bible use metaphors to express sublime ideas? The description of the creation of light comes immediately after a description of the context in which the light appeared: "And the earth was without form, and void; and darkness was upon the face of the deep. And the Spirit of God moved upon the face of the waters" (Gen. 1:2 KJV). The light seems to address the situation. The Hebrew expression *tohu wavohu,* which has been translated "without form and void," refers to a condition of emptiness or chaos. If the light of Genesis 1:3 refers to the same spiritual quality as Proverbs 8:22, then light means that God founded the universe on the basis of order in contrast to chaos. If the light of Genesis 1:3 refers to the physical light of Genesis 1:14, then its creation merely makes the chaos visible.

The identification of light as a spiritual quality in creation appears in the Gospel of John. In his introduction, John described the relationship between God and the physical universe by saying that God made everything. Without discussing any other aspect of creation, he explained that light comes from the life of God and withstands darkness. Furthermore, he explained that "the true light that gives light to every man was coming into the world" (John 1:9). Later in John's Gospel, Jesus declared, "I am the light of the world" (John 8:12). The meaning of "light" in these texts suggests that the Bible frequently uses normal aspects of sensory experience to describe a spiritual reality. Books of the Bible written centuries apart regularly use *light* to describe a spiritual situation as the familiar psalm says: "Thy word is a lamp unto my feet, and a light unto my path" (Ps. 119:105 KJV). Any effort to understand Genesis 1 must involve the determination of whether *light* refers to a physical or a spiritual situation, a scientific or a theological idea.

The Meaning of Day

Many modern people dismiss the Bible as a collection of folk- tales because it teaches that God created the universe in six solar days. Many modern Christians have rejected modern science because it teaches that the universe is fifteen billion years old. Both the scientific person and the religious person, in this context, have adopted the same understanding of the meaning of "day" in the first chapter of Genesis. The religious person may have rejected the scientific reading of the universe, but they have accepted the scientific reading of the Bible. Science understands a day to mean a consistent, measurable period of twenty-four hours, each determined by the time it takes for the earth to rotate on its axis. Metaphorical, metaphysical, or spiritual understandings of "day" do not have the validity of a "literal" scientific day, even for modern religious people. They have accepted the cultural view of the superiority of scientific knowledge over any other kind of knowledge.

The Bible, however, means several things by the term *day*. Even when speaking of a period of time related to the rising and setting of the sun, the ancient Hebrew worldview did not mean what a modern scientific view of day would mean. Perhaps the most famous example of this difference relates to the death and resurrection of Jesus Christ. Jesus predicted he would be "three days and three nights in the heart of the earth" (Matt. 12:40). The Gospels and the Epistles teach that Jesus was buried on Friday and rose again on the third day, which was Sunday. If a day is twenty-four hours, then three days would be seventy-two hours. Jesus died Friday afternoon about three o'clock (Luke 23:44–46). They rushed his body to a nearby tomb in order to bury him before the beginning of the Sabbath at about six o'clock. Seventy-two hours later would be late Monday afternoon. What happened to the missing time?

In the Hebrew understanding of time, with their respect for wholeness and completeness, any portion of a day counted as a day. On Friday Jesus lay in the tomb for no more than two hours, but probably less than one hour, but it counted for all of Friday. Saturday began at sundown on Friday and continued until sundown on Saturday, a full twenty-four hour period. Sunday began at sundown on Saturday. The women went to the tomb the next morning very early while it was still dark—at the most twelve hours later—only to find the tomb empty (John 20:1–2). Jesus could have risen any time after sundown on Saturday and it would have been the third day. In terms of solar hours, thirty-eight hours at most had passed, but in terms of Hebrew thought, three days had passed.

In the modern era, people have tended to interpret Scripture like a mathematical equation. Interpretation became a matter of finding the formula. In the equation $x + x + x = y$, one could easily find the value of y if they knew the value of x. This approach, however, assumes that x always equals x. But what happens if x does not equal x? In the example of the resurrection, x = 2 hours, x = 24 hours, and x = 12 hours. The Bible is neither a math formula to be calculated nor a riddle to be solved. Concerning the death and resurrection of Jesus x = a day, but x does not equal 24 hours. A day plus a day plus a day equals three days. If we say that a day equals twenty-four hours, then we get the wrong answer.

The problem of time and its meaning increases at each end of creation: the beginning and the end. Revelation refers to periods of time during which the final events of the cosmos will occur. It teaches that Christ will reign on earth for a thousand years (Rev. 20:1–6). The Gentiles will trample the holy city for forty-two months and the Lord's two witnesses will prophesy for 1,260 days (Rev. 11:2–3). The witnesses will be killed and their bodies thrown in the street for three and one-half days (Rev. 11:7, 9, 11). Upon the opening of the seventh seal, there will be silence in heaven for about half an hour (Rev. 8:1). Upon the opening of the sixth seal, the day of the wrath of God will come. The woman fleeing the dragon finds shelter in the desert for 1,260 days (Rev. 12:6). She is taken care of for "a time, times and half a time" (Rev. 12:14). The Beast holds sway for forty-two months (Rev. 13:5). Ten kings will receive power for one hour (Rev. 17:12). For centuries people have tried to assign a value to the different periods of time without success. The meaning of time may be different in each situation! Biblical interpreters have given wrong interpretations to Revelation because they tend to apply a number of unspoken assumptions to the Bible related to how people measure and experience the passage of time.

If one considers Genesis 1 to be revelation from God rather than merely human reflection about God, one must ask if the creation account comes from a human perspective or a divine perspective. If God views creation from a human perspective, then the concept of "day" could reasonably be understood to mean twenty-four hours. If Genesis 1 reflects a divine perspective, however, then one must consider God's experience of time and what a "day" means to God.

The Bible makes passing reference in several places to how God experiences time. Peter made the observation, "But do not forget this one thing, dear friends: With the Lord a day is like a thousand years, and a thousand years are like a day" (2 Pet. 3:8). It sounds like another mathematical formula. From the perspective of the modern person who sees everything in equal, quantifiable terms, the temptation is to substitute one thousand years for one day, which would make the first seven days of Genesis 1 equal to seven thousand years. Does this approach give us the "real" meaning of time for God? Again, the modern person who relies upon a scientific understanding of truth is tempted to conclude that either 2 Peter is true scientifically or not true at all.

Another passing reference to God's experience of time, however, also appears in the Psalms. A psalm attributed to Moses observes of God, "For a thousand years in your sight are like a day that has just gone by, or like a watch in the night" (Ps. 90:4). On the surface, it seems like another mathematical formula that allows a simple substitution of one thousand years per solar day. Yet, the statement says "like" rather than "is." How long is "a day that has just gone by"? How long is yesterday? Something that has already happened has no duration. Something that has already passed cannot be measured. And what is "a watch in the night" like? The Hebrews knew nothing of dividing time into hours. The two smallest divisions of time were day and night. In this psalm, a thousand years for God *is like* the smallest unit of time after it has already happened. This is not a formula, but it sounds like a riddle. Something that has already happened does not have duration any more. After yesterday is over, it does not exist.

The New Testament world had adopted the Greek habit of dividing days into hours, but Peter was not speaking in a formula any more than the psalm did. He also spoke in a circular riddle: a day is like a thousand years, a thousand years is like a day, which is like a thousand years, which is like a day. Any attempt at a formula here would result in an infinite mathematical equation. Einstein predicted that at the speed of light space would collapse and time would stretch out to eternity. These two biblical passages are not explaining the theory of relativity, but they share with Einstein a concept of time that goes beyond the old modern view. Time exists only as an aspect of physical space. God is not subject to time any more than he is to physical space. God is aware of physical space, and as such, he is aware of time as well. But the Creator does not experience time and space as aspects of creation in the way that creatures do.

The Timing of Creation

Relating the sequence of creation in Genesis 1 to a scientific view of the origins of the universe poses quite a problem with its sequence of six days. Modern science regards the formation of the universe to have taken billions of years. Critics and defenders of the Bible tend to share the same modern understanding of time in reading the text: The days represent six, twenty-four-hour solar days in consecutive order. The English translations of the Hebrew text support this reading, because the translators share the same assumptions. A literal reading of the Hebrew text, however, raises some interesting options on what kinds of science it will allow.

Hebrew verbs do not have a past, present, or future tense. The Hebrew mind was not concerned so much with when an action took place as with the quality of the action. Most children operate on this basis. I can ask my daughter if she cleaned her room. She may answer, "Yes." When I inspect the room and find it a mess, she will reply, "Give me time! I'm going to finish it." Hebrew verbs reflect such things as completed action or incomplete action. In the Hebrew perfect tense, action is viewed as complete even if it does not end until the future. The imperfect tense indicates an action which may have begun in the past but which has no specific ending point. The word translated "created" in Genesis 1:1 belongs to that tense of completed action but not necessarily past action. The passage begins by declaring the completeness of God's creation, even though it has not happened yet at that point in the text.

The first specifically described act of creation comes with the light in Genesis 1:3. God does not say, "Be light," which would be a command. Instead, he says, "Let there be light," which is in the *voluntative* form. The voluntative represents an exercise of the will. God willed that the light should come into being. The English translation fails to convey something else interesting about how God said it. The verbs for "said" and "be" are *imperfect,* which means the action began, but it does not end. In other words, a literal reading of the text might be, "And then God *began* to say, 'Let there *begin* to be light.'" This literal reading would suggest that God began something which he has not stopped and that the light is upheld by his word.[1]

For every new thing God does in creation, Genesis uses this same grammatical form. God says to let something begin to happen, but the action does not end. This form describes the appearance of light (v. 3), the firmament (v. 6), dry land and the seas (vv. 9–10), vegetation (v. 11), celestial bodies (v. 14), water and air creatures (v. 20), and land creatures (v. 24). This form even appears with the making of people (vv. 26–27). A literal reading suggests that God began a creative activity which he has not stopped doing.

English translations also reflect the modern worldview in how they describe the seven days of creation. Following the Greek model of sequential, measured time, the days are referred to as *the* first day, *the* second day, and so on through the seven days. For the first five days, however, the Hebrew text does not contain the definite article "the." Instead, it literally says "one day" for the appearance of light. For the appearance of the firmament the text reads "*a* second day" rather than "*the* second day." The text also speaks of *a* third day, *a* fourth day, and *a* fifth day instead of *the* third day, *the* fourth day, and *the* fifth day. In other words, the text does not refer to the acts of creation as occurring on consecutive days. Any amount of time could come between the days of creation. The days refer to particular phases of creation, but not to the timing. The world is completed in seven days, but not in one week!

The conclusion of the Genesis 1 account of creation makes the point most clearly about the continual creative activity of God. After the six days of creation, the account declares literally that "the heavens and the earth *were being finished intensively*" (Gen. 2:1, author's emphasis). The verb pattern changes from the simple indicative to the *intensive*, but at the end of the six days, creation is not finished. On the seventh day, however, the text literally says that "God *began to finish intensively* his work which he had done and he began to rest on the seventh day from all his work which he had done" (Gen. 2:2). The completion of creation occurs only when God stops, which is the meaning of the Hebrew word *sabbath*.

The Genesis 1 account begins by declaring that God created (completed action) the heavens and the earth. It then describes the variety of phases of creation, emphasizing that God began each phase and continued to call it forth. This account then ends by declaring: "These are the generations of the heavens and of the earth when they were created, in the day that the LORD God made

the earth and the heavens" (Gen. 2:4 KJV). This statement concludes the first account of creation and forms the bridge to the second account of creation. Yet, next to each other in this statement
occur two different concepts of time. The "generations" of heaven
and earth when they were created suggests vast spans of time.
Then, the text reduces creation to one day. In its totality, creation
represents a single, completed act of God.

Other Biblical Creation Accounts

In most of the accounts of creation found in the Bible, the question of time never arises. Modern people tend to ignore the other
accounts of creation when thinking about what the Bible says on
the subject. The other accounts do not contradict Genesis 1, but
they do provide a basis for understanding the point and meaning
of Genesis 1.

The Bible was written over a period of centuries in a context of
many cultures and worldviews. A few of these cultures include
Canaanite, Egyptian, Babylonian, Persian, Hebrew, and Hellenistic.
Revelation always has a cultural context in which the people who
receive the revelation live. Every culture has a worldview through
which it understands the physical world. At no point does God
require a people to change their worldview before receiving a revelation, though the revelation they receive inevitably leads to a
change of worldview. Worldview includes whatever passes for science in a culture, even the most primitive of cultures. The Bible does
not teach any particular science so much as it speaks to people in a
way that their understanding of the world (science) can receive.

Psalm 104

Psalm 104 contains an account of creation as lengthy as that in
Genesis 1, and it involves the same acts of creation. Though the
psalm describes the universe God has created, the psalm is about
God. The description merely serves to show the worthiness of God
for praise: "Praise the LORD, O my soul. O LORD my God, you are
very great; you are clothed with splendor and majesty" (Ps. 104:1).

The psalm then begins to explain why God is very great. First,
"He wraps himself in light as with a garment; he stretches out the
heavens like a tent and lays the beams of his upper chambers on
their waters" (Ps. 104:2–3a). Once again, light appears as a prel-
ude to the creation of the physical order. With what kind of light
does God clothe himself? Again, the creation of sun and moon do

not appear until quite far along (vv. 19–23). Again, the heavens appear out of the waters before the earth. Instead of a "firmament," which is a beaten brass vessel like a turkey cover, as in Genesis 1, God uses great beams to separate the waters.

Once again, God separates the waters below so that the earth appears. Instead of water covering the whole earth, God sets boundaries for the water. Just as the heavens are set on beams, the earth rests on foundations so that it can never be moved. Does this mean that the earth does not move around the sun? Or does it mean something else?

This psalm says much more about God than Genesis 1 in terms of its descriptions of creation. Here, God clothes himself in light, uses clouds as a chariot, and "rides on the wings of the wind" (vv. 2–3). God is described as having hands and a face (vv. 28–29). Does this psalm mean that God literally wears clothes, travels from place to place on a cloud for transportation, and has a physical face and hands? The ancient Greeks, Egyptians, Babylonians, Canaanites, and Philistines believed so. Or does the psalm mean something else about God? Are these statements metaphors to help people understand the wonder of how God creates?

Psalm 33

In Psalm 33 the creation of all things again forms the basis for praising God. This psalm does not give the same lengthy description of creation, nor does it expound on the breadth of creation. It does focus, however, on how God created: "By the word of the LORD were the heavens made; their starry host by the breath of his mouth" (Ps. 33:6). Again he separates the waters from the dry land, but without a firmament or beams or foundations. Instead he simply "gathers the waters of the sea into jars" (Ps. 33:7) or into a "heap" (KJV). Creation appears as effortless activity: "For he spoke, and it came to be; he commanded, and it stood firm" (Ps. 33:9).

While this psalm speaks of creation and shares the same features of creation as the other creation accounts examined, the point of the psalm lies elsewhere. The psalm focuses on the idea that God has a plan and a purpose for all of creation: "But the plans of the LORD stand firm forever, the purposes of his heart through all generations" (Ps. 33:11). The rest of the psalm discusses how the plan and purpose of God affect people. Life has meaning and purpose because a God exists who created all things with purpose in mind.

Psalm 19

Psalm 19 begins with a dramatic statement about the heavens: "The heavens declare the glory of God; and the firmament showeth his handiwork. Day unto day uttereth speech, and night unto night showeth knowledge" (Ps. 19:1–2 KJV). Creation itself tells us something about God. He made it in such a way that it gives reliable testimony about him. The same idea appears in Psalm 50: "The heavens proclaim his righteousness, for God himself is judge" (Ps. 50:6). Combining the righteousness of God with the testimony of the heavens suggests that God does not lie through what his creation declares. Chapter 2 of this book discussed the idea of revelation and God's ability to communicate as a personal being. The Bible represents a collection of specific revelations to individuals, but creation itself represents general revelation to all people. God does not lie in specific or general revelation. When a conflict appears between general revelation and specific revelation, someone has misinterpreted either creation or the Bible.

This psalm makes the clear declaration that God has "pitched a tent for the sun" in the heavens and that the sun "rises at one end of the heavens and makes its circuit to the other" (Ps. 19:4b, 6a). This statement clearly conflicts with the commonly understood scientific view that the earth travels around the sun and not the other way around. This conflict appears over and over again in the Bible. Even the Gospels say that the sun rises (Matt. 5:45; Mark 16:2) and sets (Mark 1:32; Luke 4:40).

Is this reference to the behavior of the sun a case of science being right and faith being wrong? Do the heavens declare one thing and the Bible another? Is God lying in the Bible or in the astronomical observations? It is easy to imagine this kind of conflict if one assumes that the scientific way of speaking is the way to speak about truth. Of course, every evening I turn on the television set and listen to a scientist who deals with *chaos theory* every day. (Chaos theory will be discussed in Part V of this book.) This scientist always tells what time the sun will rise and set the next day along with the weather report. Four hundred years after the Copernican Revolution, talk about a sunrise still communicates. The prevailing scientific view is irrelevant to the validity of the communication. The weather person never intended to dispute the idea of a sun-centered solar system. Neither did the Bible intend to teach a particular scientific view. Both communicate with a popularly understood image without commenting on the scientific validity of the popular image. Tremendous conflicts can arise between science and faith when either expects the creation accounts to follow the scientific method and scientific terminology as the only standard for truth.

The Point of the Creation Accounts

Throughout the Bible, the purpose of telling the story of creation is to explain who God is. The Bible begins by explaining who God is, and the explanation is simple. God is the one who made everything. When Jonah set out to run away from God and found himself on a boat in the midst of a fierce storm, the crew believed one of the gods had been offended. They asked Jonah who he was and he explained, "I am a Hebrew and I worship the LORD, the God of heaven, who made the sea and the land" (Jonah 1:9). Jonah used a way of explaining who God is that appears throughout the Bible when people who worship the God of Abraham, Isaac, and Jacob encounter people who do not know the Creator God.

On their first missionary journey, Paul and Barnabas visited the Lycaonian city of Lystra in modern Turkey. The Lystrans worshiped the old gods of the Greek pantheon. When the apostles healed a crippled man, the Lystrans prepared to offer a sacrifice to Paul and Barnabas, whom they took to be Hermes and Zeus visiting earth in human form. Paul's response to them reflects the same starting point used by Jonah to explain who God is:

> Men, why are you doing this? We too are only men, human like you. We are bringing you good news, telling you to turn from these worthless things to the living God, who made heaven and earth and sea and everything in them. In the past, he let all nations go their own way. Yet he has not left himself without testimony: He has shown kindness by giving you rain from heaven and crops in their seasons; he provides you with plenty of food and fills your hearts with joy (Acts 14:15–17).

When Paul went to Athens, he had to deal with the same problem. How does one explain who God is to people who have no background for understanding the gospel? How does one explain who God is to people who have a different understanding of spiritual reality? How does one explain who God is to people who have a different worldview? How does one explain who God is to people who have different philosophical presuppositions? In Athens, Paul talked with Epicurean and Stoic philosophers rather than with those involved in the local cult. He spoke to them at the Areopagus court where Socrates had been condemned to death four hundred and fifty years earlier for teaching that there is only one God. Paul said:

> Men of Athens! I see that in every way you are very religious. For as I walked around and looked carefully at your objects of worship, I even found an altar with this inscription: TO AN UNKNOWN GOD. Now what you worship as something unknown I am going to proclaim to you. The God who made the world and everything in it is the Lord of heaven and earth and does not live in temples built by hands (Acts 17:22–24).

The philosophical system of Epicurus accepted many gods and many universes without beginning or end. Epicurean philosophy held that knowledge arose from sensory experience. Epicurus saw no need for Plato's universal Ideals or Aristotle's universal Forms. Sense experience is "true," the feeling of pleasure is the ultimate "good," and the feeling of pain is the ultimate "evil." Epicurus denied the existence of an omnipotent, benevolent Creator God because of the presence of evil (pain) in the world.

The Stoics believed in a *monistic* universe in which everything is a single whole. "God," Zeus, the Word (Logos), and other similar expressions refer to a greater concentration of the universe but cannot be distinguished from the rest of the universe. The rest of the universe is made from God by God. The universe goes through an endless cycle of organization and destruction which replicates itself each time according to an internal law. Rationality arises with the greater concentration of the universe. The Logos is the seat of the rational law of the universe as a result of the concentration of the universe in the Logos, but people have a degree of rationality about them. For the Stoic, the highest good was to live as a responsible person (see Fig. 5.1).

In his message, Paul addressed the issues that the philosophers addressed, but he gave a perspective of the universe quite different from the universe of the Epicureans or the Stoics. The difference arises from what kind of God exists. The theological thought of the philosophers cannot be separated from their physics. The Epicureans believed in the eternal, unchanging nature of atoms. The Stoics believed that all reality is an aspect of God which takes shape through the four elements: water, earth, air, and fire. These two views represent two entirely different ways of doing science, but they also illustrate how science and faith influence one another through philosophical presuppositions. Paul did not argue with

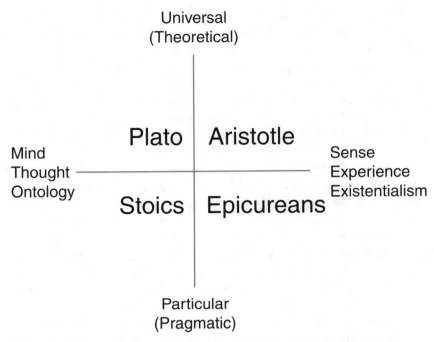

Plato and Aristotle believed in universals, but Aristotle focused
on the senses. The Stoics and Epicureans focused on the
particular, but the Epicureans focused on the senses like
Aristotle while the Stocis focused on the mind like Plato.

Fig. 5.1. Greek Philosophical Approaches to the World.

their science or their philosophy. Instead, he borrowed from the
writings of Epimenides (sixth century B.C.) and Aratus (third century B.C.) to make his point: "God did this so that men would seek
him and perhaps reach out for him and find him, though he is not
far from each one of us. *'For in him we live and move and have our
being.'* [Epimenides] As some of your own poets have said, *'We are
his offspring'*" [Aratus] (Acts 17:27–28, author's emphasis).

Remarkably, the poems refer to Zeus. This passage illustrates
the way that the Bible may contain a worldview, a philosophical
position, an understanding of science, or even a theological belief
which it does not endorse. Statements like these are included
because of the worldview of the people being addressed.

The Gospel of John represents another case in which the Bible
addresses creation in order to explain what kind of God exists.

This Gospel begins: "In the beginning was the Word, and the Word was with God, and the Word was God. He was with God in the beginning" (John 1:1–2). John used the "Word" terminology of the Stoic philosophers as he began to talk about God and creation. Unlike the Stoics, however, he claimed that the universe had a beginning. John also linked creation with the concept of light and its power over darkness (John 1:3–9). Unlike the Stoics and other monistic worldviews, John made clear that light and darkness are not two aspects of God. John emphasized also that the light associated with creation is not the physical light of science but the spiritual light of faith as he continued the theme throughout his Gospel (John 3:19–21; 8:12; 9:5; 11:9–10; 12:35–36, 46). In fact, this theme continues throughout the Johannine literature (1 John 1:5–7; 2:8–11). The Book of Revelation ends dramatically with a picture of eternity after the present world passes away, and again, it gives insight into the meaning of "light" in relation to creation:

> And he carried me away in the Spirit to a mountain great and high, and showed me the Holy City, Jerusalem, coming down out of heaven from God. It shone with the glory of God . . . . I did not see a temple in the city, because the Lord God Almighty and the Lamb are its temple. The city does not need the sun or the moon to shine on it, for the glory of God gives it light, and the Lamb is its lamp. The nations will walk by its light. . . . There will be no more night. They will not need the light of a lamp or the light of the sun, for the Lord God will give them light (Rev. 21:10–11a, 22–24a; 22:5a).

On both ends of time, for biblical writers who lived in vastly different cultures, "light" has special meaning for describing what kind of God exists and how God relates to creation. God is the source of light which was present before the creation of physical light sources (i.e., the sun) and after these sources have disappeared.

Alternative Worldviews

The conflict between science and religion about the origin of the universe relates more to a conflict between a philosophy of science and a method of biblical interpretation. From the religious perspective, any question about the origin or nature of the universe depends upon the ultimate question: What kind of God exists? The ancient people accepted common "scientific" understandings of the world in which they lived, but they had radically different understandings of what kind of God exists.

The Hebrews shared with the ancient Babylonians and Egyptians a scientific understanding of their world. Anyone who digs down deep enough will hit water. From this simple and common observation, they knew that the earth rested on the waters. But what kept the earth stable? Obviously, the earth must have a vast foundation reaching down into the fathomless deep. They also observed water falling from the sky. Reason told them that water covered the heavens, but something must hold the waters out. What could be holding the waters out? The ancients had the hypothesis that a great firmament held the waters out. So far, these are not religious views; they are simple scientific observations and hypotheses. People had different theories about the nature of the firmament. It might be a stone vault, a brass shield, or some other structure (see Fig. 5.2). This was the ancient scientific view of the world but not necessarily a science taught or endorsed by the Bible. God communicates with people at their level of understanding, not at his level of understanding.

While the ancients had general agreement about the basic structure of their world, they had dramatically different views of the nature of the world and its relationship to the divine. The waters of the sea were the domain of Dagon (Syria and the Philistines). The earth was the domain of Baal (Phoenicia). The sun which provides light was the domain of Ra (Egypt). The moon which brings light at night was the domain of Nannar (Ur). The chaos before the ordering of creation was the domain of Tiamet (Babylon). Plant and animal fertility belonged to Ishtar (Babylon) or Isis (Egypt). Order and life came about through a great struggle between Marduk and Tiamet (Babylon) or Horus and Set (Egypt). The seasons came about by the repeated murder of Osiris by Set (Egypt) or Baal by Mot (Canaan), and their revival by Isis (Egypt) and Anat (Canaan). Instead of this picture of the world controlled by competing deities at war with one another, the biblical accounts of creation tell of a single God who made everything and sustains it all through his continuing involvement.

The science of the ancient world gradually gave way to the "truth" of Ptolemy's understanding of the world. Ptolemy's world eventually gave way to the world of Copernicus. The world of Copernicus was expanded by Newton, and Newton's world was replaced by Einstein's universe. To discuss a conflict between biblical faith and science, one must first decide which science. The

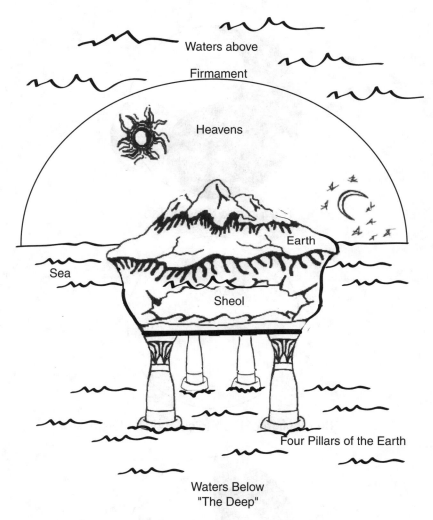

Fig. 5.2. The Hebrew Cosmology.

danger would be to assume that the current science is the true science, but that was always the problem before. We may more safely assume that the current science is not the true science, though it may be more helpful than the old science. Some new discovery and insight will come along some day to replace Einstein's universe with some new understanding of physical reality.

In the meantime, the ancient Hebrew concern for what kind of God exists is still at the center of the conversation between science and faith. In the latter twentieth and early twenty-first centuries,

The Yin and Yang of Tao

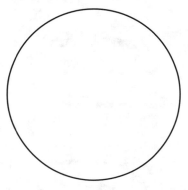

The Monism of the Stoics and Hinduism

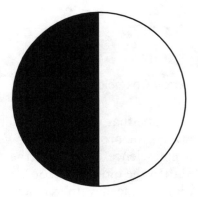

The Dualism of Zoroastrianism

Fig. 5.3. Alternative Understandings of the Divine.

the West has experienced a revival of the old nature religions that deify the earth and all aspects of nature. It has also experienced a growing fascination with the great religions of the East which have radically different understandings of the divine and how the divine relates to the physical world. The Tao of China regards darkness and light, the yin and the yang, as two equal and opposite aspects of one reality (see Fig. 5.3). Hinduism embraces a monistic view of the divine and the physical order.[2] Everything is an aspect of the One, and the One is contained within everything; thus, the divine has countless manifestations. Buddhism regards the physical world as an illusion. Only the spiritual is real.

In this climate, people of biblical faith in the West face a challenge they have not faced for a thousand years: pluralism. In the modern era empiricism, rationalism, skepticism, materialism, and existentialism had no place for God. In the postmodern era, however, it seems increasingly apparent that people have an interest in the divine, and they assume some sort of "god" exists. In this climate the relevance and point of the creation accounts appears fresh: What kind of God exists?

CHAPTER SIX

DIALOGUE ON THE COSMOS

WHEN ONE CONSIDERS THE CURRENT SCIENTIFIC THEORIES ABOUT THE origin and structure of the universe, there are several issues that cause consonance and dissonance with religion.

Critical Questions

Some of the science-and-faith issues include: Does the universe have a beginning? Is the universe static or dynamic? Does the universe have value or purpose? What is the significance of the earth? Each issue is discussed below.

Does the Universe Have a Beginning?

The Big Bang theory projects that the universe had a beginning, that it began as an infinitely small point called a singularity. Thus, there is consonance between the scientific theory and theological claims of God creating the universe. Some have carried the relationship beyond consonance to apologetics. As an example, Pope Pius XII in 1951 said that the beginning of the Big Bang provided grounds for belief in God. The problem with basing your religious proofs on science is that scientific theories are never complete and do undergo refinements; a faith based on scientific theories appears to crumble when the scientific theory changes. A classical example of this is the work of Thomas Aquinas, who blended Christian theology with Aristotelian science that included an earth-centered universe. Refinement of cosmology from an earth-centered model to a sun-centered model put a tremendous stress on the Thomist theology.

Currently, scientific understanding of the earliest part of the Big Bang cosmology is incomplete because the early universe was smaller than an atom. General relativity, which Big Bang cosmology is based on, explains the behavior of the very large but not the very small. Quantum mechanics, discussed in chapter 10, explains behavior at the subatomic level. A combination of general relativity and quantum mechanics is needed to model the very small universe. This approach is called *quantum gravity* with its cosmological model called *quantum cosmology*. At present there is no consensus on how to achieve this combination. One attempt is the work of Stephen Hawking. Hawking's calculations result in imaginary time. His calculations imply that as one approaches the singularity, time becomes imaginary. Thus, in Hawking's model the singularity can never be reached. If his model is correct, then the universe would be finite but have no beginning. Not everyone agrees with Hawking's results and more work is needed before there is a quantum cosmology. But Hawking's proposal does show the potential danger of using the singularity as an apologetic.

The idea of creation may conflict with the concept of God found in some religions or with the worldview present in some cultures or philosophies. But does the idea of creation conflict with a scientific understanding of the universe? The modern age has tended to regard the scientific explanation of things as the most accurate and reliable kind of knowledge. This view reflects a bias or presupposition about the value of different kinds of knowledge. It assumed a virtual absolute truth to scientific knowledge based on the scientific method, yet this value is one imposed from the outside rather than from within the scientific method. Science could never live up to the expectation placed upon it by the modern era. The scientific method itself actually suggests the limitation of scientific knowledge.

To ask if science conflicts with creation, one must first ask, Which science? As chapter 4 has suggested, the scientific community has adopted many explanations for the working of the universe over the last few thousand years. Must the Bible present a particular scientific understanding of the universe in order not to conflict with science? Rather than presenting a particular science, the Bible presents a scientifically neutral view of the universe. The idea of creation does not conflict with the earth-centered universe of Aristotle and Ptolemy, the sun-centered universe of Copernicus, the static universe of Newton, the dynamic universe of Einstein, or even the finite and unbounded universe of Hawking. None of these sciences may prove creation, but they do not conflict with the idea of creation either. For all of these cosmologies of the physical universe, creation cannot be excluded scientifically. The cosmologies themselves, on the other hand, have been found lacking. One after another they have given way to new cosmologies.

When religion is wed to any particular science, it is crippled. When the science fails, the religion fails with it. The science and the religion of ancient Egypt and the Celts was the same. The cosmology was the religion. When the cosmology died, the religion died. When the Christian academy wed itself to the science of Ptolemy as well as the metaphysical worldview of Aristotle, it created enormous problems for itself. When the eighteenth-century Christian academy wed itself to the mechanical cosmology of Newton, it gave up its own voice. In both cases, the content of Christian faith was abandoned to the cosmology until it was identified with the cosmology. In the modern period, process theology has created a metaphysic around evolutionary theory. This wedding of religion to science usually occurs to give religion the "respectability" of science. It leaves it, however, with nothing to say on its own. When the science eventually fails and a new science takes its place, the theologians must scramble to find a new scientific rationale. While liberals tend to rush to adopt the new scientific rationale for religion, conservatives tend to defend the old science long after it has been discredited because the old science has become so enmeshed with the old religion.

Is the Universe Static or Dynamic?

The concept of a static universe was one of the dominant ideas of science for centuries. It did not matter whether the cosmos was earth-centered or sun-centered or Milky Way galaxy-centered; in all cases the cosmos was considered to be static—the same yesterday, today, and tomorrow. Furthermore, these models gave no information about the origin or fate of the universe.

Only in the twentieth century did scientists seriously propose the revolutionary idea of a dynamic universe. The Big Bang model was a paradigm shift that caused scientists to propose that the universe has a life cycle: The universe had a beginning, has been expanding ever since, and has a predicted ending. For philosophical reasons, some scientists resisted this paradigm by reformulating the static model into the Steady State model. Although this model contains continuous creation, to these scientists its static, no-origin, no-end features were reassuring. By the end of the twentieth century, the dominant model of cosmology was a dynamic, expanding-universe model. Thus, at the beginning of the twenty-first century, religion must address the consonance and dissonance associated with a dynamic-universe model.

The deistic understanding of God grew out of the understanding of a static universe. The deists believed that God created the universe, like a watchmaker who fashions a watch. He wound it up and then left it alone. A static, mechanistic universe has no place for involvement by God. The deists, therefore, did not believe in miracles or the divine nature of Christ. Thomas Jefferson, one of the most prominent deists of his time, took scissors to his Bible and cut out all references to the miraculous!

Though the opening verses of the Bible affirm that God's creation of the physical universe is complete in its scope, the rest of Genesis 1 makes clear that creation is not a static activity of God. Creation began one day (Gen. 1:5) and is not finished until a seventh day (Gen. 2:2). If the days of Genesis 1 are meant to be understood as twenty-four-hour solar days, then all creative activity of God lies in the past as a static event. If the days of Genesis 1 have a different meaning, however, then the seventh day may lie in the future as described in Revelation as the end of the present created order and the beginning of a new heaven and a new earth in a new age.

Rather than a God who intervenes in a static universe, the Bible portrays a God who is involved in the day-to-day activity of running a universe. God appears as one responsible for and involved in each new life. God sends the rain on the just and the unjust alike (Matt. 5:45). Such passages may mean that God determines by a decisive act where each drop of rain will fall. Such passages could also mean that God continually calls the process into being which makes rain possible. As we saw in chapter 5, the form of the Hebrew verbs in Genesis 1 suggests that God began to call all of creation into being, but that the action is not completed.

The Book of Hebrews probably gives the clearest interpretation of the meaning of time in creation and the dynamic involvement of God in creation across time. Hebrews follows the New Testament pattern of attributing the work of creation to the Son:

> But in these last days he has spoken to us by his Son, whom he appointed heir of all things, and through whom he made the universe. The Son is the radiance of God's glory and the exact representation of his being, sustaining all things by his powerful word (Heb. 1:2–3).

The choice of the term *universe* represents an interesting interpretation of this text by the translators for a modern audience since the ancients had no word for what we call today the universe. The Revised Standard Version translates the Greek word as "world" which would imply cosmos rather than the planet Earth. The King James Version of 1611 translated the word as "worlds." The word in the text is actually the word *aionas* (eons) which means "ages." Hebrews suggests that the Son made the ages and that he sustains or continues to uphold creation by the same word by which he began creation (see also John 1:1–3). Paul also affirmed the dynamic nature of Christ's involvement with creation in his letter to the Colossians when he said, "He is before all things, and in him all things hold together" (Col. 1:17). The continued existence of the created order depends upon the exercise of the will of God (Rev. 4:11).

Does the Universe Have Value or Purpose?

As we discussed in chapter 1, questions about purpose are really outside the realm of the scientific method. However, this has not stopped some scientists from making statements about purpose. Since the latter part of the nineteenth century, more and more scientists have assumed that the universe has no purpose; it just is. They assumed that the universe arose from matter, developed by natural laws, and that nothing else was involved. As Jacques Barzun wrote, "Matter and Force . . . explain our whole past history and presumably would shape our future."[1] How would one test Barzun's assumptions? Scientists check their assumptions by changing the value of a variable and then repeating the process to see what will happen. For example, a chemist could check the effect of temperature on a reaction by running a series of reactions while the temperature is increased by ten degrees over that of the previous run. These experimental runs would reveal whether the outcome of the reaction depended upon the temperature.

Likewise, to test Barzun's assumption, one would need to "build" a series of universes with different values for certain fundamental variables and then observe if life develops in any of these universes. Until the advent of supercomputers, there was no way to "build" other universes. With supercomputers, scientists have been able to perform "if" calculations on the universe. If the size of the Big Bang were larger or smaller or if the fundamental force of gravity were weaker or stronger, would life still develop? If the universe and life were just the result of purposeless natural forces, scientists had assumed that life could exist even with a lot of variance in the values of these variables. They had assumed that under the new conditions life would exist; it might not lead to life with the intelligence of humans, but life would form.

As shown in Figure 6.1, very small changes in the fundamental forces will result in a universe in which life does not develop. Scientists were surprised to learn from these calculations that the universe seems to be fine-tuned for the existence of life; seems to be fine-tuned for mankind. As the astronomer Fred Hoyle, who was an atheist, wrote, "A common sense interpretation of the facts suggests that a superintellect has monkeyed with physics, as well as with chemistry and biology, and that there are no blind forces worth speaking about in nature. The numbers one calculates from the facts seem to me so overwhelming as to put this conclusion almost beyond question."[2] These fine-tuned variables are called the Anthropic Principles. The word *anthropic* refers to anything related to humans; thus, to some scientists, these variables were fine-tuned so life and humans could be present in the universe. At least twenty-six of these variables are known.[3] Three of these are listed in Figure 6.1.

Size of Big Bang	*If smaller:* Big Crunch occurs before life can form.	*If larger:* universe expands too fast to form stars, planets, and galaxies.
Size of Gravity	*If weaker:* stars do not ignite.	*If stronger:* stars too big, burn too fast for life to develop.
Size of Strong Nuclear Force	*If weaker:* only the atom hydrogen would form and no other elements would be formed which are needed for life.	*If stronger:* all hydrogen would be converted to helium. Life, as we know it, needs hydrogen to make biological molecules.

Fig. 6.1. Life-Supporting "Coincidences" Concerning the Universe.

Size of Big Bang. The size of an expanding universe results from the interaction of an outward force due to the size of the Big Bang and inward force due to gravity. An everyday analogy of this is a paddleball which involves a ball attached to a paddle by a rubber band. Hit the ball with the paddle and it flies away, stretching the rubber band. At some point, the outward motion of the ball equals the inward pull of the rubber band. The ball stops moving outward and then the pull of the rubber band causes the ball to fly inward toward the paddle. The distance the ball flies before stopping and returning to the paddle depends upon how hard the ball was originally struck. Likewise, the larger the Big Bang the longer the space-time fabric of the universe will expand before it could be stopped by the gravitational force.

Calculations have shown that if the Big Bang were slightly smaller (one part in a billion trillion), the time taken for gravity to stop the expansion of the universe and recompact the universe would be less time than it took for life to develop in the current universe. If the Big Bang were slightly larger (one part in a million), the expansion would be too fast for gravity to collect matter into stars and planets which, according to the current model, are needed for life to form.

Size of Gravity. According to current cosmological theory, a star begins as a cloud of hydrogen gas held together by gravity. The force of gravity gradually pulls the hydrogen gas toward the center of the cloud, causing the temperature of the gas to increase. As the contraction continues, the hydrogen gas reaches a temperature large enough for hydrogen atoms to fuse into helium atoms. The star "ignites" and expands outward due to the forces released by the fusion. The size of the star is determined by the interaction between the force of gravity (inward force) and force of fusion (outward force).

Calculations reveal that if the force of gravity is slightly smaller, the collapse of the hydrogen cloud never results in a temperature large enough to cause fusion to occur. According to current theory, stars are needed for life to exist. Other calculations reveal that if gravity were slightly larger, the resulting hydrogen clouds would be larger, thus forming larger stars. The larger a star, the faster it "burns" its nuclear fuel and the shorter its life span. Thus, in a universe with a stronger gravity, the life span of stars would be too short for life to develop.

Size of Strong Nuclear Force. As discussed previously, the strong nuclear force is the strongest of the four fundamental forces and is responsible for the binding of protons and neutrons to form atomic nuclei. The strength of the strong nuclear force will determine which combinations of protons and neutrons in the nucleus are stable. For example, in the carbon atom, a nucleus containing six protons and six neutrons is stable, while a nucleus containing six protons and eight neutrons is unstable.

Calculations have revealed that if the strong nuclear force were slightly weaker, only the nucleus of the hydrogen atom would be stable. All other atomic nuclei (combinations of protons and neutrons) would be unstable. Thus, with a weaker strong nuclear force, elements such as carbon, nitrogen, and oxygen would be unstable. Since these elements are needed for life as we know it, life would not develop in a universe with a weaker strong nuclear force. Further calculations have revealed that if the strong nuclear force were slightly larger, the helium nucleus would be much more stable than the hydrogen nucleus. Under these conditions, all hydrogen would be converted to helium. Again, life as we know it requires hydrogen to exist; and life would be impossible within a universe having a larger strong nuclear force. Further issues concerning life and the fine-tuning of the universe for life will be discussed in chapters 7, 8, and 9.

What Is the Significance of the Earth?

The earth orbits a "typical" star in the outer arm of its galaxy. In addition, the earth is one of many planets. It is not the largest planet or the smallest. Assuming a materialistic explanation of the earth's origin, there does not seem to be anything special about the earth. However, these "insignificant" facts about the earth and sun actually are interesting "coincidences" that imply that the earth is in the right place for life to flourish. Figure 6.2 lists some of these life-supporting coincidences.

Worldview and Interpretation

In the dialogue between science and faith, a person's basic assumptions have a great deal to do with how they interpret the Bible in areas related to science and how they interpret the physical world in areas related to the spiritual domain. When does the biblical text speak literally and when does it speak allegorically, figuratively, or metaphorically? Was Jesus serious when he said, "If

Size and mass of sun	*If larger:* sun would burn out too quickly for life to flourish.	*If smaller:* life supporting distance from sun would be much closer than now. At this closer distance, gravitational tidal forces would disrupt a planet's rotational period, making life support difficult.
Distance of sun from center of galaxy	*If closer:* radiation from other stars would be too great for life to exist. Also, the stellar density gravitational forces would destabilize the earth's orbit.	*If farther:* there would not be a large enough concentration of heavy elements to form rocky planets like the earth.
Distance of sun from closest galactic spiral arm	*If closer:* radiation from other stars would be too great for life to exist. Also, the stellar density gravitational forces would destabilize the earth's orbit.	*If farther:* there would not be a large enough concentration of heavy elements to form rocky planets like the earth.
Distance of earth from sun	*If closer:* earth would be too warm for liquid water to be found on surface of the planet. This is not good for human life as about 60 percent of a human's body is composed of liquid water.	*If farther:* earth would be too cool for liquid water to be found on surface of earth. In other words, all water would exist as ice.
Size of earth and strength of earth's gravity	*If larger:* earth's atmosphere would retain too much ammonia and methane (both toxic) for life to flourish.	*If smaller:* earth's atmosphere would lose too much water.

Fig. 6.2. Life-Supporting "Coincidences" Concerning the Earth and the Sun.

thine eye offend thee, pluck it out?" Baptists claim the Bible as their only religious authority and Catholics add the tradition of the church to the Bible. Yet Catholics take Jesus literally when he said of the bread at the last supper, "This is my body," while Baptists regard Jesus as speaking metaphorically.

The interpretation of the Bible always carries a grave responsibility for those who view it as the Word of God. The responsibility becomes complicated if a person does not realize he is interpreting the Bible. As one well-meaning preacher remarked, "I never interpret the Bible—I just preach the truth!" This preacher is unaware of the presuppositions, biases, assumptions, and prejudices which color his reading of Scripture. The worldview of a person will color how he or she reads and understands the Bible. Liberals and conservatives alike fall victim to this same problem, primarily when they are unaware of imposing a standard for interpreting Scripture which comes from their background.

Nowhere is the problem of interpretation more pronounced than in understanding the biblical idea of creation. In chapter 5 we have seen how the timing of creation has tended to cloud the real issue of the fact of creation. From the perspective of worldview, the fact of creation is the point of the biblical accounts of creation. The fact of creation involves the objective reality of the physical order as well as the goodness of this physical creation.

Religion, Philosophy, and Cosmology

Major worldviews take contrary positions about the physical world. In his quest to understand suffering, the Buddha concluded that suffering comes from desire. If we had no desire, there would be no suffering. Desire results from living in a physical universe where things and circumstances to desire exist. The Buddha concluded that the physical universe does not really exist. It is merely a bad delusion. Most forms of Hinduism would say that the physical world does have a form of existence, but only as an extension or manifestation of the divine. The world has no creator because it has no separate existence from the divine itself. While people may experience differentiation between themselves and the rest of the world, this difference is an illusion.

As we saw in chapter 1, science as it is known today emerged within a Christian worldview. Peoples within every culture, however, regardless of worldview, develop some kind of science or knowledge of the world around them. These approaches to the world around them among primitive people involved sophisticated astronomy capable of predicting eclipses of the sun accurately. The science of primitive peoples involves a knowledge of the medicinal value of many plants. The great cultures of India and China made scientific discoveries far earlier than western Europe, yet none of these cultures produced the methodology or the systematic industry known to modern people of all cultures as science.

In the West, science grew out of the church as a systematic examination and description of what God has done. Science, as such, has no particular worldview. It either subsists or flourishes within the context of the prevailing worldview of a culture. Science existed in China for thousands of years, but it did not flourish, just as international commerce did not flourish, because in the traditional worldview of Confucian society, it had no contribution to make. It was interesting and entertaining, but not a part of tradition. Within Buddhist societies, science involved the observation of a world which was only an illusion. There was no point to it. It distracted people from reality. So we can see that worldview has as much to do with how one interprets nature (science) as with how one interprets the Bible (theology).

Alongside science in the modern West, a philosophical worldview has developed which has often been confused with science. *Materialistic naturalism* is a philosophical worldview which believes that the physical world is all that exists and that everything can be explained by natural processes. This view is not a logical conclusion from scientific observation. Rather, it is a philosophical perspective imposed on the data from the outside, like any other worldview. Naturalism represents in many ways the opposite of a Buddhist perspective of reality. To the Buddhist the physical world is an illusion, but to the naturalist the spiritual world is a delusion.

Christianity and Cosmology

Modern science developed within a Christian framework as a subdivision of theology. The Christian perspective affirms both the physical world and the spiritual world, yet it does so without *dualism* because physical and spiritual reality are both aspects of creation. The affirmation of the unity of creation occurs, however, without the *modalism* of Taoism which sees opposites as the totality of reality. Christianity affirms a creator God who made both spiritual and physical reality and who has power over them. Instead of viewing the material world as evil, which frequently occurs in Eastern religion, the Bible calls the created world good. Instead of the cause of human sin, the physical world is the victim of human sin, having suffered under human mismanagement (Rom. 8:19–22).

The church of the Middle Ages believed that the physical world deserved the same systematic study as the Bible, because creation itself spoke of God, just like the Bible. The psalmist declared in antiquity:

> The heavens declare the glory of God;
> the skies proclaim the work of his hands.

Day after day they pour forth speech;
　　night after night they display knowledge.
There is no speech or language
　　where their voice is not heard.
Their voice goes out into all the earth,
　　their words to the ends of the world (Ps. 19:1–4a).

The heavens themselves say something about God. The created order itself says something about what kind of God exists. The apostle Paul observed in his letter to the Romans that "since the creation of the world God's invisible qualities—his eternal power and divine nature—have been clearly seen, being understood from what has been made, so that men are without excuse" (Rom. 1:20). Therefore, the study of nature became an acceptable academic discipline, particularly after the time of Thomas Aquinas, who adopted Aristotle's view of knowledge through sensory perception.

Christianity presented a world of substance that could be known. Unlike the world of nature religion, it was not a host of hostile deities to be appeased. It was an obedient servant which followed the "laws" of its master. The biblical image of the king of creation who ordains laws for nature persists in the language of science, which continues to think of the "laws of nature." At the same time, however, philosophical views affected how people interpreted the Bible and nature. Augustine, the great theologian of the fifth century who laid the foundations for the medieval world, followed Plato's philosophy as a basis for his theological system. Thomas Aquinas, the great theologian of the fourteenth century who laid the foundations for the modern world, followed Aristotle's philosophy as a basis for his theological system. Thus, philosophy imposed on both Scripture and nature an acceptable way to be read. Galileo's troubles did not represent a conflict between Christianity and science. Rather, his troubles came as a result of the conflict between Aristotle and science. Galileo's observations of the moon and the planets of the solar system did not contradict Scripture so much as they contradicted an Aristotelian interpretation of Scripture.

Our Place in the Universe

Modern naturalists have argued that Galileo created a crisis by taking man out of the center of the universe and relegating him to a secondary status. When the sun and the planets ceased to revolve around man, then the human race ceased to have its place of importance. This line has proven quite popular with modern people because it sounds consistent with the modern worldview. In the modern world, people have placed themselves at the center of the universe. Through the combination of technological advances, economic prosperity, and the exaltation of the "self," the modern world has become a great mass of individuals seeking their own interests.

Removing man from the center of the universe would have seemed a foolish notion to the people of Galileo's day. No one thought man was at the center of the universe for several reasons. At that time, the universe did not exist! Rather, no one yet understood that anything went beyond the observable planets. The universe was limited to the solar system. Second, the order of importance was hierarchical, not concentric. Whether the sun revolved around the earth or the earth revolved around the sun was immaterial to one's place in the created order. God sat enthroned over all creation. God was the point of reference. Humanity's place within creation is in relationship to God.

Modern naturalists have also suggested that humanity's location within the universe makes a statement about the likelihood of the existence of God. The inference goes something like this: People live on a minor planet circling a third-rate star in a corner of an unexceptional galaxy on the back side of the universe. The inference drawn is that if God really exists, people would have a much more important place in the universe.

The naturalistic interpretation of nature with its religious conclusions has an interesting corollary in the Bible. Throughout the Bible, over centuries and cultures, in many books written by different prophets, God continually used the most unlikely people whom he found off to the side. The naturalist preoccupation with the insignificance of humanity in the grand scheme of things is a major theme of the Bible. The perception of insignificance says more about a person's perception than it says about the activity of God.

The Bible suggests that God has a preference for the unexpected. Abraham stands as the father of faith for Muslims, Jews, and Christians, yet what did Abraham do? He founded no religion, wrote no books, established no kingdom. He pales in comparison with the great figures of antiquity. He was a wandering Bedouin. Yet four thousand years later, we still talk about him as the model for what it means to believe God. He believed God in the two great earth-shattering events of his life: he moved, and his wife had a baby. So the most insignificant and commonplace of events which are easily overlooked take center stage as of prime importance.

Who would ever have chosen the slaves of Egypt over the great Egyptian culture as the people through whom God would reveal himself? In that corner of the world, the Babylonians, the Phoenicians, the Greeks, or the Hittites could have offered the flower of culture through which to reveal divine truth. The choice of slaves seems unlikely, but the unlikeliness of it says more about our own value system through which we judge events.

God chose unlikely servants throughout his dealings with Israel. He chose as his greatest prophet Moses, a man who could not speak well. He chose as his greatest general Gideon, a coward who hid from the enemy. Instead of choosing the eldest sons in a culture based on primogeniture, God regularly chose the younger sons: Jacob instead of Esau, Joseph instead of his ten older brothers, David instead of his seven older brothers. In coming into the world, God did the unlikeliest thing of all. Instead of a palace, he was born in a stable.

Conclusion

The Bible does not contain scientific explanations in the sense that modern science understands them. God does not tell people in the Bible what they can learn for themselves. The nature of gravity, the spherical shape of the earth, the process of photosynthesis, the behavior of atoms, and electrical currents are not discussed. Because the Bible talks about some things that science discusses, people have a tendency to think that the Bible has made a scientific statement. Because the Bible refers to the cosmology of the ancient Middle East, people may assume that the Bible teaches this cosmology as the true science. This assumption becomes more complicated when one finds the Bible referring to Persian and Greek cosmologies as well. This assumption would come within the same category as assuming that the Bible teaches polygamy because it refers to the practice of polygamy found in the ancient Middle East.

During the modern period, the desire to conform the Christian faith to the most current science resulted in a situation called "the God of the gaps." This phrase refers to the habit of crediting God with those things science cannot explain. If it can be explained, then God did not do it. As science made broader and grander advances in knowledge, this view of the activity of God squeezed God out almost entirely. In contrast to this approach, "the God of creation" is involved in the very things science describes.

In what sense can the Bible be accurate if it does not speak scientifically? This question betrays a surrender to the naturalistic view of the superiority of scientific knowledge in the modern era. Nevertheless, it is not necessary for the Bible to make scientific statements for it to correspond to the world described by science. One must ask if the Bible is consistent with the world described by science. The Bible talks about the kind of world in which scientific knowledge is possible because of the order established by the God who created order out of chaos. The Bible talks about a "real" physical world which can be known.

As we will see in the chapters on quantum theory and chaos theory later in the book, contemporary science faces a major challenge of uncertainty as the old science has failed. The metaphysical worldview of naturalism which denied metaphysics built an arrogant but unsustainable expectation of absolute certainty which quantum mechanics and chaos theory have dashed. The temptation has been to retreat into subjectivism and a new metaphysical worldview that denies an objective universe. Biblical faith speaks most directly to this issue in affirming a real universe caused by a creator.

As we saw in chapter 5, the grammar of the creation accounts leaves a wide door for understanding the timing and sequence of creation. This whole line of discussion, however, assumes that the Bible is intending to explain how creation occurred. This assumption grows out of the same modern preference for scientific explanations. Since the time of Thomas Aquinas in the late Middle Ages, Christian theology in the West has had a preference for literal, concrete understanding in keeping with Aristotle's emphasis on the physical, sensory road to knowledge. For more than a thousand years, however, Christians had a preference for an allegorical interpretation of Scripture that focused on the spiritual meanings of things. Perhaps as the modern era draws to a close, we may conclude that the allegorical interpretation is not always wrong and the literal interpretation is not always right.

PART III

WHERE DID WE COME FROM?

THIS SECTION EXAMINES CURRENT THINKING ABOUT EVOLUTION IN relation to the Christian concepts of *imago Dei* and salvation. This section will explore such issues as purpose and meaning, varieties of views of evolution, cultural presuppositions about the meaning of biblical texts, and God's relationship with and way of relating to people.

Is there a purpose for humanity? Are people the pinnacle of the natural order? One is struck by the rich diversity in the living world, over one million species of animals alone. Many species are connected in a symbiotic relationship; for example certain plants can only be pollinated by a single species of insect. One also discovers that there is fossil evidence that many species became extinct before many species living today appeared in the fossil record. Finally, humans are apparently the only species conscious of its existence. This section reviews the current scientific theories concerning the origin of life, the development of life, and the place of humans in the chain of life. The development of the current understanding of life will be traced back to the Greek philosophers.

The Bible makes clear that all life comes as a result of the creative activity of God. Intentional rather than accidental force caused life. The nature of people depends upon this origin of life and relationship to God as "creature." As creatures made in the image of God our ultimate goal depends upon the experience of "re-creation" as expressed in the Christian understanding of salvation.

Must a biblical perspective of creation be static, or may it be dynamic (continuous creation)? Does the presence of dynamic emergence in the natural order preclude creation? How does

evolutionary theory relate to the Christian concept of "adoption"
and "indwelling" by the Holy Spirit? How does evolutionary theory
relate to Eastern religious ideas about the relationship between people and the divine?

CHAPTER SEVEN

ORIGIN OF LIFE

How do we know if an organism is alive? It is difficult to come up with a precise definition of life, but a broad definition would be that something is considered alive if it has the following properties:

- Organization: Living things consist of one or more cells (complex assemblies of molecules enclosed in membranes).
- Sensitivity: Living things respond to internal and external stimuli.
- Homeostasis: Living things maintain relatively constant internal conditions despite changes in the environment.
- Growth: Living things change during their life.
- Importation: Living things take energy and materials from their environment.
- Reproduction: Living things produce offspring like themselves.
- Adaptation: Structures, physiology, and behaviors of living things are suited for their survival in a particular environment.

Any theory about the origin of life and about life today has to explain the diversity of living organisms, the similarity of living organisms, and the fossil record. *Diversity* is reflected in living organisms, ranging from microscopic bacteria to visible organisms such as roses, redwoods, dogs, whales, and people. On earth, life is found in diverse locations: the cold of the Antarctic, the heat of hot springs, the temperate climate of Tennessee, the tropics of Brazil.

At the same time, scientists also observe *similarities* in living organisms. These similarities allow scientists to develop taxonomic classification systems. Classification systems result from the exam-ination of the anatomy, biochemistry, genetics, ecology, and fossil record of organisms. Today, scientists classify living organisms by using a system of seven categories: kingdom, phylum, class, order, family, genus, species. (A memory aid my son learned in seventh grade for remembering the relationship of these divisions is "Kelly played checkers on Fred's green stage.") Scientific names for organisms are given by the genus and species classification for the organism. For example, a common bacteria in the human intestine is commonly called "E. coli" which is an abbreviation of its genus and species names of *Escherichia coli.*

Aristotle, in his classification systems, divided life into two kingdoms of plants and animals. Most scientists today divide life into five kingdoms: animals, plants, fungi, protista, and monera. The kingdom *monera* contains unicellular organisms without a nucleus; bacteria belong to this kingdom. Most *protista* are unicellular and microscopic, containing a nucleus; examples of the kingdom protista are algae and amoebas. When one thinks of a type of organism today, one usually thinks in terms of the species classification. This is because the species label gives one a unique group, a biological group containing biologically related organisms that can interbreed. Figure 7.1 lists the current estimates of the number of species in each kingdom. Scientists estimate that there are ten million different living organisms.

Kingdom	Number of Species
Monera	10,000
Protista	68,000
Fungi	100,000
Plants	275,000
Animals	1,000,000

Fig. 7.1. Number of Species in Each Kingdom.

Figure 7.2 reveals how as one moves down the classification scheme, the organisms become more and more similar until finally a unique classification is reached at the species level. Let us use the domestic dog as an example. The dog belongs to the animal kingdom as do starfish, beetles, and fish. At the kingdom level there is a lot of difference between these organisms. Once one reaches the family level, there is much more similarity. Finally at the species level, we have only one choice: the dog.

	Classification	Possibilities			
Kingdom	Animalia	starfish	beetle	fish	dog
Phylum	Chordata	snake	lizard	bird	dog
Class	Mammalia	monkey	whale	elephant	dog
Order	Carnivora	skunk	cat	seal	dog
Family	Canidae	red fox	African hunting dog	jackal	dog
Genus	Canis	timber wolf	coyote	dingo	dog
Species	Familiaris	dog	dog	dog	dog

Fig. 7.2. Classification of Domestic Dog.

Fossils are remains of plants and animals preserved in sedimentary rocks and other material (asphalt, amber, and ice). For our purposes, three points about fossils are important: their age, their relationship to living organisms, and their distribution in the geological record. The age of fossils ranges from 3.5 billion-year-old traces of blue-green bacteria to 10,000-year-old ice age remains. Many fossils look like animals and plants that exist today; an example of this is an insect. Anyone who has collected amber jewelry can recognize that amber often has an insect trapped inside. In other cases, the fossil does not resemble anything alive today; an example would be the dinosaurs. An examination of the distribution of fossils in the geological record reveals that a species starts and stops, only to be followed by other species. An example is the trilobite. The first trilobites are found in the geological record about 570 million years ago, with the last trilobite fossils being found about 250 million years ago. Another observation about the fossil record is, in general, the lower strata have simpler organisms, while the higher strata have more complex organisms.

Responses to Observations

As we have discussed, when a scientist observes life on earth, he or she observes a diversity of life forms, similarities between organisms, and a fossil record. The worldview of the scientist affects how he or she interprets these observations. These interpretations also laid the foundation for modern biology. Although we have used the terms *scientist* and *biology* in our discussions, these terms did not appear until the 1800s. A person who studied nature was a *natural philosopher* or a *naturalist*. The word *biology* was coined by the Frenchman Jean Baptiste Lamarck in the early 1800s while the word *scientist* was coined by the Englishman William Whewell in the 1830s.

One group of scientists interpreted their observations of nature from a Protestant worldview. The English naturalist John Ray (1628–1705) pioneered the systematic classification of organisms. He was the first to define a species as a group of interbreeding organisms. The orderliness he observed in nature revealed to him a Great Designer who created the universe. The Swedish naturalist Carolus Linnaeus (1707–1778) developed the current system of *binomial nomenclature* (genus and species) to label organisms. His inspiration for a classification system was his belief in God's original creation of fixed "kinds." Although he originally believed that the fixed kinds of Genesis were at the species level, he later revised it to the genus and finally to the order level. Both Ray and Linnaeus wrote essays in natural theology, using the order of nature to provide information about God.

The French naturalist Georges Cuvier (1769–1832) was of a Huguenot background. He expanded Linnaeus' classification system by adding phylum and family to Linnaeus' class, order, genus, and species. Cuvier also applied this classification system to fossils. The fossil record convinced him that extinctions had occurred and that life was ancient. Since he believed in fixed species, he proposed catastrophes and re-creations to account for the fossil record. In 1813 the Scottish geologist Robert Jameson (1774–1854) published an English translation of Cuvier's *The Theory of the Earth*. In Jameson's preface to this translation, he proposed the "age-day theory" of creation; the six days of Genesis represented six long periods of time. The Rev. William Buckland (1784–1856), the first Oxford professor of geology, responded to Cuvier's catastrophes by proposing the "gap theory." In his work *Relics of the Flood* (1823), Buckland proposed that there were millions of years between the creation and the first day of Genesis. During this gap, all the geological catastrophes proposed by Cuvier would have occurred.

Parallel to and interacting with the previous group of scientists was a group of scientists who took a more materialist interpretation. The French naturalist Georges Leclerc, Comte de Buffon

(1701–1788), presented one of the first modern accounts of history that was not based on the Bible. In 1779, he published *Epochs de la Nature* in which he divided the history of the earth into seven epochs. Physical laws were used to describe the origin of the solar system as well as the origin and development of life. He proposed that the earth was seventy-five thousand years old. The English physician Erasmus Darwin (1731–1802) was influenced by the English ideas of progress and free enterprise. He believed that an inner force drives organisms to higher forms. The new forms would result from accumulation of experiences. Erasmus was the grandfather of Charles Darwin.

The French naturalist Jean Baptiste Lamarck (1744–1829) in 1809 proposed the first comprehensive theory of organic evolution. He proposed that life arose by spontaneous generation. Through the inheritance of acquired characteristics new species are formed. He also believed that an inner force was at work improving the species. The Scottish geologist Charles Lyell (1797–1875) was a student of Buckland. Unlike Buckland, Lyell proposed natural causes for the geological formations. During 1830–33 he published the three-volume work, *The Principles of Geology: Being an Attempt to Explain the Former Changes of the Earth's Surface by Reference to Causes Now in Operation*. As stated in the book's title, Lyell proposed that the same geological forces have always been at work. Assuming long periods of time, these forces have shaped and reshaped the earth. This is *uniformitarianism* in contrast to Cuvier's *catastrophism*.

Charles Darwin and Alfred Russel Wallace

When a person speaks of evolution today, one name always comes to mind: Charles Darwin. Actually, both Darwin and Alfred Wallace simultaneously and independently arrived at the concept of evolution by natural selection. They reached this conclusion based on the work of the previously discussed scientists as well as their own field work. The word *evolution* is derived from a Latin word that means "unrolling." The meaning of evolution ranges from a process of change to a theory that current plant and animal species developed from preexisting plant and animal species. *Natural selection* is a natural process by which populations of plants and animals become adapted to their environment.

Charles Darwin (1809–1882) graduated in 1831 from Cambridge, where he had developed a love for natural history.

After graduation, he signed on as the naturalist for the voyage of the H.M.S. *Beagle*. The purpose of the five-year (1831–1836) voyage of the *Beagle* was to explore the coast of South America and the islands of the Pacific. Darwin took on this voyage Lyell's *Principles of Geology*, which introduced him to uniformitarianism. In South America Darwin observed fossils of extinct animals that closely resembled modern species. He also observed the effect of natural forces on the earth's surface. On the Galapagos Islands off the coast of Ecuador, Darwin observed that each island supported its own tortoise, mockingbird, and finch. Each was different in structure and habitat from island to island. After Darwin returned home, he began studying the diversity of species.

In 1838 he read the Rev. Thomas Malthus' (1766–1834) *Essay on the Principles of Population*. This work was the key to his understanding of how nature selects species for extinction and survival. Malthus had observed that populations increase faster than their food supply does. This population increase results in either famine, disease, or war. Darwin thought that a similar struggle for food must hold for all forms of life. The part of the population that survived the struggle would be the most fit (best able to compete for food). This struggle for existence was what Darwin labeled "natural selection." Thus, Darwin had arrived at the theory of evolution by natural selection. For the next two decades, he continued to refine his theory.

In 1858 he received a communication from Alfred Russel Wallace (1823–1913) asking for Darwin's comments on Wallace's theory of evolution by natural selection! Darwin had Wallace's letter as well as one of his own published together in the *Journal of the Linnaean Society* in 1858. In 1859 Darwin published *On the Origin of Species by Means of Natural Selection, or the Preservation of Favoured Races in the Struggle of Life*. In 1871 he published *The Descent of Man* in which he argued that no special design or creation was needed to explain the human mind. Upon his death he was buried in Westminster Abbey.

Alfred Russel Wallace explored the Amazon Basin from 1848 to 1852. From 1854 to 1862 he explored the Malay Archipelago. He noted fundamental differences between the animal species of Asia and Australia. He observed that the mammals of the Malay Archipelago are divided into two groups separated by an imaginary line currently called the Wallace Line. West of the line are Asian mammals, with Australian mammals east of the line. Wallace wrote *The Malay Archipelago* (1869), *Contributions to the Theory of Natural Selection* (1870), and the *Geographic Distribution of Animals* (1876). Wallace established the principle of *animal geography* or the study of the geographic distribution of animal species. He differed with Darwin in regard to the human mind. While Wallace proposed natural selection as the means for the development of life forms, he did not believe that natural selection could explain the development of the human mind.

The Triumph of Darwinian Evolution

Most modern biologists are Darwinian evolutionists. However, Darwinian evolution did not immediately sweep through biology. By 1900 there were many who did not support evolution. Of those who did support evolution, there were as many Lamarckian evolutionists as Darwinian. This was because Darwin could not explain changes that occurred in the characteristics of organisms from parent to offspring. Lamarck's idea of inheritance of acquired characteristics made more sense to many. During the early 1900s, the work on genetics by the Austrian monk Gregor Mendel (1822–84) was rediscovered. Genetics could explain the variation in characteristics. The current theory of evolution was finalized by the end of World War II and is called *neo-Darwinism* or the *synthetic theory*. The current theory is a synthesis of Darwin's theory of natural selection with modern population genetics.

A synopsis of the current prevailing thought on the origin and evolution of life would begin with the formation of the earth about 4.5 billion years ago. About 3.5 billion years ago, life appeared with the chemical synthesis of biological molecules (DNA, RNA, proteins) that self-assembled into a reproducing cell. About 700 million years ago multicellular organisms appeared. Marine algae flourished about 500 million years ago which would have been instrumental in creating the current oxygen atmosphere. During this time, the first vertebrates appeared. About 400 million years ago, land plants appeared, followed by insects and amphibians. Reptiles appeared about 350 million years ago and mammals about 250 million years ago. Dinosaurs flourished from about 200 to 65 million years ago. Modern flowering plants appeared about 35 million years ago. Finally, hominids appeared from 6 to 2 million years ago.

According to the theory of evolution, the following factors are involved in one species changing into a new species (*macroevolution*). Variation in the members of a species is introduced by sexual reproduction and mutations. *Mutation* refers to random changes in genes which introduce new traits to the species. Sexual reproduction generates an enormous amount of variation within a population. Sexual reproduction leads to new combinations of traits; and at a given time, it is probably much more important than mutations. When a part of a species' population is isolated from the rest of the population, then these variables can become important to survival. *Plate tectonics* (the theory that the earth's crust is divided into thirteen mobile plates) can result in geographic isolation. At the boundary between colliding plates, mountain ranges can arise, changing the climate from wet to dry, from hot to cold. In these new environments, certain members of the population may have traits that allow them to survive the new conditions better: they reproduce more efficiently; and ultimately, a new species should form. This natural selection results in the *survival of the fittest*.

Today there is a philosophical triumph of Darwinism in all sciences. Most scientists work from an assumption that only naturalistic processes can be used to explain observations. In biology adaptation to the environment has replaced design. Chance, within the constraints imposed by the physical world, has replaced purpose. Is this triumph justified? Let us examine the evidences given to support Darwinian evolution to answer this question.

Evidences for Darwinian Evolution

Below are listed some observations that have been used to support Darwinian evolution. After each observation, the interpretation to support Darwinian evolution will be given, followed by an alternative interpretation.

1. Fossil Record

Observations. Most organisms preserved as fossils were buried under layers of mud or sand that later turned to rock. Relatively few species are preserved. Oldest rocks contain the simplest forms of life that differ from species living today. Essentially all extinct and living body forms (phyla) emerge in the fossil record at the base of the Cambrian rock layer about 570 million years ago. Of the about one hundred new body forms that appeared in the Cambrian period, only thirty phyla remain today. After the diversification of the body forms in the Cambrian, younger rocks have fossils that show a "top-down" pattern of diversification in the fossils. Using the established body forms, there is an increase in the number of classes, followed by an increase in the number of orders, followed by an increase in the number of families, and so on.[1]

The fossil record indicates the occurrence of mass extinctions. For example, the Permian extinction some 200 million years ago resulted in about 96 percent of species becoming extinct. After such extinctions, no new phyla (body forms) appear in the fossil record. Rather, the fossil pattern again shows the "top-down" pattern of diversification based on the established body forms. The fossil record also contains what appear to be transitional forms between the taxonomic categories. Examples are *Archaeopteryx,* which has reptile and bird properties, and *Basilosaurus,* which has the body of a whale with hind legs. Although the previous discussion concerned changes in the fossil record, in other cases there appears to be little change (*stasis*) in the fossil record. For example, some species are *living fossils* since they seem to be little changed from their earliest fossil records. Examples, with the earliest date of their fossils, include: horseshoe crabs (500 million years ago), crocodiles (200 million years ago), and coelacanth fish (350 million years ago).

Darwinian Evolutionary Interpretation. There are two interpretations for the fossil record. Evolutionists favoring *gradualism* say that the fossil record shows a progression from the earliest simple organism to complex organisms alive today. Transitional forms reveal a common ancestry between groups of animals such as reptiles and birds. A second interpretation is *punctuated equilibrium,* which assumes that evolution occurs in spurts between long periods showing little evolutionary change. Both of these views would agree that these changes occur only by natural processes.

Alternative Interpretation. The fossil record seems to indicate variations on the theme of a few body forms. Since these body forms do not appear to overlap in the fossil record, these body forms could indicate intelligent design. Once these body forms were established, life seems to have some plasticity (ability to adapt and change) to fill all available ecological niches.

2. Geographic Distribution of Species

Observations. Oceanic islands arose from the sea floor and have never been connected to the mainland. Hawaii, Tahiti, and the

Galapagos Islands are examples. Native species found on oceanic islands are those that can easily travel over long stretches of water: flying insects, bats, birds, plants whose seed can float. For example, the Galapagos Islands do not have any native land mammals or amphibians (frogs and toads). The species of oceanic islands are most similar to those on the nearest mainland, even if the climate is different. The Galapagos Islands are dry and rocky, while Ecuador has a wet tropic coast, yet there are similar organisms on each. The Galapagos Islands have thirteen species of finches, which is more than any continent. All these species are unique to the Galapagos Islands.

Darwinian Evolutionary Interpretation. A limited number of species came to the island and developed into new species to occupy all environments.

Alternative Interpretation. This could be an example of variation on a design with adaptation to fill all available ecological niches.

3. Embryology

Observations. Embryology is the study of the ways organisms develop during the earliest stages of life. The appearance of the early embryos of all vertebrates are very similar in appearance during some stage of their development. As an embryo, mammals form three types of kidneys in succession. In mammals, the first two perform no function and break down. In the embryos of fish, amphibians, and reptiles, one of these first two types of kidneys becomes the mature kidneys of these animals. A human fetus grows a coat of hair that is usually shed before birth.

Darwinian Evolutionary Interpretation. The interpretation is stated as "ontogeny recapitulates the phylogeny," or the developmental stages of an organism reflects its evolutionary history. Thus, mammals are retaining some of the developmental features of their evolutionary ancestors.

Alternative Interpretation. Even though the vertebrate embryos have similar appearance and developmental stages, they always end up as the expected vertebrate. They are developing according to a genetic plan. A plan implies a planner.

4. Homologous Structures

Observations. Comparative anatomy studies have revealed that vertebrates have a fundamental likeness in body architecture. The appendicular skeletons of frogs, horses, and humans have similar arrangement of bones. The major muscles of vertebrates are similar and perform the same function. Both of these cases are examples of *homologous structures.*

Darwinian Evolutionary Interpretation. Homologous structures imply a common ancestor.

Alternative Interpretation. The homologous structures are the result of a common design that has been changed by natural or supernatural modifications.

5. Vestigial Organs

Observations. A *vestigial organ* is a bodily part or organ that is small or degenerate in comparison to one more fully developed in other animals. Examples are cavefish, which are blind but still have eyes; porpoises and pythons with a pelvic girdle; humans with a rudimentary tail with a complete set of muscles for wagging it; and humans with an appendix.

Darwinian Evolutionary Interpretation. The vestigial organs reflect some earlier evolutionary stage for the organism at which time the organ had a function.

Alternative Interpretation. In some cases, so-called vestigial organs have been shown to have a function; for example, the appendix has some immune system function. Other cases could again indicate a common design with modification.

6. Biochemistry

Observations. All organisms use the same biochemical molecules, including DNA (genetic code), ATP (energy storage molecules), and enzymes (catalysts). Comparison of structures of biochemical molecules between species reveals some interesting relationships. Cytochrome c is the molecule used to synthesize the energy molecule ATP. The following number of amino acid sequence differences are noted between the cytochrome c molecule of a human and monkey (1), duck (11), and yeast (51). Analysis of the DNA sequences reveals the following differences between a human and chimpanzee (2.5 percent) and lemurs (42 percent).

Darwinian Evolutionary Interpretation. The similarity between the biochemical molecules implies a common ancestry. The more similar the chemical structure of the molecules, the more related are the two animals. Thus, humans would be more related to chimpanzees than lemurs. Comparison of biochemical molecule structure differences can be used to create an evolutionary tree.

Alternative Interpretation. This is another example of common design.

7. Current Observation of Evolution

Observations. Certain species undergo physiological changes due to humans causing disturbances in the environment. Disease-causing bacteria can develop a resistance to drug therapy. Before the industrial revolution, most peppered moths in England were white with black spots. This caused the moth to blend in with the lichens that covered the tree trunks. There were only a few black peppered moths. During the industrial revolution, most trees became blackened. The number of light-colored moths declined, while the number of black moths increased.

Darwinian Evolutionary Interpretation. This is an example of rapid change in response to an environmental change. "Natural selection has favored the dark form of the peppered moth in areas subject to severe air pollution, perhaps because on darkened trees they are less easily seen by moth-eating birds."[2]

Alternative Interpretation. These are examples of microevolution or changes within a species. The peppered moth example has been in biology textbooks for decades.[3] Recently a book was published which showed that the heart of the pepper moth example is incorrect.[4] The peppered moth does not rest on trees, and thus the change in distribution between black-and-white varieties has nothing to do with the color of the trees. Also, pictures of the peppered moth resting on trees have been shown to be staged. At present, scientists do not understand the change in the distribution of the peppered moth varieties.

8. Artificial Selection

Observations. Animal and plant breeders can produce many different varieties. An example is the many different breeds of dogs which have been developed.

Darwinian Evolutionary Interpretation. Darwin used this as an example of artificial selection which corresponds to natural selection. He believed that this artificial selection would eventually lead to enough change to produce a new species (macroevolution).

Alternative Interpretation. This is another example of microevolution. No new species has ever been produced. Also, these breeds have been guided by an intelligence, man.

Major Problems for Darwinian Evolution

Darwinian evolution is the attempt to explain the origin and development of life by materialistic means. Darwinian evolution proposes that everything about life, from the function of DNA to the structure of the largest dinosaur, resulted from the nature of matter and the laws of nature. As discussed in chapter 9, Darwinian evolution also denies a purpose to the development of life. There are at least three problems for the materialism and purposelessness of Darwinian evolution: information, irreducible complexity, and anthropic principles. It must be remembered that even if these three problems remove the materialistic basis for Darwinian evolution, they do not eliminate the possibility of evolution, of change in living organisms. It would mean that scientists would have to consider modifying evolution to include Intelligent Design.

Information

DNA (deoxyribonucleic acid) is a double helical molecule found in the nucleus of cells. DNA contains the master blueprint, in coded form, of an organism. The code is written with a four-letter alphabet called the bases. The bases are projected from the double helical backbone. The four bases and their one-letter designation are adenine (A), cytosine (C), guanine (G), and thymine (T). DNA carries instructions for the synthesis of proteins. Proteins, made of amino acids, serve as muscles, enzymes, hormones, antibodies, and structural elements in organisms. A gene is a specific portion of the DNA molecule that codes for a particular protein. Combinations of three bases, called a codon, specify for one amino acid. A segment of DNA might look like this: CGTTACCCTCAG . . . ATTCAC. In this example, the triplet TAC is the codon for a chain initiation signal, while the triplet ATT is the codon for a chain termination signal. The triplet CCT is the codon for the amino acid valine, which is the first amino acid in the protein insulin, which is made of 51 amino acid units. The code has to be in the correct order so that the 51 amino acids are assembled in the right sequence or something other than insulin will be synthesized. Insulin is a small protein; on the other hand, a large protein like hemoglobin contains a total of 574 amino acids.

What is the source of this information? What determined that a certain codon triplet would be a start signal or a stop signal?

How are the codons arranged in the right order to make a particular protein? What was the source of the information? Information is different from (independent of) matter. As an example, let us consider the information in this chapter. First an intelligence (the author) came up with the information which was stored in his brain. This information was then transferred to a yellow pad, was transferred from the yellow pad to a computer chip, subsequently to this book, and is now being transferred to the reader's brain. Thus, the information is independent of the medium. Changing the medium does not change the value of the information. Darwinian evolution has not successfully answered the question, "How can information only arise from matter and physical laws?"

Irreducible Complexity

Charles Darwin stated, "If it could be demonstrated that any complex organ existed which could not possibly have formed by numerous successive, slight modifications, my theory would absolutely break down."[5] Michael Behe in his book *Darwin's Black Box* presents biochemical structures which he believes are too complex to function unless all the parts are present. Behe proposes that the biochemistry involved with vision, blood clotting, and cellular transport are systems that are too complex to develop piecemeal. As a mousetrap can only function when all its parts are present, Behe proposes that these biochemical systems can only function as a complete unit. If he is correct, then how did these irreducibly complex systems arise only from matter and physical laws? Behe says that Intelligent Design must be included to explain these irreducible complex systems.

An argument against "irreducible complexity" is the paradox that because we cannot explain something does not mean that it does not have a physical explanation. A preindustrial person looking at a Boeing 747 might conclude that no one could conceive of something so complex, yet the plane arose from only ninety years of progressive design. Nature has had 3.5 billion years to tinker with living organisms. Of course, this argument does involve an intelligence (mankind) in the progressive development of the 747. Biochemists are beginning to propose "reasonable" solutions to some of Behe's examples. These proposals represent the greatest danger of irreducible complexity—the tendency for it to become another "god-of-the-gaps" theory. The supporters of irreducible complexity must formulate it in such a way that a biochemical explanation for one or more examples will not undermine the whole process.

Anthropic Principles

The Anthropic Principles or coincidences were discussed in chapter 6. At least twenty-six anthropic coincidences have been identified. These imply that the universe was fine-tuned for the existence of life. The challenge to scientists who propose a purposeless, natural cause for life is to explain this fine-tuning of the universe. Why does the universe appear to be fine-tuned for the appearance of life and humans?

Evolution: Another Look

It is difficult to write about something as emotion-laden as evolution. Hopefully, the reader will not leave this chapter thinking either that evolution perfectly explains everything or that evolution explains nothing. Why is evolution so emotional-laden? There are many ways to use the word *evolution:* (1) change over time, (2) relation of organisms through a common ancestry, (3) a theory giving a mechanism to explain all the change, (4) naturalistic tenet that everything is the result of purposeless and natural process.

At its simplest, evolution means change through time. One speaks of evolution of a political party, evolution of automobile design, or evolution of a star. Yet the fossil record shows stasis as well as change. Thus, one cannot say that everything changes.

Evolution is also a hypothesis that all organisms are related through a common ancestry. This is an attempt to interpret the observed common characteristics of organisms. Although the genetic code of all organisms is similar, that observation is not the same as establishing the common genetic ancestry of all life. Expressing evolution as this hypothesis is not an established fact but an inference.

Evolution is also a theory to provide a mechanism to explain similarities and diversities observed in organisms. Since mutations and natural selection have been shown to produce some biological variations, Darwinian evolutionists have proposed that mutations and natural selection are the mechanism that produced the similarities and diversities observed in organisms. The mechanism of evolution is the area where serious debate continues among most biologists; the debate is not over whether evolution occurs but over how it occurs.

The word *evolution* is also used in a philosophical manner when it is stated that everything is the result of purposeless and natural process. As discussed in chapter 1, such a statement moves out of the realm of science and cannot be analyzed by the scientific method.

The usage of the word *evolution* today usually includes a combination of one or more of these meanings. In many instances, one person may be using one meaning of evolution while the other person replies using another meaning. No wonder conversations involving evolution can become so emotional.

A final thing to remember is that evolution is considered a very successful scientific theory. Evolution, with its concepts that "things change with time" and "organisms are related," has been very successful in organizing a lot of scientific observations. As Ernst Mayr explained, "The theory of evolution is quite rightly called the greatest unifying theory in biology. The diversity of organisms, similarities and differences between kinds of organisms, patterns of distribution and behavior, adaptation and interaction, all this was merely a bewildering chaos of facts until given meaning by evolutionary theory."[6] The observations and themes of many different disciplines are linked by evolutionary theory: genetics, animal geography, plate tectonics, radioisotope dating, taxonomy, cosmogony, and so on. Evolutionary theory allows scientists to put all these disciplines together into one "big picture." Evolution is viewed as one of the most successful theories of modern science, in terms of unification, problem-solving strategy, and fecundity.

Summary

We have observed that any theory about life on earth must deal with the diversity of life, the similarity of organisms, and the fossil record. Most scientists feel that the theory of evolution adequately explains all of these variables. Most biology textbooks present the theory of evolution as a materialistic, purposeless process. We saw that there was room for design and purpose in all the observations that evolutionists use to support their theory. We also saw that the materialistic, purposeless presentation of evolution does not satisfactorily address how genes contain information, the irreducible complexity of biochemical structures, or the Anthropic Principles. Finally, we observed that evolution is viewed as a very successful concept in linking together ideas from many different disciplines.

CHAPTER EIGHT

MADE IN THE IMAGE OF GOD

THE ACCOUNT OF CREATION IN GENESIS 1 CONTAINS SEVERAL repet-titive patterns. Perhaps the most striking pattern is the phrase, "And then God began to say, Let [something] begin to be" (see Gen. 1:3, 6, 9, 14). God willed the light, firmament, land and sea, and heavenly bodies into existence. God expressed the idea, and it took shape. Centuries before Plato, the Hebrew Scriptures expressed the priority of the Idea over the Image.

When the creation account moves from inanimate matter to life, however, a startling change in the pattern occurs. God does not say, "Let there be grass on the earth," or "Let there be moving creatures that have life in the waters," or "Let there be living creatures on the earth." Instead of following the established pattern, God creates life in a different way. He involves what he has already created in the bringing forth of life: "And God said, Let the earth bring forth grass, the herb yielding seed, and the fruit tree yielding fruit after his kind, whose seed is in itself, upon the earth: and it was so. And the earth brought forth grass, and herb yielding seed after his kind, and the tree yielding fruit, whose seed was in itself, after his kind: and God saw that it was good" (Gen. 1:11–12 KJV).

God brings a prior creation into responsibility for cooperating to accomplish his purpose. Instead of willing plants into existence, God wills that the earth produce the plants, and the earth complies. The will of God also included provision for the continuing appearance of life through reproduction signified by seed, and later by procreation of animals.

The creation of plants establishes a new pattern for the creation of life forms. God wills for the earth to produce plants. Likewise, he wills for the waters and the earth to produce animal life. It does not happen as a spontaneous, natural occurrence. It happens as a result of the earth and the sea responding to the will of God. Though the waters brought forth animal life (1:20), God created that life (1:21). In other words, Genesis emphasizes that regardless of the circumstances under which life appeared, it happened as a result of the creative activity of God.

Some translations of the Bible make a careful distinction between the Hebrew words for "make" and "create" which are found interspersed throughout Genesis 1. The word for create (*bara*) refers to the exclusive activity of God (Gen. 1:1, 21, 27; 2:3–4). The word for make (*asah*), on the other hand, does not imply the exclusive activity of God (Gen. 1:7, 16, 25–26, 31; 2:2). Nonetheless, even when God is one step removed, Genesis emphasizes that even his "making" is "creating." For instance, God determines to *make* man in his image, but when it happens, Genesis gives a threefold emphasis that man as male and female was *created* by God (Gen. 1:26–27).

The Genesis 1 account of creation lays out a series of phases of creation which involve qualitative differences, beginning with the difference between light and darkness, air and water, water and earth. Plant life represents another significant qualitative difference in creation from inanimate matter. The introduction of animal life represents another qualitative distinction from plant life. The creative activity of God described in Genesis 1 concludes with another qualitative distinction. God determines to "make" an animal in his own *image*.

What is the image of God? What is any image? Again, Genesis 1 anticipates a central element of Plato's thought by several centuries. Plato taught that an Image is a mere representation of an Ideal. It is not necessary to pursue Plato's development of the distinction between an Ideal and its Image to appreciate the qualitative distinction between God and people. A statue is an image of a person. By viewing a statue, someone can develop an impression of some of the aspects of the person the statue represents. Yet the statue cannot move, think, talk, feel, or experience the host of other experiences essential to being a person. To say that people are made in the image of God is to say that a gigantic qualitative gulf exists between people and God.

To say that people are made in the image of God is to say they are not God. This statement may seem simplistic to many who read the Bible from a Christian perspective, yet over a billion people believe they are inseparable from God. Major forms of Hinduism and Buddhism would hold such a view. The Genesis 1 account of creation speaks to this theological issue by making two distinctions with respect to people. They are made qualitatively different from other animals because they are made in the image of God. But because they are made in the image of God, they are qualitatively different from God.

The word for "people" or the "human race" in Hebrew reflects the relationship of people to the rest of creation. The collective Hebrew noun for male and female humans is *adam*. The Hebrew word *adam* comes from the Hebrew word for "dirt," the feminine noun *adamah*. The relationship of people to the earth raises another serious theological issue. From the earliest times until the present, groups of people in various cultures have believed that the earth itself is divine and living, as the Great Mother. Forms of this belief have involved ancient religion in India and Canaan, the Artemis worship of the Ephesians, the Druid worship of the Celts, animistic religions of Africa and the Americas, and contemporary feminist and ecologist religion in the United States and western Europe.

While God may create life from earth and water, the Genesis 1 account makes clear that the earth is not among the living, reproducing work of creation. The earth takes no initiative, nor does it "give birth." Genesis 1 does not concern the scientific dimension of the nature of life so much as it establishes the theological understanding of the origins of life. In the presence of many rival religious explanations of the origin of life, Genesis 1 emphasizes that people and all other living things are the result of the creative work of God, regardless of how he may have used the earth and the sea in the process.

In a culture dominated for fifteen hundred years by a Christian worldview, one might easily suppose that the account of the creation of people is about people. In a much larger world with many competing worldviews, however, the striking feature of the account of the creation of people focuses on what it tells us about God. It is only about people because people are made in the image of God. When these lines were written in a Hebrew community thousands of years ago, the world had numerous explanations for the origins of life, and more numerous explanations of what kind of God or gods exist. As the West enters a post-Christian era, the old Western worldview that assumed a Creator-creature relationship between God and people has begun to fade as Christianity loses its favored religion status. In this context, the ancient focus of the creation accounts once again speaks directly to the religious pluralism of society. It emphasizes that people are not an aspect of God. Rather, they are creatures made by God.

Whether people are an aspect of God or creatures of God has profound implications for human existence on earth. If people are the result of the creative activity of God based on God's intentional, self-conscious decision to make people, then creation results from the purpose of God. People have a purpose, and this purpose emerges from the Creator-creature relationship. If, on the other hand, people are aspects of a single spiritual unity of which all things are a part, but which lacks self-consciousness, then life has no purpose. It merely exists.

The creation account establishes the basis for human purpose and value. The will of God exercised in creation establishes purpose, while the judgment of God exercised in the evaluation of each aspect of creation establishes value. God decided to make something ("Let us make . . ."). God made what he envisioned ("Let there be . . ."). Finally, God evaluated what he made ("God saw that it was good"). Purpose and value suggest a destiny. The accounts of the creation of people lay the foundation for understanding the purpose and destiny of the human race, which is tied inseparably to the relationship of people to God.

The second chapter of Genesis begins to develop the idea of the purpose and destiny of humanity in relationship to God and in relationship to one another. The second account of creation in Genesis stands in remarkable contrast to the first account and must be understood to make an intentional contrast, because the two accounts appear side by side. Chapter 2 reverses the order in which God creates life and separates the creation of male and female humans. In chapter 1, man is created as male and female in a single act of creation, but in chapter 2 several events come between the creation of the two.

Both chapters acknowledge the creation of the heavens and the earth as coming before the creation of life. Chapter 2 makes no mention of the creation of light, the separation of light and darkness, and the separation of waters and dry land. Rather than presenting a different view on these matters, however, chapter 2 appears to assume the work of creation and separation which establish the order of the heavens and the earth. Chapter 2 is not concerned with the origins of the universe or even the origins of life. Chapter 1 has clearly established the origins. Instead, chapter 2 is concerned with the meaning and purpose of life. With the heavens and the earth established, the accounts of life follow these sequences:

Chapter 1	Chapter 2
1. Plants (v. 11)	Man (v. 7)
2. Sea creatures and birds (v. 20)	Plants (vv. 8–9)
3. Land creatures (v. 24)	Beasts and birds (v. 19)
4. People (v. 26)	Woman (v. 22)

Some translations of the Bible try to resolve the contrast by changing the tense of the English verbs in chapter 2. For instance, after the creation of the man, the New International Version (NIV) states that "the LORD God *had planted* a garden in the east" (2:8, author's emphasis). This translation suggests that plant life had been arranged before the formation of the man. Later, the NIV states that "the LORD God *had formed* out of the ground all the beasts of the field and all the birds of the air" (2:19, author's emphasis). Once again, the use of the past perfect verb translation suggests that the animals had been made prior to the creation of the man. This approach makes it possible to harmonize the sequence of creation in chapter 2 with the sequence of creation in chapter 1. Unfortunately, this approach does damage to the explanation in chapter 2 itself which states that no plants existed when God made the man (2:5–7) and that the man had no living company (2:18–20).

The King James Version took an entirely different approach. It gives a more literal translation of the Hebrew verbs. After the creation of the man, it states that "the LORD God *planted* a garden eastward in Eden" (2:8, author's emphasis). After God decided that it was not good for the man to be alone, the King James Version states that "out of the ground the LORD God *formed* every beast of the field, and every fowl of the air" (2:19, author's emphasis).

Although the New International Version is recognized as a conservative translation of the Bible, it reflects the attitude of the modern era with respect to science and faith. The attitude affects conservative Christians as much as liberal Christians. Conservative Christians believe that the Bible is the Word of God. They also live in a culture that venerates the success of modern science and that views scientific knowledge as the most reliable and valid form of knowledge. Therefore, the Bible must be accurate scientifically to be valid. When the Bible and science make different statements about an issue, liberal Christians will tend to dismiss the biblical statement as the culturally biased opinion of a person who lived a long time ago, while conservative Christians will tend to dismiss the scientific view as the wrong science. Conservative Christians will adopt the biblical statement as the correct scientific statement, because for the Bible to be true, they reason that it must be scientifically accurate. Oddly enough, this attitude makes scientific knowledge the criteria for judging the validity of biblical revelation. Both liberals and conservatives tend to operate from the bias that for the Bible to be true, it must be scientifically accurate. This bias reflects the view of modernity.

The translators of the King James Version did not operate under the biases of the modern world with its veneration of scientific discovery. The validity of the Bible rested in its being revelation from God. It could make statements about reality without these statements necessarily dealing with the scientific dimension of reality. The fact that chapter 1 and chapter 2 of Genesis contain dramatic reversals of sequence does not suggest an error. For one who believes in revelation, it suggests that God is making a point.

It is inconceivable that the difference between chapter 1 and chapter 2 escaped the notice of the one who originally placed them next to each other as the beginning of the Hebrew Scriptures. Rather than harmonizing the difference, perhaps one can find in the difference a clue to the meaning of the passages. The two passages suggest that the timing and sequence of creation are not the point of the accounts since the two accounts cancel each other out with respect to time and sequence. In the first passage, humanity represents the culmination of creation. In the second passage, the world is made hospitable for the man. Both passages declare what kind of God exists and explain the relationship of humanity to God and the rest of creation. The Genesis accounts explain how people fit into the universe. They provide the basis for human purpose, and this purpose centers in relationships of the most intimate kind between male and female and with God.

Formed of Clay

The Bible describes life as having a beginning. At some point in time, life appeared for the first time in physical reality. There was a point in time before which physical life did not exist. In terms of the development of life, there was a point before which animal life did not exist. Sea life appeared before mammals, or "the beasts of the field." At the tail end of the complexity of life, God made people.

Despite the idea of a definite beginning to each form of life, however, the Bible does not contain a static view of the creation of life. Though the Bible speaks of God creating the initial life forms and the process of reproduction, it also indicates that God remains intimately involved in the creation of life. In fact, the same description of the making of the first man in Genesis 2 is used throughout the Bible as a description of God's involvement in the procreation of every person. While Genesis 1 contains no description of how God created human life "in his own image," Genesis 2 pictures God forming mankind from the red clay like a potter fashioning a pot. Throughout the Bible, this same picture appears to describe God's creation of every other human. All people are made of clay by God (Job 4:19; 10:8–12; Isa. 29:16; 45:9; 64:8; Lam. 4:2; Rom. 9:20–21; 2 Cor. 4:7), yet the Bible just as steadfastly asserts that God made each person within his or her mother's womb (Job 10:18; Ps. 139:13–16; Isa. 44:2; Jer. 1:5).

Contemporary readers take the reference to the continuing creation of people from clay as a metaphor, while they would tend to take the reference to creation of people within their mother's womb as literal. The references to human formation from clay harken back to Genesis 2, but one must ask if the Genesis 2 account was ever intended to be taken as anything more than a metaphor for the creation that occurred in Genesis 1. The reversal of the order of the creation of life in the two accounts strongly suggests that Genesis 2 has made the same use of the clay/dust image as the rest of the Bible, yet simply calling Genesis 2 a metaphor dismisses it as not truthful or real knowledge for people disposed to think of metaphors as merely poetic opinion.

Chapter 2, and all the other references to people as clay who will return to the dust, makes a dogmatic statement about the nature of people and their tenuous hold on life. People are composed of the same kind of matter as the rest of the earth and have the same breath of life as the other animals (Eccles. 3:18–21). People have a brief, transitory existence from dust to dust. Unlike Greek thought or Eastern thought, the Bible teaches that people do not have an eternal origin before their physical life. They are born and they die. The "breath of life" is not a "spark of the divine." Yet this frail life differs from all other animal life in one respect: It is made in the image of God.

In the first three chapters of Genesis may be found the three great issues that *existentialist philosophy* has identified as the cause of humanity's greatest anxiety: the dread of meaninglessness, the dread of loneliness, and the dread of death. These are not scientific concerns but spiritual concerns. Oddly enough, many adherents to existentialism, particularly that form which developed in France and Germany, do not believe in God. It is not necessary to believe in the cure, however, to be aware of the problem. Chapter 1 of Genesis describes a purposeful creation. Chapter 2 describes the basis for relationship. Chapter 3 describes the alienation that destroys the relationship of people with God and with each other.

Chapter 3 explains that the problems of humanity derive from a broken relationship with the Creator, a condition the Bible refers to as *sin*. Sin describes the nature of humans in contrast to the nature of God. Sin is a condition unique to religions that recognize God as the Creator. Islam, Judaism, and Christianity understand sin as a category in relation to God. Sin includes what humans do to injure relationship with God. Cut off from God, people are cut off from their purpose. Life such as this ends in death. Finally, we have a scientifically verifiable condition.

Instead of accepting the condition of death, however, the Bible is concerned with the restoration of the relationship with God which provides meaning and purpose for individuals, and the healing of relationships between people. Ultimately, the restored relationship with God leads to a quality of life that transcends death.

One of the most familiar psalms of David explores the meaning of life in the context of the enormity of creation:

> O LORD our Lord, how excellent is thy name in all the earth! who hast set thy glory above the heavens. Out of the mouths of babes and sucklings hast thou ordained strength because of thine enemies that thou mightest still the enemy and the avenger. When I consider thy heavens, the work of thy fingers, the moon and the stars, which thou hast ordained; What is man, that thou art mindful of him? and the son of man, that thou visitest him? For thou hast made him a little lower than the angels, and hast crowned him with glory and honour. Thou madest him to have dominion over the works of thy hands; thou hast put all things under his feet: All sheep and oxen, yea, and

the beasts of the field; The fowl of the air, and the fish of the sea, and whatsoever passeth through the paths of the seas. O LORD our Lord, how excellent *is* thy name in all the earth! (Ps. 8:1–9 KJV).

The question, "What is man, that thou art mindful of him?" poses the purpose question in terms of identity and relationship to God. In other words, David asks, "Who am I in this great big universe?" The answer to the question involves the purpose for which God created humanity, giving people a stewardship responsibility to care for the earth and everything in it. David realizes his identity and purpose in relationship with God.

Divine Incarnation

For the early church, this passage took on new meaning. In Christ they saw the ultimate fulfillment of what it meant to be made "a little lower than the angels" and "crowned with glory and honor." They regarded the passage as more than a statement about humanity in general or even David in particular. They saw it focusing on the Messiah for whom God "put all *things* under his feet." The writer of Hebrews explores the passage as the ultimate intersection of God and humanity. The destiny of humanity is tied to the manifestation of God in the created order. Human destiny is tied to relationship with the Creator. In Christ, God became one of his creatures.

In describing the *incarnation,* or the coming of God in the flesh, Hebrews interprets a portion of Psalm 8: "In putting everything under him, God left nothing that is not subject to him. Yet at present we do not see everything subject to him. But we see Jesus, who was made a little lower than the angels, now crowned with glory and honor because he suffered death, so that by the grace of God he might taste death for everyone" (Heb. 2:8b–9).

Aristotle would have been at home with this way of talking. Aristotle believed that knowledge comes through what we can experience through our senses. This passage from Hebrews explains that the incarnation makes knowledge of God possible. We cannot see or understand in what sense the exalted Lord has all of creation under his control. It certainly does not look this way, unless God is some sort of demon. Rather than speculating on what kind of God exists, Hebrews points to Jesus and says that the physical manifestation of God gives the most profound clue as to what kind of God exists.

The apostle Paul would discuss the same issue in similar terms. In his letter to the Philippians Paul said:

> Let this mind be in you, which was also in Christ Jesus: Who, being in the form of God, thought it not robbery to be equal with God: But made himself of no reputation, and took upon him the form of a servant, and was made in the likeness of men: And being found in fashion as a man, he humbled himself, and became obedient unto death, even the death of the cross. Wherefore God also hath highly exalted him, and given him a name which is above every name: that at the name of Jesus every knee should bow, of things in heaven, and things in earth, and things under the earth; And that every tongue should confess that Jesus Christ is Lord, to the glory of God the Father (Phil. 2:5–11 KJV).

Paul used the language of Aristotle to speak of the two natures of Christ. For Aristotle, *Form* represented the perfect, eternal reality. Christ had the form of God. He then took on the form of a servant. In Aristotelian thought, the idea of being the Form rather than the Substance would suggest that Christ took the nature of what humanity was intended to be. By being in the form of a servant, but also in the likeness of men, his physical manifestation could point to his spiritual nature.

The Image of God

The Ten Commandments begin with a strong declaration about who God is, followed by the commandment not to make idols, or physical representatives of the divine (Deut. 5:6–8). This disgust for the physical depiction of God finds reinforcement throughout the Hebrew Scripture as well as in the New Testament (cf. Acts 17:24–31). God is not physical. God created the physical order, but God does not belong to the physical order. God relates to the physical order, but God is not subject to the physical order. In contrast with the physical world of creation, Jesus said that God is Spirit. In whatever sense people are made in the image of God, this image or likeness refers to the sense in which people are like God. People are like all other animals in many respects related to the physical world, but people are like God in many respects related to the spiritual world.

Most English translations of the Bible draw a distinction in Genesis between the forms of life that God created. The King James translation refers to the sea animals as "the moving creature" (1:20), land animals as "the living creature" (1:24), and human life as "a living soul" (2:7). The NIV follows the practice of most modern translations and speaks of sea and land animals both as "living creatures" (1:20, 24). It refers to the human, however, as a "living being" (2:7). The Hebrew text does not make this distinction. All animal life, whether human or beast or fish, is *nephesh hayah* (literally "a breathing being").[1] With respect to physical life, the Bible teaches that people are like all other animals. English translations have attempted to make the theological distinction between people and other animals based on the animals being made "creatures" while people were made "souls." The original Hebrew of the Genesis accounts, however, makes the distinction based on "the image of God."

The Jewish rabbis of Alexandria translated the Hebrew Scriptures into Greek following the conquests of Alexander the Great. In this version known as the Septuagint (LXX), they translated *nephesh* with the Greek word *psyche*. *Psyche* originally meant "breath" as *nephesh* did, but Plato and other philosophers used the word to represent the philosophical/theological idea of an immortal, preexistent aspect of human life which returned to merge with God at death. This concept of the human *psyche* being a part of God dramatically conflicts with the biblical teaching of created life which has a beginning and an end.[2]

The Greek philosophical idea has had a confusing influence on theology in the West and especially in the English-speaking world. The English word *soul* has served to translate the Greek word *psyche*. In early English, the soul refers to "the principal of life in man or animals" and represents a good translation of the Hebrew *nephesh* and the early Greek *psyche*.[3] Unfortunately, "soul" also came to represent the Platonic idea of the immortal preexistent aspect of people that returns to God. When theologians insert the Greek philosophical idea into the text, they tend to arrive at the notion that people *possess* souls. In Genesis, people *are* souls. A soul is not a part of divinity implanted into a person. A soul *is* a person.

In areas which have preserved a strong linguistic connection with English without significant influence by immigration from other language groups, the plain meaning of soul still remains. It is not uncommon in the South to hear someone remark of an event which has poor attendance, "Not a soul was there." The statement is not complicated by the philosophical concept of the *psyche* in Platonism.

The distinction between people and the other animals does not lie in an artificial distinction between "souls" and "creatures." It lies in what it means for God to make people in his image. People are souls who have a body and a spirit. The human body and human spirit exist alive as a unity. A body without a spirit is a corpse, while a spirit without a body is a ghost. While each may theoretically exist without the other, the prospect is most unattractive. The spirit at death is but a shadow consigned with its body to the pit. The body decays to dust in the earth. The body allows people to experience the physical world, while the spirit allows them to transcend it. The body affects the spirit, and the spirit affects the body. Through the human spirit, people have the capacity to relate to God who is a spirit. The human spirit is like the Spirit of God, but it is not God. It is like God in the same sense that my photograph is like me. It is an image of something far more.

Theologians and philosophers have tried to reduce the uniqueness of humans to a single dimension, the essential thing that separates people from the animals: language, love, laughter, shame. The idea of the image of God represents a far more complex matter, however, than one essential thing. In describing the human spirit, the Old Testament presents a variety of dimensions as different as taste is from sight. These different dimensions or domains of experience make up the complexity of the extent to which people bear the image of God.

While the domains might be described differently, since the Old Testament does not organize them into a single list, one may speak of six general domains. The human spirit involves emotions, intellect, character, will, imagination (or ability), and vitality. Each of these domains interacts dynamically with the others and with the physical body as a unity that defies reduction. Emotions influence the intellect in terms of how we think. Character influences our decisions. Vitality influences how well the other aspects of the spirit work. When we are tired or sick, our emotions fray or our intellect cannot concentrate.

Though people have physical substance through which the senses allow knowledge of the physical world, they experience life primarily through the spiritual dimension. Falling down the stairs is a physical experience, yet how we cope with the fall is a spiritual experience. Eating a meal is a physical experience that people share with the amoeba and the oyster. The physical process of nourishment to sustain life operates for all animals, but for humans it moves into the spiritual realm. Many animals prefer one food to another, but for humans it goes beyond preference. It becomes art. Humans ask questions about how they perform their animal functions in a physical world: how they provide shelter, food, and clothing. People reflect, evaluate, and create. People interpret and assign value to their physical experiences.

The Western philosophical worldview tends to separate the emotions from the intellect, the heart from the mind. The biblical worldview teaches that both emotions and intellect are aspects of the spirit. In the Bible, "heart" is used as a metaphor for "spirit." This connection appears in such passages as King David's psalm of repentance: "Create in me a clean heart, O God; and renew a right spirit within me" (Ps. 51:10 KJV). This connection does not necessarily mean that the Bible teaches that the intellectual functions take place in the heart. Rather, it emphasizes that the spiritual dimension has a dynamic relationship with the body. Today, we would say that the brain is the locus of activity for the spiritual dimension which modern people often call "the mind." Mind and brain are intimately related, but they are not the same.

While sin manifests itself in the physical world, it resides in the spiritual dimension. Sin describes the flawed aspect of the human spirit. Sin operates in each domain of the spirit and may affect another domain in a domino effect. Sin expresses itself through character in such ways as deceit, malice, jealousy, envy, unfaithfulness, and irresponsibility. Though these characteristics abide within a person, they have an impact on how people relate to others. Sin expresses itself through the intellect as bigotry, prejudice, narrow-mindedness, close-mindedness, and self-deceit. These characteristics have a profound impact on human behavior. To confuse matters, all of these expressions of sin may be localized so that a person is not always narrow-minded or jealous. Instances may be localized, which makes them easier to rationalize. Sin expresses itself through the will in terms of the failure of the will. People may know what to do and not do it. Conversely, they may resolve not to do something, yet do it anyway. Sin expresses itself through talents and abilities in terms of how people put those talents and abilities to use. People with the ability to stir the hearts of people may do it like Mother Theresa or Adolf Hitler.

In all of these cases, the difference lies in an external value imposed on creation from the outside. It is a value with which people agree or disagree. This value emerges from the purpose of God in creation and the evaluation of God in establishing the criteria for "the Good" (Gen. 1:4, 10, 12, 18, 21, 25, 31). Through the spiritual domain, people have the capacity for establishing their own sense of value in violation of God's established valuation of creation. This capacity results in the human behavior described as sinful acts. The third chapter of Genesis explores how sin manifests itself in the simplest fashion from a flawed thought process, to a revised value system, to a failure of the will, to a form of behavior that injures a relationship. Because of God's relationship to creation and because people are made in the image of God, all sin is a matter between people and God.

Regeneration

Nineteenth-century classical Protestant liberalism adopted a view of the inevitable progress and perfection of the human race through science, technology, and education. The civilized West had a mission to civilize the rest of the world and bring in the kingdom of God on earth. This understanding came crashing down in World War I with the slaughter of millions of people by the educated, civilized West, which had learned that science and technology could make mass murder economical on a large scale. Classical liberalism did not take the problem of sin seriously.

According to Jesus, people are not essentially divine; they are essentially physical even though they have a spiritual dimension. In order to have a meaningful existence beyond physical life, people must be born again (John 3:3). People in their present form are not finished, nor is their completion inevitable. Just as physical life must change to meet the challenges of a changing physical environment, spiritual life must change to meet the challenge of a changing spiritual environment. The Bible teaches that God is responsible for whatever twists and turns different physical organisms may take. It also teaches that God brings about the change that humans must undergo in order to live beyond physical death. Jesus explained that the same Spirit who caused creation in the beginning is the one who will transform a human spirit in a way that can be called a new birth.

Though God has entered his rest from the perspective of eternity, the Book of Hebrews teaches that humans have not yet reached this rest (Heb. 4:3–11). From the perspective of eternity, God looks back on the present and forward to the beginning. He has completed his work, yet the creation in time and space is not finished. The Bible teaches that the God who created people waits at the end of time as the destiny of people who agree to accept God as their destiny.

CHAPTER NINE

DIALOGUE ON THE ORIGIN OF LIFE

DURING THE MODERN AGE, DISCOVERING THE SECRET OF LIFE HAS replaced the medieval alchemists' search for the lodestone that would change base metal to gold. Long before Charles Darwin published his *Origin of the Species*, Mary Shelley published her *Frankenstein* (1818) in which she explored the horror of man-made life which has no connection with the rest of life created by God. Later in the nineteenth century, *Dr. Jekyll and Mr. Hyde* explored the idea of solving the problem of human evil through scientific means. During the latter twentieth century, we have seen science fiction close in on reality with test-tube babies, cloning, and genetic engineering of DNA molecules. Still, these ventures manipulate life; they do not create life.

What Is the Origin of Life?

The question of life is not simply a question about another feature of the physical or even the spiritual universe. It is a question about me. For every person, the question of the origin of life is a question about themselves.

Scientific View

Darwin speculated little on the origin of life. Since then, neo-Darwinism has postulated that life arose completely from natural chemical reactions. In the 1920s the Russian Alexander Oparin and the Englishman J. B. S. Haldane postulated that the early earth's atmosphere contained what chemists call "reducing gases" such as hydrogen, ammonia, and methane. They also assumed that the atmosphere contained practically no free oxygen. They further stated that the presence of energy (lightning, ultraviolet radiation, or volcanic eruptions) would cause these chemicals to combine to form the chemicals of life: sugars, amino acids, fatty acids, and nucleic acids (RNA or DNA). In 1950 Stanley Miller and Harold Urey at the University of Chicago sought experimentally to reproduce these conditions. In a closed glass container, they placed water (ocean), the gases hydrogen, methane, and ammonia (atmosphere), and an electric arc (lightning). After letting the reaction run for a week, they analyzed the contents of the reaction vessel. Among the many compounds formed, they found the biological molecules amino acids, fatty acids, and urea. At the 1959 Darwinian Centennial celebrations, the Miller-Urey experiment was touted as the triumph of neo-Darwinism.

The Miller-Urey experiment was also the high-water mark of origin-of-life experiments. Very little progress has been made since. Much criticism has developed about the experimental design and results:

- Geochemical studies suggest that the earth's early atmosphere was not reducing but contained gases such as carbon dioxide, nitrogen, and water vapor. Further studies indicated that oxygen was present, probably as a result of volcanic eruptions. If oxygen was present, it would cause the biomolecules to degrade (decompose).

- Human intervention is apparently needed for the Miller-Urey experiment to work. One thing that experimenters do is stop the reaction before the biological molecules react further to form nonbiological products. Another intervention involves using only short-wavelength ultraviolet radiation. Long-wavelength ultraviolet radiation degrades the products.

- The molecules of life can be made in two forms which are mirror images of each other. Chemists call these forms *optical isomers* and label one isomer as left-handed with the other labeled right-handed. In the Miller-Urey experiment, an equal amount of the left-handed and right-handed molecules are produced. Yet, nearly all naturally occurring amino acids are left-handed. No one has devised a natural way for only the left-handed amino acids to be synthesized.

- No one has devised a natural, spontaneous way for the amino acids to combine to form functioning proteins. Proteins are the actual biochemical molecules found in living organisms and are used for structure (collagen in bone), contraction (muscles), catalysts (enzymes), hormones (insulin), antibodies (gamma-globin), and transport (hemoglobin). Proteins have four different structures called primary, secondary, tertiary, and quaternary. The *primary structure* is the sequence of the amino acids which makes a long chain. A protein is a polymer containing up to twenty different amino acids that must be linked in the right sequence for a protein to function properly. For example, hemoglobin contains 574 amino acids. Sickle-cell hemoglobin differs from normal hemoglobin in only two out of these 574 amino acids.

- The *secondary structure* of a protein results from the chemical interactions between amino acids in the chain which creates a three-dimensional structure. One such structure is the alpha helix, a three-dimensional structure in the form of a right-handed screw. A *tertiary structure* results from further chemical interactions with the secondary structure components. This tertiary structure gives the protein a lock-and-key relationship to other molecules. By having a certain tertiary structure, the protein acts like a lock that only certain molecules can fit into like a key. Without the correct tertiary structure, the protein cannot catalyze specific chemical reactions. A *quaternary structure* results if the protein is composed on two or more chains of amino acids. Each chain has its own primary, secondary, and tertiary structure. In the quaternary structure, the chains are held together by chemical attractions. Both insulin (two chains) and hemoglobin (four chains) have quaternary structures. The change of two amino acids in sickle-cell hemoglobin affects all structural levels. To degrade or denature a protein is to change one or more of these structural levels.

Although chemical origin-of-life proposals are still being made, some scientists have concluded that the origin of life is beyond the reaches of the scientific method.

The Religious View

For the Christian, the question of the origin of life is quite simply answered: God made all living things. The creation of life came about as an intentional act of God. All life, not just human life, was created with a purpose. The Bible links life with value; in Genesis God declares life to be "good" (Gen. 1:12, 21, 25). Life is valuable to God in and of itself without the necessity of accomplishing something to justify its existence. The different orders of life also came into being as an intentional act of God. In broad strokes, Genesis describes the intentionality of God in creating all kinds of life in the three possible realms in which they can live: on land, in water, and in the air.

While the fact of God's creation of life is quite plain in the Bible, the manner of God's creation of life remains veiled. God planned it and caused it to happen, yet he used the earth and water he had already created to bring forth life. Was there something about the way earth and water and the rest of creation were planned that at the impulse of God, life would spring from them? Was the creation of life already planned in the very way God prepared the heavens and the earth beforehand?

The Bible also says that life did not appear all at once. The creation of life involves a sequence in which plant life preceded animal life and water life preceded land life. The Bible is silent about the relationship of forms of life to one another. The question does not appear to arise except in distinguishing between forms of life that exist, as Paul does in 1 Corinthians when he declares: "All flesh is not the same: Men have one kind of flesh, animals have another, birds another and fish another. There are also heavenly bodies and there are earthly bodies; but the splendor of the heavenly bodies is one kind, and the splendor of the earthly bodies is another" (1 Cor. 15:39–40). In this passage, however, Paul describes the change that takes place in humans at resurrection when they are transformed by God from one form of life (a child of the dust) to another form of life (a child of God). By analogy, Paul's example suggests that any changes which God brings about in creatures on earth would provide evidence for resurrection.

What Is the Origin of Human Life?

Does humanity differ from other forms of life in any qualitative way? We tend to see ourselves as the highest form of life. Yet, we wonder if we are alone in the universe as superior beings. What is our origin and how do we relate to the rest of life?

Scientific View

Neo-Darwinism views humans as any other animal and says that humans evolved from a common ancestor. Evidence for the evolution of humans, such as fossils and tools, is rare and often fragmented. In many cases, only part of a skull and a few other bones are found; nearly complete fossil skeletons are very rare. Thus, scientific theories about the evolution of humans is based on limited evidence. Although museum reconstructions may indicate otherwise, there is at present no detailed picture of early human life.

Physical anthropology, the study of human origins, probably involves a lot more speculation than other areas of science. For example, when a fossilized fragment—say a pelvic bone—is found that does not fit an idealized version of the pelvic bone of an ape or a human, can we say whether this fragment comes from an ape, human, or ape-human? Does this pelvic fossil indicate an evolutionary intermediate between apes and humans? If one "knew" that the specimen whose fossil had been found did evolve from ape to man, then the feature would represent an intermediate. But there is no way of knowing with the same certainty that a chemist "knows" that sodium plus chlorine changes to table salt. Physical anthropology will never have the certainty of chemistry. Thus, the basic assumptions of the scientist cloud what he or she sees.

Also, fame may cloud the conclusions. It is a lot more prestigious to announce the discovery of another human ancestor than another ape ancestor. As Alan Mann, professor of paleoanthropology at the University of Pennsylvania, said, "Human evolution is a big deal these days. Leakey's world known, Johanson is like a movie star, women moon him and ask for his autograph. Lecture circuit. National Science Foundation: big bucks. Everything is debatable, especially where money is involved. Sometimes people deliberately manipulate data to suit what they're saying."[1]

Keeping the above caveats in mind, the following is a summary of current thinking on human evolution. Because of the similarities in the physical structure, genetic material, and blood of humans and apes, anthropologists assume that human beings and the apes, such as gorillas and chimpanzees, share a common ancestor. It is proposed that between 10 million and 5 million years ago the line leading to humans split from the line leading to the great apes. The classification *hominids* includes both modern humans and fossil species. Most anthropologists believe that the first hominids were the *australopithecines*. The australopithecines are thought to have lived between 5.5 million and 1 million years ago in Africa. Their facial features may have resembled chimpanzees, and anthropologists believe that they walked upright. The australopithecines had canine teeth that were less ape-like in appearance and had brains that were about one-third the size of modern human brains. The australopithecines, classified in the genus *Australopithecus* (southern ape), are divided into five species: (1) *A. anamensis,* (2) *A. afarensis,* (3) *A. africanus,* (4) *A. boisei,* (5) *A. robustus.*

A. anamensis is thought to have evolved into *A. afarensis* about 3,700,000 years ago. The most famous *A. afarensis* fossil find is "Lucy," which was discovered by Don Johanson in Ethiopia. At 40 percent complete, "Lucy" is the most complete australopithecine specimen. "Lucy" was about 3.5 feet (107 centimeters) tall and weighed about 60 pounds (27 kilograms).

It is estimated that about three million years ago *A. afarensis* evolved into *A. africanus,* whose fossils have been found in South Africa. *A. africanus* had rounder and slightly larger skulls than *A. afarensis.* Many scientists believe that *A. africanus* split into two lines: gracile (slender) and robust. The robust line probably led to *A. boisei* and *A. robustus,* which became extinct about one million years ago. The gracile line is thought to have evolved into the genus *Homo* about two million years ago.

Homo habilis (handy human being) is currently considered the oldest human species. Its fossil remains were discovered by Louis Leakey in East Africa. The brain of *H. habilis* was one-half the size of modern human brains, and *H. habilis* has smaller molars and a less protruding face than the australopithecines. Most anthropologists believe that *H. habilis* was the first toolmaker.

It is thought that about 1.75 million years ago *H. habilis* evolved into *H. erectus.* The *H. erectus* species had thick skulls, sloping foreheads, browridges, and chinless jaws. Their brain size eventually reached the size of modern human brains. This species eventually migrated out of Africa into Asia and Europe. *H. erectus* was thought to be the first to master the use of fire.

Between four hundred thousand and three hundred thousand years ago, it is thought that *H. erectus* evolved into *Homo sapiens* (wise human being). The first *H. sapiens* skulls were higher and rounder than the *H. erectus* skulls. Early *H. sapiens* were about as tall as modern human beings. The early *H. sapiens* skulls do not look exactly like modern human beings; they have larger faces that protrude around the mouth and eyes, browridges, low sloping foreheads, and no chin.

The first fossils with modern human features are thought to have appeared about one hundred thousand years ago. These fossils are classified as *Homo sapiens sapiens.* They had a chin, high forehead, a less protruding face, and no browridge.

Scientists have developed two theories to explain the origin of modern human beings: multiple origins theory and single origin theory. The *multiple origins theory* postulates that *H. erectus* in each geological area of Africa, Asia, and Europe, evolved into a form of *H. sapiens* unique to that area. These types of *H. sapiens* could then have developed into the modern human races. The *single origin theory* postulates that modern humans (*H. sapiens sapiens*) arose once in Africa and then spread throughout Africa, Asia, and Europe, replacing the older populations of *H. sapiens* already living there. Some scientists use genetic research to support the single origin theory. Each cell contains two locations for genetic material (DNA). In addition to the cellular nucleus, there is also DNA in a cellular structure called the mitochondria. The *mitochondria* contains enzymes responsible for converting food to usable energy. The mitochondrial DNA only comes from one's mother.

By comparing the mitochondrial DNA of different women and by assuming a rate for mitochondrial DNA evolution, Rebecca L. Cann, Mark Stoneking, and Allan C. Wilson of the University of California at Berkeley concluded that all women have a common ancestor who lived in Africa about two hundred thousand years ago.[2] Robert L. Dorif, Hiroshi Akashi, and Walter Bilbert of Yale University, University of Chicago, and Harvard University, respectively, did a similar study of the Y chromosome only found in men and concluded that all men have a common ancestor who lived about two hundred and seventy thousand years ago in Africa.[3] The two ancestors have been dubbed "Eve" and "Adam." Many scientists do not accept the assumptions required to obtain the results.

Religious View

The Bible teaches that humans resulted from an intentional act of God whereby God made an animal which conforms to his image. The image of God is the distinguishing feature of humans from other animals. Not only did God begin the human race; God also continues to create every person. Procreation may be the mechanism through which life begins, yet life only begins in procreation when God creates a new life. God established a physical process as strong as gravity to provide for the continuity of life, yet he remains intimately involved with these lives. God is not an absentee landlord.

In spite of the strong declarations in the Bible about the fact of God's creation of people, the Bible does not say exactly how God did this creation. An explicit description appears in Genesis 2, but as we have seen from the discussion in chapter 5, the reversal of the order of creation in Genesis 2 suggests an allegorical understanding of that chapter which veils from our sight what God actually did. Frankenstein notwithstanding, the secret of life is withheld from us, but the source of life is proclaimed.

The presence or absence of allegory in Genesis adds a sense of gravity to its interpretation in deciding if a passage should be understood literally—which has been the preference of the modern scientific world—or allegorically—which was the preference of the early Christians. Paul referred to the figures of Sarah and Hagar in Genesis as an allegorical representation of the two covenants (Gal. 4:21–31). Likewise, Hebrews stresses the typological significance of Melchizedek (Heb. 6:20–7:28).

The presence of allegory in Genesis would raise a question about the intention of Scripture regarding when the creation of people took place. At the beginning of the modern period, Archbishop Ussher of Armagh in Ireland calculated the date for the beginning of the world as 4004 B.C. Ussher was highly regarded as a biblical scholar by his Puritan contemporaries in early seventeenth-century England. His calculations are based on the ages of men given in the genealogical tables in Genesis 5:1–32 and 11:10–26. The 4004 B.C. date arises from the view that the numbers in the genealogical tables should be taken as literal numbers. The question of allegory arises, however, because of the location of the numbers in a text that would appear to fix the precise date of the creation. The Book of Genesis and the Book of Revelation mirror each other as they frame the entire Bible. God laid down an allegorical veil on the timing of the end in Revelation while revealing what would happen at the end. At the other end of time, God may have done the same thing with regard to the timing of the beginning while revealing the fact of creation.

The most compelling argument for an allegorical interpretation of Adam and his descendants to Abraham comes from the text itself. The literalist skeptic will invariably ask, "Where did Cain get his wife?" Though smugly posed, the question cannot be ignored. The Bible does not answer the question, nor does it suggest an answer. Only an individual exhibiting a naive arrogance, however, would believe that the ancient writer did not notice the problem. A wife for Cain represents one other person not mentioned in the genealogy of Adam, but the wife for Seth represents a second person unaccounted for. The fear of Cain that someone would kill him because he had killed Abel raises an even larger question: Who are these others that Cain fears? He does not appear to be afraid of his

mother or father, but of some other group. The text not only suggests but assumes that other people were living.

The text does not conflict with itself, but it does conflict with
both liberal and conservative modern interpretations of the text
based on assumptions that do not necessarily hold. One problem
arises in assuming that the Adam and Eve of Genesis 3 and the
Adam and Eve of Genesis 4 are the same people. Could they be different couples living an indeterminate number of years apart?
Another problem arises in assuming that Eve's name means she was
the mother of everyone who ever lived instead of the mother of all
those living at the time Genesis was written (Gen. 3:20). The text
suggests that a number of people were alive by Genesis 4.

Some have suggested that Adam and Eve had many more children than Cain, Abel, and Seth. This suggestion proposes that Cain
and Seth married their sisters. It also proposes that the people Cain
feared were other brothers, who also would have married more sisters. This solution has the disadvantage of suggesting that God's
plan for procreation involved incest. While incest was a feature of
Egyptian and Canaanite religion, it was repugnant to Hebrew faith
and the revealed will of God in Scripture, even though Abraham
married his half sister Sarah.

All of these solutions represent an attempt to make the text of
Genesis fit a modern, scientific understanding of time, sequence,
and history. The conservative position would be that if a literal
reading of the text conflicts with science, then science must be
wrong. The liberal position would be that if a literal reading of the
text conflicts with science, then the story is just a legend made up
a long time ago to teach a lesson. One position denies the validity
of scientific knowledge, while the other denies the reality of divine
revelation. They both cling to a modern rationalistic understanding
of what constitutes truth.

By raising the question of where the other people came from,
the Book of Genesis deliberately places a veil over how God popu-
lated the earth and the relationship of people to one another. All
solutions to the problem from a theological perspective require the
kind of speculation which has been suggested here. We always
tread on dangerous ground when we add to Scripture by "filling in
the gaps" where the Bible is silent. We always fill in the gaps or create our own scripture by appeal to reason. The variety of positions
from conservative to liberal that arise from the appeal to reason,
however, suggests how frail a standard reason may be.

Does Human Life Have Purpose?

The existential philosophers have said that people suffer from an overpowering "anxiety" over the need for purpose and the threat of death. How do science and religion deal with these issues posed by the philosophers?

Scientific View

As we discussed in chapter 1, questions about purpose are really outside the realm of the scientific method. However, this has not stopped some scientists from making statements about purpose. In the nineteenth century, many scientists did see human beings as the purpose or pinnacle of evolution. They saw evolution as progression from the simple to the complex. Those scientists holding these views were more likely Lamarckian evolutionists rather than Darwinian evolutionists. With the triumph of neo-Darwinism, a new attitude about purpose developed. The results of neo-Darwinian evolution are viewed as arising from "the unpredictability of variations and the opportunistic character of selection."[4] The following are some neo-Darwinian thoughts on purpose:

> Man was not the goal of evolution, which evidently had no goal. He was not planned, in an operation wholly planless.[5]
>
> The denial of purpose is Darwin's distinctive contention. . . . The sum total of the accidents of life acting upon the sum total of the accidents of variation thus provided a completely mechanical and material system by which to account of the changes in living forms. . . . To advance natural selection as the means of evolution meant that purely physical forces, brute struggle among brutes, could account for the present forms and powers of living beings. Matter and Force. . . . explain our whole past history and presumably would shape our future.[6]
>
> Man is the product of causes which had no provision of the end they were achieving. His origin, his growth, his hopes and fears, his loves and beliefs are but the outcome of accidental collocations of atoms.[7]

They believe that if evolution were run again, human beings would not necessarily appear but that some similar type of bipedal species would appear. Maybe a dinosaur or large flightless bird would fill this niche; this theme can be found in many science fiction stories.

According to neo-Darwinism all species eventually evolve into another species or become extinct as they do not successfully adapt to a changing environment. Thus, *Homo sapiens sapiens* should disappear either through extinction or evolution. However, some scientists believe that *Homo sapiens sapiens* may be the first species to escape from the effect of natural selection. *Homo sapiens sapiens* is the first species that can drastically modify the effect of the environment on itself. Thus, some scientists say that how *Homo sapiens sapiens* evolves is much more difficult to understand and predict. However, humans may not be in as much control of their environment as we think. We may be depleting our environment and thus destroying ourselves.

Religious View

Christians believe that people have a purpose because of the kind of God who exists. The idea of planned, involved creation suggests that God made people with a purpose in mind. The purpose for people is found in relationship with the Creator. Scripture describes God's relationship to people in terms of bringing an eternal purpose to completion over a period of ages. In the course of time and relationships, people have a purpose to fulfill in terms of the grand design God has planned.

Each life has value and each life is significant in terms of the purpose of God. Likewise, except in relation to their Creator, people cannot know their purpose. More often than not, purpose is found in the little, ordinary moments of life rather than in grand but transitory achievements. Abraham, the father of faith for all three of the great monotheistic religions, discovered his purpose and exercised his faith in the simplest of life experiences. He moved, and his wife had a baby. In those two events, he realized his purpose.

In the medieval period, Thomas Aquinas developed a proof for the existence of God based on the idea of purpose. Because we see purpose in the world, it must have some source; therefore, God exists. The "proof" did not prove the existence of God so much as it expressed faith. The people of the Middle Ages saw the purpose. The people of the modern age, as the existential philosophers have suggested, struggle to find if there is any meaning and purpose. In the modern period, we might turn the proof upside down and say that because a Creator God exists, we have a purpose.

People also have a destiny because of the existence of God. Everyone has a destiny, but not everyone has the same destiny. Some will experience eternal life, while others will experience eternal death. We may think of eternal life as presence with God, while eternal death is separation from God. Eternal death does not mean extinction. Christians believe that God entered time and space through Jesus Christ to make known how we can have relationship with him. Those who want to spend eternity with Christ will do so. Those who do not want to spend eternity with Christ will not. Eternal life is not inevitable, evolutionary, or a natural extension of physical life, even though it begins during physical life. It comes as a by-product of uniting with Christ, who is life itself (1 John 5:11–12).

PART IV

WHAT CAN WE KNOW
WITH CERTAINTY?

THIS SECTION EXAMINES THE CURRENT SCIENTIFIC THOUGHT ABOUT quantum physics in relation to the Christian doctrines of the Incarnation and the Trinity. Quantum physics raises the question of certainty and objective reality for both science and religion.

Beginning with Newton's laws of motion, a mechanistic view of nature developed. Newtonianism stated that given the position and velocity of an object, one could calculate its past travel as well as its future travel. This certainty ended when scientists began to probe the inside of the atom. Scientists discovered that the act of measuring changed properties of an object. Certainty is replaced with probabilities.

The idea of creation includes more than the idea of origins. It also includes the idea that God sustains and governs the universe and all of its substructures. As a result of this situation, Christians can speak of "objective reality." Monotheistic and Eastern religious views of reality differ dramatically at this point.

How does God relate to the world of sensory perception? The idea of God intervening in the world in a fashion that might be seen as a violation of the laws of nature offends many modern people. To what extent are the arguments against intervention actually emotional and philosophical arguments rather than conclusions of scientific inquiry?

CHAPTER TEN
_____

THE QUANTUM WORLD

THIS CHAPTER DEALS WITH THE SCIENCE OF THE SUBATOMIC WORLD. In a chemistry class, a student learns that atoms are the basic building blocks of matter. The physical and chemical properties of everyday objects result from the interactions of their atoms. For example, the interactions of the atoms of wood make it combustible; the interactions of the atoms of gold make it shiny, malleable, and ductile; the interactions of the atoms of grass make it green; the interactions of the atoms of a particle of food with the atoms on the tongue begin the sensation of taste. In the twentieth century, it was discovered that atoms are made of even tinier parts: *electrons, protons, neutrons*. Later it was realized that there are many additional subatomic particles. We identified a few of these subatomic particles in chapter 4.

The challenge to science was how to model and understand these invisible atoms and subatomic particles. Were subatomic particles and their interactions like ordinary particles and their interactions? For example, were atoms like billiard balls colliding with one another? Were subatomic particles just small balls within larger balls? This subatomic world is called the *quantum* world. As we shall see in this chapter, the quantum world is not a miniaturized version of our *macroscopic* world. In this chapter, we will also examine how our understanding of the quantum world affected our philosophical understanding of the macroscopic world.

We live in a macroscopic world of golf balls, cars, trees, and stars. Our understanding of the motion of objects in this world is due to the work of English scientist Isaac Newton (1642–1727). Newton determined a key concept that helps us organize all the varied information about motion. For centuries before Newton, it was

154

believed that one set of rules governed motion on earth; another set governed motion in the heavens. On earth objects seemed to move a while and then come to rest, while in the heavens the stars seemed to move forever. Newton's key concept was that one set of laws governed all motion. What is today called Newton's three *Laws of Motion* along with the *Law of Universal Gravitation* explains the fall of the apple and the orbit of the moon. Using Newton's key concept, modern scientists can calculate the position and speed of a planet thousands of years into the future or the path of a rocket sent from earth to explore that planet. To carry out these calculations, the scientist needs to know the current position and momentum (*mass* and *velocity*) of the object plus this information about any other objects interacting with the original object.

The success of explaining motion by Newton's laws led to development of the philosophy of *determinism*. Determinism is the theory that all action, including human, is caused entirely by preceding events. The French astronomer and mathematician Pierre Simon de Laplace (1749–1829) believed that an omniscient Intelligence could use Newton's laws to calculate all future events based on the position and motions of all particles in the universe. If Laplace was correct, then there can be no *free will* (which would present challenges to Christian doctrines). Until the development of quantum theory (mechanics) in the twentieth century, many thought that science left no room for *indeterminacy*. With the development of quantum mechanics, indeterminacy would again enter into the scientists' models of the universe.

Why do we need quantum mechanics? Quantum mechanics makes it possible to describe the interaction of light and matter at the subatomic level. Quantum mechanics arose at a time (the end of the nineteenth century) when physicists thought they had answered all the problems in physics. Yet in this utopia there were a few clouds. The best minds could not explain the following phenomena that arose in experimentation: black body radiation in 1859, photoelectric effect in 1887, solar model of the atom in 1911, and wave-particle duality of light in 1704. As scientists examined these problems, a new view of nature would emerge.

Black Body Radiation

One source of light is *incandescence* in which an object is heated to a temperature high enough to cause its excited electrons to emit light. In an incandescent light source, heat causes atoms to vibrate more and collide with one another. During these collisions energy is transferred to electrons. When the electrons release this energy, they emit light. Burning candles emit light from the excited electrons in the hot atoms of the soot in the candle flame. An incandescent lightbulb emits light from the excited atoms in the thin wire (filament) that is heated when an electric current passes through it. A metal pan in the kitchen oven or an iron poker in a fireplace emits light from the vibration of its atoms. Scientists model real incandescent light sources by studying an idealized incandescent light source called the *black body*. Unlike a real incandescent light source, a black body's light emission only depends upon its temperature, not on the material of the source.

As you may have observed, when an iron pan or iron poker is heated, we gradually notice a change in the appearance of the object and the emission of heat from the object. While the object is at a relatively low temperature, its appearance has not changed but we can feel it radiate heat. As the temperature continues to increase, we begin to notice a change in the object's appearance. The object becomes dull red, then bright red, and finally blue-white. Note that the radiation output is moving from infrared (heat) to the visible spectrum (red to blue). Note also that, as the temperature is increased, the amount of radiation emitted also increases; the object feels hotter and looks brighter. The next part of the spectrum is ultraviolet. If we continue to increase the temperature, does the radiation output move into the ultraviolet and does the amount of radiation emitted continue to increase? Classical physics, using the black body model, indicated that the output would move into the ultraviolet and the radiation output would go to infinity. Fortunately, this does not occur in our ovens, fireplaces, or incandescent lightbulbs or we would all acquire skin cancer from the ultraviolet flux. This failure of the classical physics prediction is known as the "ultraviolet catastrophe." It may be a catastrophe, but at first no one could explain why it was not observed.

In 1900 the German physicist Max Planck (1858–1947) proposed a solution for the theoretical problem for the ultraviolet catastrophe. He discovered a formula whose output reproduced the black body radiation output exactly. Planck's formula was *empirical*, which means it had been modified to fit the experimental data and that it had no theoretical basis. Planck found that he could theoretically explain the black body radiation output if he made two radical assumptions. First, he assumed that vibrating atoms can vibrate only at certain energies or that the energies are *quantized*. Previously, classical physics had no limit on the energies of the vibrating atoms; their energies could be any of an infinity of values. Planck's second assumption was that the atoms only radiated energy when they moved from one energy state to another. This means that the energy is radiated in discrete bundles that Planck called *quanta*.

At the time Planck was studying black bodies, the current scientific theory of light stated that light was emitted as a wave. A wave is a series of crests and troughs that is *continuous;* it is uninterrupted as it extends through space. Consider a wave traveling across a surface of water; the wave is a continuous series of crests and troughs. Waves are characterized by their wavelength and frequency. The *wavelength* is the distance between two consecutive wave crests. The *frequency* is the number of crests that pass a point in a given time. In contrast to a wave, Planck was proposing that black body radiation could be understood if light were a particle. A particle is *discrete,* not continuous. A particle is located by a position in space, not by a wavelength and frequency. Particles and waves are mutually exclusive. The second finding of Planck was that the energy of the emitted light depended upon the frequency of the light rather than the intensity of the radiation. The energy is related to the frequency by a universal constant, now called Planck's constant. The numerical value of Planck's constant is very small, 6.63×10^{-34} joule-seconds. Planck received the Nobel Prize in physics in 1918 for his work.

Planck's relating energy of the quanta to the frequency raises a quantum paradox: Frequency is associated with wave, a continuous phenomenon, while the quanta are discrete particles! Could nature be this strange at the subatomic level? Or was Planck's observation just a mathematical calculation that worked? Or did the epistemology reflect the ontology? Planck, himself, was concerned by all of this. As he wrote, "My futile attempts to fit the elementary quantum of action [Planck's constant] somehow into the classical theory continued for a number of years, and they cost me a great deal of effort."[1] Scientists would not have to wait long before the quantum was used to explain another phenomenon (the photoelectric effect).

Photoelectric Effect

Certain metals will liberate electrons when light is shined upon the metal's surface. This phenomenon is called the *photoelectric effect*. This effect is the basis of the photoelectric cell or phototube or electric eye used in burglar alarms, door openers, and traffic-light controls. The wave theory of light could not explain certain features of the photoelectric effect. Wave theory predicted that the energy of the emitted electrons should increase as the intensity of the light beam is increased; but the energy of the photoemitted electrons are independent of the light intensity. Wave theory predicted that the photoelectric effect should occur at any light frequency; but for each metal surface, there was a frequency below which no photoelectric effect is observed, no matter how intense the illumination. Wave theory implied that there should be a time delay as the wave is "soaked up" by the metal surface; no such time delay is observed.

In 1905 Albert Einstein (1879–1955) used Planck's insights to explain the photoelectric effect. Einstein proposed that light is propagated through space in discrete particles called *photons* and that the energy of the photon depends upon the frequency of the light. Photons are different from other particles, such as a baseball or a train. Photons are massless and always travel at the speed of light.

Einstein's photon hypothesis successfully addressed the features of the photoelectric effect that wave theory could not explain. The first problem was that the energy of the emitted electron is independent of the light intensity. The energy of the emitted electron depends only on the energy with which the photon strikes the electron. The photon's energy depends on the light's frequency, not the light's intensity. The intensity only measures the number of photons striking the metal. The second problem was that a minimum frequency was required for electrons to be emitted. The electron is held in the metal by an electrostatic attraction. A certain energy is required to break this attraction. Since the energy of the photon is dependent on the frequency of light, only photons above a certain frequency will have enough energy to dislodge an electron. The third problem was no time delay. The photon is a concentrated bundle. A photon is not spread over a large area like a wave would be. Thus, as soon as the photon hits the metal's surface, an electron can be emitted.

Like Planck, Einstein had again created a quantum paradox of relating the continuous property (frequency) with a discrete property (photon). Einstein received the Nobel Prize in physics in 1921 for his work. We can ask the same question about Einstein's work that we asked about Planck's. Does the epistemology reflect the ontology? Confirmation of the concept that the photon is a bundle of energy came in 1923 from the work of the American physicist Arthur Holly Compton (1892–1962). Compton allowed a beam of X-rays of a sharply defined wavelength to fall on a block of graphite. The X-rays are scattered by the electrons in the surface of the block. Compton observed that the scattering causes a change in the wavelengths of the X-rays. Wave theory cannot explain this change, while the photon postulate can. Compton won the Noble Prize in physics in 1927.

Solar System Model of the Atom

In 1911 Ernest Rutherford (1871–1937) proposed that an atom consists of a very small, positively charged nucleus surrounded by negatively charged electrons that revolve around the nucleus. Classical physics stated that these moving electrons should emit energy and eventually fall into the nucleus. Thus, Rutherford's atom should be unstable. In 1913 Niels Bohr applied the quantum concept to the Rutherford atom. He proposed that the electrons' orbits around the nucleus were quantized or that only orbits of certain diameters were allowed; the allowed orbital diameters were related to Planck's constant. In classical physics, any orbital diameter is allowed. Bohr could not explain why the orbits were quantized; he only knew that this proposal resulted in a stable atom.

Bohr also postulated that electromagnetic radiation is emitted from an atom if an electron moves from a higher energy orbit (farther from nucleus) to a lower energy orbit (closer to nucleus). Absorption of radiation occurs, Bohr proposed, when the electron moves from a lower energy orbit to a higher energy orbit (see Fig. 10.1). These electron movements are called *quantum jumps*. These quantum leaps are easy to observe. When one burns the Sunday comics or special fire logs in the fireplace, the colored flames that result come from the emission of quanta of radiation as electrons move from higher Bohr orbits to orbits closer to the nucleus. Bohr won the Nobel Prize in physics in 1922 for his work.

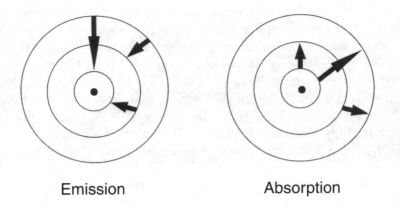

Emission   Absorption

Fig. 10.1. Bohr Model of the Atom, Explaining the
Emission and Absorption of Radiation by an Atom.

Wave-Particle Duality of Light

Since the time of Newton, scientists have been debating whether light is a wave (continuous) or a particle (discrete). Visible light is a small part of the *electromagnetic spectrum* which ranges from low-energy radio waves, to microwaves, to infrared light, to visible light, to ultraviolet light, to X-rays, to gamma rays. So the question should be stated: Is electromagnetic radiation a particle or a wave? Certain experiments imply a wave: interference, diffraction, polarization. Other experiments imply a particle: photoelectric effect (Einstein), X-ray scattering (Compton). As we shall see, we may be asking the wrong question when we ask if light is a wave or a particle.

Wave-Particle Duality of Matter

In 1924 Louis de Broglie (1892–1987) turned the question on its head by asking if particles of matter behave like waves! Or does the electron (a particle) have a wavelength? Assuming that the electron does, de Broglie discovered that he could explain why certain distances from the nucleus of the Bohr atom were stable for an orbit while others were unstable. He explained the stability of the orbits in terms of interference of waves. *Interference* occurs when two waves overlap. If the crest of one wave overlaps with the crest of another wave, a new wave is produced that has crests that are the sum of two overlapping crests. This is called *constructive inter-*

ference. If the crest of one wave overlaps with the trough of another wave, the two waves cancel each other, producing no wave at all. This is called *destructive interference*. An example of these types of interference is a concert hall that has areas with enhanced sound (constructive interference) and no sound (destructive interference). De Broglie observed that stable orbits had circumferences that allowed for constructive interference of the electron wave (see Fig. 10.2). The electron wave will be reinforced and stable. Unstable orbits had circumferences that produced destructive inferences of the electron wave. The electron wave would be unstable. De Broglie won the Nobel Prize in physics in 1929.

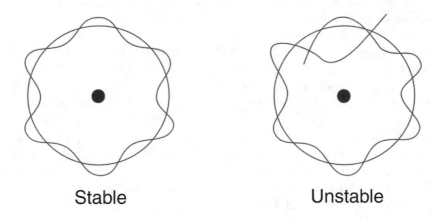

Stable   Unstable

Fig. 10.2. De Broglie's Wavelength for Electrons.
A whole number of crests would be stable, while
a non-integer number of crests would be unstable.

The epistemology and ontology question was bad enough when quantum results implied wavy light was a particle. Now quantum results are implying that particles have waves. Can this be correct? Think about it. For centuries physicists had observed that energy was carried by either waves or particles. Waves carried energy over water and a particle like a stone carried energy from the top of a mountain to the bottom. Physicists extended these models into the invisible realm of nature. Sound was explained as a wave while subatomic particles were particles. Protons, neutrons, and electrons have mass. Thus, in a beginning chemistry course, one learns that the atom is made of three particles: proton, neutron, and electron—not that an atom is made of a proton, a neutron, and a wave!

However, experimental confirmation of de Broglie's idea came quickly. Two independent groups used diffraction of electrons to test de Broglie's idea. *Diffraction* is a wave property where waves spread as they pass through a small opening or around a barrier. One example of diffraction is a person's ability to hear a radio in a room adjacent to the room where the radio is located. Sound waves diffract through the doorway into the adjacent room. Another example is the behavior of water waves as they pass a boat dock. The waves that pass the dock's supports diffract into the area behind the dock's supports which is directly blocking the waves. A microscopic example is the atoms in a crystalline solid, such as table salt. The atoms act as an array of barriers that can diffract electromagnetic waves. X-ray diffraction has been used for about one hundred years to determine the structure of crystalline solids.

Using diffraction, de Broglie's idea that electrons had a wave property was independently tested by the American physicist Clinton Davisson (1881–1958) and the British physicist George Paget Thomson (1892–1975). Davisson diffracted electrons from nickel, while Thomson diffracted electrons from gold. The success of their experiments revealed the wave properties of the electron. The electron microscope is an application of the electron wave property. Davisson and Thomson shared the Nobel Prize in physics in 1937. There is an irony in Thomson's winning the Nobel Prize for showing that the electron is "a wave." In 1906 his father, J. J. Thomson (1856–1940), won the Nobel Prize for experimentally establishing that the electron is "a particle." If it was not upsetting enough that the electron was wavy, scientists soon were observing diffraction for protons, neutrons, hydrogen atoms, helium atoms, and hydrogen molecules, revealing that all these particles had wave properties. Recently, the research group of Anton Zeilinger[2] in Vienna performed the double slit experiment on a fullerene molecule containing sixty carbon atoms. Even this large molecule was shown to exhibit wave as well as particle properties. The fullerene experiment is an important extension of the wave/particle duality toward a genuinely macroscopic region.

Quantum Wave Mechanics

The work of de Broglie led the Austrian/English physicist Erwin Schrödinger (1887–1961) to develop quantum *wave equations* to describe the behavior of electrons in atoms. The quantum wave equations were similar to classical physics equations used in optics to describe the waves of light or used in music to describe the standing waves in a violin string. The Schrödinger wave equation is a mathematical expression consisting of an operator and a wave function. The *operator* is a mathematical expression that tells one what to do with whatever follows it. For example, in the expression "1/3," the "1/" is an operator telling one to take the inverse of what follows, in this case 3. The *wave function,* usually represented by the Greek letter psi, ψ, is a mathematical expression describing the physical system, in this case the nucleus of an atom and its electrons. Operation on the wave function yields *eigenvalues,* or characteristic values for the system. Different mathematical expressions are used as operators on the same wave function to yield eigenvalues for the electron's characteristics, such as energy or momentum. Another way of saying this is that the observed properties of an atom can be calculated by the appropriate operator and wave function.

Solving the Schrödinger wave equation for the hydrogen atom yielded the same energy levels for the electrons as found in the Bohr model. What information did the wave equations give about the trajectories (paths or orbits) of the electrons? In 1926 the German-English physicist Max Born (1882–1970) suggested that the mathematical squaring of the wave function (ψ^2) gives a representation of the probability of finding an electron at a certain distance from the nucleus. Rather than a sharp line for the trajectory of the electron, the quantum mechanical treatment yields probabilistic predictions of the electron's position. Figure 10.3 shows these probability distributions. The maxima of the curves labeled 1s, 2p, and 3d correspond to the radius of the orbits predicted by the Bohr model. Figure 10.4 shows the three-dimensional shapes of these probability distributions. In quantum wave mechanics, the Bohr orbits are replaced by probability distribution *orbitals*. One of these orbitals has a spherical shape and is labeled the "s" orbital; orbitals of a dumbbell shape are labeled a "p" orbital; and those of a four-leaf clover shape are labeled a "d" orbital. The electron can no longer be located with precision. One now speaks of a certain probability that the electron is at a particular location. Schrödinger won the Nobel Prize in physics in 1933 for his work, while Born won the Nobel Prize in physics in 1954.

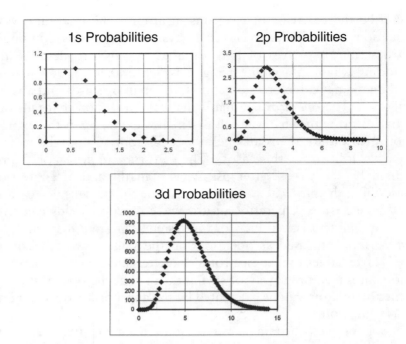

Fig. 10.3. Probability Densities for Electron Positions around the Nucleus.

Heisenberg's Uncertainty Principle

Max Born further interpreted the work of de Broglie and Schrödinger to say that photons and electrons are particles associated with probabilities that interfere as waves. The German physicist Werner Heisenberg (1901–1976) extended the indeterminacy

Fig. 10.4. Shapes of Atomic Orbitals.

further by stating that it is impossible to know exactly both the position and momentum of a particle at the same time. The theory also states that the more certain one determines one quantity, the less certain one can determine the other. The product of both uncertainties will never be less than Planck's constant. For macroscopic, everyday objects this limitation on simultaneous measurements of position and momentum is not important when compared to ordinary experimental error. However, for objects, such as an electron, these uncertainty restrictions are significant. Heisenberg won the Nobel Prize in physics in 1932.

Is this indeterminacy only due to experimental limitations? When I see a car (determine its position and speed), I use light photons as my probe. Photons are very small compared to the car. Thus, bouncing the photons off the car has no measurable effect on the car's position and momentum. When I try to "see" an electron (determine its position and speed), I use electrons as the probe. But now the probe and the object are the same size. The probe electrons can cause the object electron to move. An example from the macroworld would be to use rockets tipped with explosives to determine where airplanes are over an airport; this probe would no doubt affect the speed and position of the airplanes!

Heisenberg's insight goes beyond experimental limitations. Suppose we could find a new smaller probe to discover the position and momentum of electrons. We would still not be able to obtain simultaneous exact position and momentum values for the electron because of the electron's wave probabilities. Thus, the Heisenberg Uncertainty Principle has raised uncertainty to a universal principle. Even if there were no errors in a measurement, it would still be impossible to obtain a precise value for both the momentum and position at the same time. The more precisely we can determine one variable, the less precise would be our simultaneous measurement of the other. Before Heisenberg's statement, it had been assumed that one could, in theory, do these measurements without any uncertainty.

The Strange Quantum World

I am not sure that the reader has grasped how strange the quantum world really is. Two experiments, the double slit experiment and the particle twins experiment, will be used to give us a "glimpse" of this strangeness.

A

B

A. Apparatus that allows marbles to roll down an inclined
   plane and pass through a single slit.
B. Distribution of the marbles after passing through the slit.

Fig. 10.5. Marbles Passing Through a Single Slit.

Double Slit Experiment

Before examining the double slit, consider what happens when particles and waves pass though a single small opening, the *slit*. As shown in Figure 10.5, marbles are allowed to roll down an incline and pass through a slit. Once the marbles pass through the slit, they are collected in boxes. After the marbles pass though the slit, most

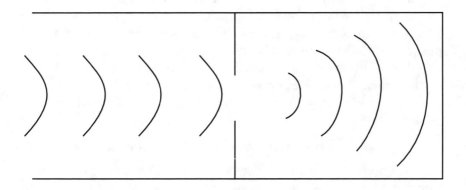

Fig. 10.6. Wave Passing Through a Single Slit.

of the marbles collect in the center boxes with fewer marbles toward the sides.

What happens when a water wave passes through a slit? In Figure 10.6, water waves approach a slit. The waves spread out behind the barrier. Using detectors for wave intensity, one discovers that the greatest wave intensity is right behind the slit as seen for the marbles. Although the maximum intensity is the same for both the particle and the wave, the particles strike localized spots on the detector while the wave covers the whole detector.

What happens when we send particles through two parallel slits, the double slit experiment? In Figure 10.7, marbles are allowed to roll down an incline and pass through two slits. Once again the marbles are collected in boxes. As with the single slit, the largest concentration of marbles is directly behind each slit.

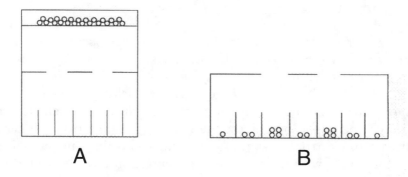

A. Apparatus that allows marbles to roll down an
   inclined plane and pass through a single slit.
B. Distribution of the marbles.

Fig. 10.7. Marbles Passing Through Two Slits.

Will the wave behavior in the double slit experiment parallel the particle behavior? The answer is no because of wave interference. In Figure 10.8, one observes that waves emerging from each of the slits interfere with each other, creating regions of constructive and destructive interference. The interference creates a pattern of alternating regions of wave, no wave, wave, no wave, wave or a

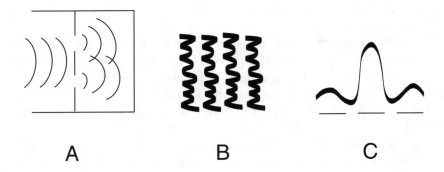

A

B

C

A Interference pattern as waves exit from two slits.
B. Light/Dark/Light (zebra) pattern that results from interference.
C. Wave intensity distribution.

Fig. 10.8. Waves Passing Through Two Slits.

zebra pattern. The maximum intensity of waves occurs at the mid-point between the two slits. The double slit experiment clearly distinguishes between particles and waves.

Now, consider a quantum object, the electron. Figure 10.9 shows the apparatus for the single slit experiment with an electron source and a photographic plate to detect the electrons. When a stream of electrons pass through a single slit, they hit the photographic plate with their greatest concentration directly behind the slit, as we saw for the experiment with the marbles and water.

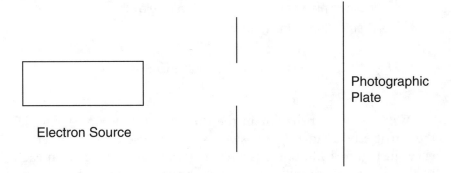

Photographic
Plate

Electron Source

Fig. 10.9. Electron Single-Slit Experiment.

What would you expect if a beam of electrons were sent through the double slit apparatus? Would the electrons behave like the marbles (particle) or water (wave)? The electrons behave like the water waves, creating both the interference pattern of zebra stripes and the greatest intensity midpoint of the two slits. Maybe this interference is occurring because we are sending electrons through both slits simultaneously? De Broglie did "show" that electrons had a wave property and it is not too farfetched to imagine the wave of one electron interfering with the wave of another. Let's modify the experiment and send only one electron through the apparatus at a time. We will also wait until this electron has passed through a slit and hit the photographic plate before sending the next electron through the apparatus. Under these conditions, will the behavior be like the marbles (particle) or water (wave)?

As we watch the individual electrons arrive at the photographic plate, they seem to be random at first. But as more and more individual electrons arrive at the photographic plate, the wave interference pattern results. Even though only one electron at a time is sent through the apparatus and only one electron is detected on the plate, the electrons are interfering with one another as waves. How can the electrons interfere with one another when they pass through the apparatus one at a time? It may not make sense, but it is how nature works in the strange quantum world.

But wait, there is more. If during the double slit experiment, we close one of the slits, the individual electrons now hit the photographic plate as particles. How does the electron "know" when the second slit is closed? Reopen the second slit and the interference pattern begins again. Somehow the electron "knows" if two slits are open and "acts" as a wave or if one slit is open and "acts" as a particle. De Broglie called the electron a matter wave, which is a holistic system that always contains information from the particle side as well as the wave side. A very strange world indeed.

Particle Twins Experiment or the EPR Paradox

Further insight into the idea of a holistic system resulted from an experiment proposed in 1935 by Einstein, Boris Podolsdy (1896–1966), and Nathan Rosen (1901–1995).[3] Einstein believed that the results of the proposed experiment would reveal that quantum mechanics was incomplete and that there are yet undiscovered hidden variables that remove the uncertainty of quantum mechanics. In 1962 the physicist John Bell developed a theorem, called

Bell's Theorem, which showed that the predictions of the hidden-variable theory would be different from the predictions of quantum mechanics.

The experiment proposed by Einstein is called the EPR Paradox. In this narrative, the experiment is also called the particle twins because two particles are formed simultaneously. The EPR Paradox involves the following ideas. Subatomic particles, such as electrons and protons, contain a rotational property called *spin*. A model of spin would be the rotation of the earth on its axis. The particle spin orientations are quantized; this is, they are restricted to only two values, called spin up and spin down. If two particles are formed simultaneously (like twins), then the system of the two particles will have a total spin of zero with the two particles having opposite spins. If we experimentally cause the spin of one particle to change, say from up to down, then the spin of the other particle will immediately change from down to up. These changes maintain the zero value for the total spin of the system.

Scientists wondered if there was a limit on how far apart the two particles could be and still maintain the coupling between their spins. If, once the particles are formed, the two particles are sent in opposite directions, will the left particle always change spin when the spin of the right particle is changed? Also as the particles get farther and farther apart, how do they "know" what is happening to each other? If they "communicate" with each other, would the theory of relativity's limit that nothing can move faster than the speed of light apply? This experiment was performed in 1972 by the physicists John Clauser and Stuart Freedman and later in a more sophisticated version in 1982 by the physicist Alain Aspect.[4] Aspect designed his experiment so that he was able to change the orientation (change or do not change) of his right detector while the particles were in flight and with the particles too far apart to signal each other. Yet the particles behaved as if they were communicating. Even under these extreme conditions, when one particle changed spin, the other "knew" and changed its spin. Guided by Bell's Theorem, scientists observed that the results of the particle twins experiment followed the predictions of quantum mechanics rather than the hidden-variable theory.

How did one particle "know" what the other particle was doing? Some say the problem is viewing our example as two separate particles. Rather, this example should be viewed as a whole, a single system. The quantum wave function of the example is not two separate wave functions for two particles but a single wave function including both particles. The physicist Paul Davies said, "The system of interest cannot be regarded as a collection of things, but as an indivisible, unified whole."[5] Again as in the case of the double slit experiment, the matter waves are providing "information" about the whole. A very strange world indeed.

Responses to Quantum Mechanics

Quantum theory has been very successful in helping scientists explain atomic structure, chemical bonding, and radioactivity. It led to the development of the electron microscope, transistor, and laser. Yet the uncertainties and probabilities of quantum mechanics raise many philosophical questions and concerns. The following are some of the more common responses to quantum mechanics.

We Have Not Seen the Big Picture: Hidden-Variable Theory

Although Planck, Einstein, and de Broglie were instrumental in developing quantum mechanics, they believed that there was an underlying determinacy to nature. De Broglie wrote, "It is possible that looking into the future to a deeper level of physical reality we will be able to interpret the laws of probability and quantum physics as being the statistical results of the development of completely determined values of variables which are at present hidden from us."[6] This view is sometimes called the "hidden variables interpretation." They believed that once the hidden variables were found, all the quantum uncertainty would vanish. Einstein said, "Quantum mechanics is very impressive. But an inner voice tells me that it is not yet the real thing. The theory produces a good deal but hardly brings us closer to the secret of the Old One. I am at all events convinced that He does not play dice."[7] At first Einstein tried to show that quantum mechanics was inconsistent; after all his challenges were met, Einstein admitted that quantum mechanics was consistent. Einstein then changed his attack to say quantum mechanics was incomplete, that hidden variables would remove the quantum uncertainties. Many believe the results of the EPR Paradox show that quantum mechanics is complete and there are no hidden variables.

Noncausal and Nonlocal: The Copenhagen Interpretation

This interpretation is the most common interpretation of quantum mechanics and was developed under the leadership of Bohr with input from Heisenberg, Born, and Wolfgang Pauli (1900–1958). Bohr held that the wave functions do not represent the reality of nature but rather what we can know about nature. Or we do not know the quantum reality, only our observations on the quantum reality. As Bohr wrote, "We meet here in a new light the old truth that in our description of nature the purpose is not to disclose the real essence of the phenomena but only to track down, so far as possible, relations between the manifold aspects of our experience."[8] The observation (the collapse of the wave function) changes our knowledge of the world, not the reality itself.

Some postulates of the Copenhagen Interpretation are complementarity, indeterminism, no event-by-event causality, and nonlocality. *Complementarity* says that quantum objects have contradictory properties: wave/particle duality. Our choice of experiment determines what we observe with loss of information about the complementary property. The Copenhagen Interpretation says that the quantum world is truly indeterminate. The Heisenberg Uncertainty Principle represents a new universal principle. The Copenhagen Interpretation says that we cannot know anything about the trajectory of the electron. There is no causality. The electron is in one energy level and then in another energy level; the collapse of the wave function gives us no information on the path the electron took or even if there is a path. It is as if the electron disappears from one energy level and reappears in another energy level. *Locality* is the assumption that an event in one part of space cannot immediately affect another event separate from the first. The Copenhagen Interpretation says that a change in one part of the system causes the wave function to change immediately everywhere.

Causal but Nonlocal: The Pilot-Wave Interpretation

Building upon the proposal of de Broglie, the physicist David Bohm developed the Pilot-Wave Interpretation. Bohm assumed that the electron is a particle accompanied by a wave. Thus, one can know the path the electron takes, which is causality. The wave directs the path that the particle takes. If there is one slit, the wave directs the electron on a path like a particle. If there are two slits, the wave directs the electron on a path that involves wave interference. The paths the electrons take depend upon knowing precise initial conditions. Since these initial conditions cannot be precisely known, the best one can do is to obtain a statistical prediction of the path. The Heisenberg Uncertainty limitation sets the lower limit on the accuracy of knowing the path of the electron. Although this interpretation has causality, this interpretation contains the concept of nonlocality, like the Copenhagen Interpretation. Thus, Bohm has causality with nonlocality. Since there is no way to distinguish mathematically between the Copenhagen Interpretation and Bohm's interpretation, most scientists have followed the earlier Copenhagen Interpretation.

What We Choose to Observe Is What We See

The idea that what we choose to observe is what we see is a radical interpretation of the Copenhagen Interpretation. Not only does the choice of instrument result in what we observe (wave/particle), but the act of observing creates the reality. As physicist John Wheeler says, "No elementary phenomenon is a real phenomenon until it is an observed phenomenon."[9] What makes something observed: the click of a Geiger counter, the image in a photograph, or the mind of a human? The mathematician John von Neumann argues that since all instruments contain atoms (quantum events), only the human mind can do the observing. Thus, the most extreme view would be that the universe was in an indeterminate state until a human mind observes it.

A Seamless Whole

Experiments such as the double slit and the particle twins led to the view that the universe is a unified, seamless whole. The observer and observed are not separate. They are part of the same experiment. As physicist David Bohm says, "One is led to a new notion of unbroken wholeness which denies the classical analyzability of the world into separately and independently existing parts."[10] Physicists who blend physics and Eastern religions have adopted this interpretation.[11]

Many Universes

Hugh Everett first proposed the "many universes" interpretation of quantum theory while a Princeton graduate student. He suggested that when the wave function collapses, it collapses to all possible outcomes. When one runs the particle twins experiment, in one universe the spin of the right particle is changed, in the other universe the spin of the right particle is unchanged. Thus, the universe is forever splitting into universes on top of universes.

Apparently there is no way to communicate between the universes. This idea was the basis of Frederik Pohl's science fiction work, *The Coming of the Quantum Cats,*[12] which is an appropriate place to treat this view.

Summary

Once scientists began exploring the subatomic world, they discovered that the causal determinism of their Newtonian worldview could not explain the subatomic world. Quantum mechanics stated that subatomic particles are associated with probabilities that interfere as waves. This led to the realization that uncertainty was a universal principle. Responses to the implications of quantum mechanics have ranged from a denial of quantum uncertainty, to fundamental concept of uncertainty, to mysticism. If at the end of this chapter you still feel that you do not understand quantum theory, you are in good company. As Richard Feynman, one of the leading physicists of the twentieth century and Nobel Prize winner (1965) said, "We have always had a great deal of difficulty understanding the worldview that quantum mechanics represents. At least I do, because I'm an old enough man that I haven't got to the point that this stuff is obvious to me."[13]

CHAPTER ELEVEN

CONTRADICTION AND THE TRIUNE GOD

LONG BEFORE SCIENTISTS PONDERED THE IMPLICATIONS OF QUANTUM physics, people wrestled with the determinacy or indeterminacy of the universe. Does God determine everything that happens, or do humans have free will about their behavior? The Bible speaks quite clearly to the issue, but the philosophical interpretation of Scripture in the West has tended to cloud the issue. First of all, terms like *determinate*, *indeterminate*, *sovereignty*, and *free will* are not biblical terms. These terms come from the philosophical consideration of religion, and now science. Rather than pre-determine the argument, it may be more helpful to disregard the levels of philosophical speculation and restate the question: How does God relate to the physical world?

Each religion has its own understanding of the nature of God and how God relates to the physical world and especially to people. Some religions view God as an unconscious and nonpersonal being or force. Others view God as many beings of a capricious and unreliable sort. The three monotheistic religions view God as a personal, self-conscious being who orders the inanimate matter of the universe and guides the course of the personal lives of people. The quantum existence of subatomic particles which have mutually exclusive qualities (discreet and continuous) has implications for one of the most incomprehensible features of the Christian faith. In relating to the physical world, God manifests parallel, mutually exclusive qualities that Christian theology refers to as the *Incarnation* and the *Trinity*. The Incarnation refers to the coming of God into physical time and space through Jesus Christ. The

Trinity refers to the relationship between God the Father, God the Son, and God the Holy Spirit.

The Spirit of God and the Physical World

The Bible begins with a description of God's involvement in the beginning of the time-space continuum that we call the physical world. It states that "the Spirit of God moved upon the face of the water" (Gen. 1:2). In Hebrew, the word for "spirit" (*ruach*) also means "wind" or "breath." It has the power to move and cause an effect. The Hebrews were not speculative, metaphysical thinkers. Instead, they expressed ideas in concrete terms which often represented a nonphysical idea. The Greeks were highly speculative and would use as many as four different words to distinguish carefully between different kinds of love. The Hebrews did just the opposite. They would use one word, *ruach,* to describe "breath," and by extension "wind" because it blew like breath. *Ruach* also meant "spirit" because it could not be seen like breath or wind, but its power could be felt. The Spirit of God moving upon the face of the waters before the formation of the earth represents a concrete way of describing God's power over nothingness for a people who did not use philosophical language. Instead of the language of rationalism, the prophets used the language of poetry. Nonetheless, they described the work of God graphically.

The Spirit of God caused the elements to exist and continues to act upon them. God engages the elements and they respond. God engaged the elements, and the earth began to appear, as had the waters. God engaged the earth and the waters, and life began to appear. This description of God's involvement in the physical world operates at the micro level. It suggests that God engages the molecular and subatomic strata of the universe. Viewing God's realm of activity as that realm just beyond scientific explanation has been known as "the God of the gaps." This approach regards those realms of reality which have scientific explanations as outside the activity of God, which leaves those unknown areas of the physical world as the only spot for God. At one time, the gaps were much larger before science made such dramatic new discoveries in cosmology and subatomic particles.

Before pushing God out of the picture entirely, however, perhaps a reassessment of fundamental assumptions is in order. The assumption has been that if a phenomenon can be described scientifically, then it is not the result of the activity of God. This assumption has neither scientific nor biblical basis, but it has a strong philosophical tradition that has influenced theological thinking.

Instead of stopping at the micro level, the Bible goes on to describe God's involvement in the physical world at the macro level. God operated within nature to bring a series of plagues upon Egypt and to open the Red Sea in order for the Hebrew slaves to escape from Pharaoh's army. Besides engaging objects, God also engaged people to bring about a desired end. The effect of engaging Pharaoh was to "harden his heart." The meaning of this phrase has further fueled the discussion about how God relates to the physical world. Beyond this level of engagement, however, the Bible describes the encounter between God and people in which God makes himself clearly known.

Theology speaks of these encounters as *revelation* or *inspiration*. In revelation, God reveals what could not be known any other way. In revelation, knowledge comes to people without their effort. This experience is related to the idea of *grace*. Grace involves a gift that comes unearned, unmerited, and unsolicited. In the Bible God reveals himself first, but never his entirety. He gives glimpses of himself. He reveals his plans for people, but never all of his plans. He reveals his expectations of people, though not all at the same time. He reveals what he intends to do, but not all of what he intends to do. He reveals the coming end of time and space, but not when it will end.

Inspiration describes the way in which revelation takes place. The term comes from the Latin phrase *in spiritus,* which has the sense of the spirit coming inside a person. The Oracle at Delphi in ancient Greece breathed in sulphur fumes which were believed to allow her to see the future. This pagan activity is quite different from the biblical picture of inspiration. Over and over throughout the Old Testament, the Spirit of the Lord "came upon" or "moved upon" a person who at that moment became a prophet. The same description of God's Spirit moving upon the elements is the picture given of the Spirit moving upon people.

Rather than a God of the gaps, the Bible describes God as involved in the physical world at every level of complexity. Yet, at every level of complexity, God relates in a different way. For many years it was popular to think of this ongoing relationship of God to his creation as an intervention into nature. Such an intervention

represents a "miracle" that would further be described as a violation of the laws of nature. The philosophers of the Enlightenment
regarded such an idea as repugnant to their reason, and theologians
who followed their lead became *Deists*. Deists believe that God
created the universe and established its physical and moral laws,
but was not involved in it—like a watchmaker who winds up a
clock and leaves it.

Instead of a mechanical, static picture of creation, however, we
have seen in previous chapters that the Bible presents a dynamic
picture of God's ongoing involvement in creation over a long
period of time and including the present moment.

Revelation

Revelation involves not only the engagement of the natural
order at a higher level of complexity; it also involves a qualitatively
different kind of engagement. The major world religions have different concepts of God. The great Eastern religions of Hinduism
and Buddhism tend to view God as the totality of all things, though
in some forms of each of these religions God may have a specific
manifestation. In the great monotheistic religions of Judaism,
Islam, and Christianity, however, God is totally separate from all
else. In the Eastern religions, a person may experience enlightenment by which they transcend themselves and engage ultimate reality, but God does not take the initiative in reaching out to the
person. In the monotheistic religions, a person may seek and experience the spiritual, but this is not revelation. All people may have
spiritual experience because all people have a spiritual dimension.
Revelation only occurs, however, at the initiative of God.

When both Eastern and monotheistic religions have sacred
books, what is the difference? The books of the East do not claim
to be revelation from God but accounts of those who experienced
the sublime inexpressibility of transcendence. The books of
monotheism, on the other hand, claim to be the result of the Spirit
of God taking hold of people and giving them a message to share.
The essential difference in the two relates to the two major views
of God represented by the two religions that emerged on the Indian
subcontinent, and the three religions that emerged in the Middle
East. The former sees God as impersonal, of which all things are an
aspect, including people and the vastness of the universe. The latter sees God as personal and everything else the creative work of
God. In the former, the transcendent is real and the physical is an

illusion. In the latter, the transcendent is real, but so is the physical. These ideas are summarized in Figure 11.1.

	Eastern Religions	Monotheistic Religions
God	Impersonal	Personal
Transcendent Realm	Real	Real
Physical Realm	Illusory (physical realm is actually part of God)	Real (physical realm was created by God)
Sacred Texts	Insight or Enlightenment	Revelation from God

Fig. 11.1. Comparison of Eastern and Monotheistic Religions.

Revelation is communication between two persons. Because humans are created in the image of God, they are persons. As persons, humans have a certain capacity for personal relationship, though this capacity is severely damaged, retarded, and inhibited by sin. At the heart of personal relationship lies communication. If God is a personal being, then the kind of personal communication described as revelation would be quite reasonable. The communication depends upon the ability of the superior being to make the communication clear to the inferior being rather than upon the ability of the inferior being to comprehend the superior. Since I can make my dog understand me, then the kind of God who created me would likely know how to communicate with me in a way I would understand. In this divine-human communication, revelation depends upon God's ability to make himself known, while prayer depends upon God's ability to understand. From the human perspective, people do not need ability so much as desire for the communication. God's relating to people in this way is superior to the method he uses in relating to less complex levels of animal life and inanimate matter.

Incarnation

From the picture of God in the Bible expressed in creation and God's continuing engagement of the physical world, we may speak of God as all-powerful, all-present, and all-knowing. God is eternal rather than finite. God is immortal rather than mortal. People, on the other hand, are limited in time and space, knowledge, power, and life span. God and people are not the same. They appear to have mutually exclusive natures, though they share the quality of personhood.

Into this neat differentiation between God and people comes Jesus Christ, who threw a quantum problem into the philosophical understanding of his generation and many generations since. Jesus represented himself as equal with God (John 10:30). Instead of calling himself "son of God," which would have been the appropriate title for a king of Israel about to reinstitute the royal throne of David, he called himself "Son of Man." The Son of Man was the foretold divine being who shared the glory, authority, and worship of God who would reign forever over all creation (Dan. 7:13–14). Jesus was condemned by the Sanhedrin for claiming to be the Son of Man (Matt. 26:63–66; Mark 14:61–64; Luke 22:67–71).

At the heart of faith in Jesus Christ lies a logical impossibility. Christians believe that Jesus Christ is both fully God and fully man. Perhaps the most beautiful picture of this sublime contradiction appears in Revelation 22:3 when the fulfillment of Daniel's prophecy of the Son of Man is complete at the end of time and the beginning of something else: "No longer will there be any curse. The throne of God and of the Lamb will be in the city, and his servants will serve him. They will see his face, and his name will be on their foreheads. There will be no more night. They will not need the light of a lamp or the light of the sun, for the Lord God will give them light. And they will reign for ever and ever" (Rev. 22:3–5).

Notice how the grammar violates the basic principles of logic. The throne (singular) of God and of the Lamb (plural) will be in the city. A single throne belongs to two. One would then expect to hear that "their servants will serve them." Instead, we are told that "his servants will serve him." Who is this individual? God and the Lamb. The servants will see his face. Whose face? God and the Lamb. His name will be on the forehead of his servants. Whose name? God and the Lamb. The two expressions or persons of deity take a single personal pronoun until the end when the ground shifts to focus on the unity of the Lord God. In focusing on the Lord God, however, we are told that *they* will reign forever and ever. Who are they? The Lord God.

The whole scene draws attention to the remarkable nature of the person of God with respect to the Father and the Son, but it also demonstrates the inability of certain traditions of philosophical logic to deal with the Incarnation. This contradiction of logic also appears earlier in the passage when the river of life flowing from the throne of God appears. The text remarks in passing that "on each side of the river stood the tree of life." This is a remarkable statement in itself. A single tree stands in two places at the same time.

Entering into physical reality and relating to people as a man is what one might expect of a personal God who seeks relationship with people. God must take the initiative to make himself known. From the perspective of eternity, beyond the limits of the time-space continuum of the physical world, the assumptions of the universe may be quite different from what one would expect from daily experience in the physical world of sensory perception. If the universe is being created by a person called God who can exist in physical form and metaphysical form at the same time, then the discoveries of quantum mechanics are not surprising. The substructure of atoms, the building blocks of the universe behave as discrete and continuous entities. These are mutually exclusive behaviors. This capacity reflects the nature of the Creator. It is not surprising that quantum mechanics exists as it has been defined so far. What would be surprising is if it does not prove to be even more complex and inconsistent with traditional ways of conceiving the physical world.

The Trinity

What must happen for God to have full relationship and communication with people? The spiritual experiences of the prophets in the Bible represent an important initiative in relationship by God. The visitations by the Spirit of God resulted in powerful personal experiences and messages shared by entire communities that related to God over centuries. The Incarnation represents a substantially and qualitatively different kind of initiative in relationship and communication by God.

Because of the problem of sin, people have the capacity to distort, misuse, misrepresent, and violate the truth of God as expressed in spiritual experience. The professional prophets of Israel were as guilty as the prophets of Baal in focusing on the ecstatic experience of spiritual bliss rather than the person who caused it. By entering into creation in order to relate to people, God affirmed creation in its goodness as a medium for truth. The physical bodies of people presented a way of knowing Christ, and the physical body of Christ presented a way for people to know God.

The Incarnation, however, represented a discreet human life in a moment of time and space. The Incarnation may have presented a way for people a long time ago to know God in a profound way, but what good does this do people who live in different places and different times? Does the Incarnation need to be repeated in every place and every time? The Incarnation does not represent the final stage of development in the relationship between God and people. It represents more a hinge between two different ways of relating.

Instead of the limitations of time and space that inhibit a relationship with God, Jesus Christ came to extend the capacity of spiritual experience from mere visitation to unity with God. In this regard, Christianity differs from the other major religions of the world. Unity with God is not a prospect of Judaism and Islam. The Eastern religions would tend to view people and all other aspects of what we call physical reality as already a part of God. The focus of Eastern religion would be to lose the illusion of differentiation in merging with God. Christianity, on the other hand, views the physical world as created by God and separate from God. Union with God forms as dramatic a stage in the development of life as the progress from nonliving matter to living matter. When union occurs, however, separate identity and uniqueness continues to be preserved as the gift of personhood and the basis for perfect relationship.

The hinge created by the incarnation represents the transition from the old covenant of law to the new covenant of the Spirit. A *covenant* is an agreement between two or more parties, but it involves much more than a mere contract. It involves promises and commitments that are regarded as too important to break. A covenant forms the basis for a relationship. Christian marriage represents a covenant for life. Civil marriage represents a contract which can be nullified by suing for divorce.

The kind of revelation which resulted in the Law, the Prophets, and the Wisdom of Israel resulted in the development of a cultural identity, a national consciousness, and a religious system. This community of faith went through a series of crises that centered on whether they actually believed that God had revealed his will through the Law, Prophets, and Wisdom. The crises of faith occurred over a period of centuries and involved rival interpretations of spiritual reality. At the heart of the issue lay the question, "Would Israel remain faithful to the covenant relationship with God as it had been offered through Moses?"

In the crisis times of unfaithfulness, God spoke to prophets. They delivered the message to Israel that the people should remember the blessings of God and return to the covenant. With these messages, the prophets also spoke of a golden age at some indeterminate time in the future when God would make a new covenant with Israel. A classic statement of the new covenant was made by Jeremiah:

> "The time is coming," declares the LORD,
> "when I will make a new covenant
> with the house of Israel
> and with the house of Judah.
> It will not be like the covenant
> I made with their forefathers
> when I took them by the hand
> to lead them out of Egypt,
> because they broke my covenant,
> though I was a husband to them,"
>   declares the LORD.
> "This is the covenant I will make with the house of Israel
> after that time," declares the LORD.
> "I will put my law in their minds
> and write it on their hearts.
> I will be their God,
> and they will be my people.
> No longer will a man teach his neighbor,
> or a man his brother saying, 'Know the LORD,'
> because they will all know me,
> from the least of them to the greatest."
>   declares the LORD (Jer. 31:31–34a).

The new covenant would involve immediate knowledge of God rather than mediated knowledge of God. This immediate knowledge of God within the human heart and mind (spirit) would occur because of God's promise, "I will pour out my Spirit on all people . . . before the coming of the great and dreadful day of the LORD" (Joel 2:28a; 31b).

All four Gospels begin their accounts of the public ministry of Jesus with his visit to John the Baptist to be baptized (Matt. 3:13–15; Mark 1:9–11; Luke 3:21–22; John 1:19). John the Baptist gave the following testimony of that baptism to his own follower John, who then began to follow Jesus and would eventually write the Gospel of John: "I saw the Spirit come down from heaven as a dove and remain on him. I would not have known him, except that the one who sent me to baptize with water told me, 'The man on whom you see the Spirit come down and remain is he who will baptize with the Holy Spirit.' I have seen and I testify that this is the Son of God" (John 1:32–34).

During the public ministry of Jesus, he brought healing to every dimension of life: physical, emotional, social. At the conclusion of his ministry, he celebrated the Feast of Passover with his disciples. The Passover meal memorialized the night that the angel of death had passed over the homes of all the faithful Hebrew slaves who had marked their doorways with the blood of a lamb before eating the lamb as a family meal. From the time of the first Passover in Egypt when Pharaoh finally let the slaves go free until the night Jesus led the Passover meal over a thousand years later, the same story of deliverance had been told. The meal celebrated the beginning of the old covenant with God.

That last night he was with his disciples, however, when Jesus took the cup to share it with his disciples, he said something startling which had never before been heard: "This cup is the new covenant in my blood, which is poured out for you" (Luke 22:20). He then went on to explain briefly what the new covenant would mean.

As the Spirit of God provided the connection between the eternal, transcendent God and the finite, physical creation, the Spirit of God provides the connection between God and people that makes relationship and communication possible. This Holy Spirit provided the continuity between the infinite Father and the finite Son from the moment of conception in Mary's womb through the death and resurrection (Luke 1:35; Eph. 1:18–20). Although the Son shared the glory and unity with the Father before the Incarnation, upon entering the physical world as a human, Jesus accepted all of the limitations of time, space, and mortality that all other people experience. Ultimately this emptying meant sharing death with people (John 1:1–3, 14; 17:5; Phil. 2:6–8). Jesus pointed out that the power he exerted over creation and the things he knew did not happen because of himself, but because his Father living in him did the work (John 14:10; 8:28–29; 7:16; 6:57; 6:38; 5:19, 30).

The new covenant provides a similar union between people and God that God modeled through the Incarnation. The Holy Spirit provides people with a connection to the eternal. The Christian teaching about the Trinity arises most clearly in terms of how people enter into the new covenant and the difference this new relationship makes. The *Trinity* is not a term found in the Bible, but it is a theological term that describes the relationship between the Father, the Son, and the Holy Spirit.

Through the new covenant, God accomplishes *regeneration* of people by filling them with the Holy Spirit, who transforms them by analogy in the same way that he transformed inanimate matter into living matter. The Holy Spirit engulfs people and prepares them for the change from living as a physical creature to living as a spiritual creature. By analogy, the change corresponds to the changes of environment and nature that a frog goes through from life underwater as a polliwog to life above the water as a frog.

After sharing the Passover meal, his Last Supper, with his disciples, Jesus went on to explain the implications of the new covenant. It involved a quality of life that embodied love (John 13:34–35; 15:9–17), joy (15:11; 16:20–24), and peace (14:27; 16:33). Jesus also described how the Father, Son, and Spirit are one although they represent the multidimensional way in which the one God relates to people.

Jesus began by reinforcing the point that he had made so frequently in the past: "Believe me when I say that I am in the Father and the Father is in me; or at least believe on the evidence of the miracles themselves" (John 14:11). He then renewed the ancient promise of the coming of the Spirit. Jesus described the Spirit as a *paraklete,* which is translated "Counselor" or "Comforter." The word literally means "one who stands beside," and Jesus promised the Spirit would be with his followers forever (John 14:16). Jesus then made clear his own relationship to the Spirit by saying that "you know him, for he lives with you and will be in you" (John 14:17b). To erase any doubt of what he meant, he added, "I will come to you" (John 14:18b).

After identifying himself with the Spirit, Jesus then explained how he and the Father relate to the Spirit: "If anyone loves me, he will obey my teaching. My Father will love him, and we will come to him and make our home with him" (John 14:23). Jesus moves in his description from *the Spirit* will come, to *I* will come, to the *Father and I* will come. This curious way of expressing the coming of the Spirit results because of the relationship to the Father that Jesus emphasized: "I am in the Father and the Father is in me" (John 14:11). In this sense, Jesus could also say that the Father would send the Spirit in the name of Jesus, and that Jesus would send the Spirit from the Father (John 14:25–26; 15:26). In describing the transformation that the Spirit brings to a life, the apostle Paul made clear that this transformation "comes from the Lord, who is the Spirit" (2 Cor. 3:18).

Implications for Sovereignty

The Christian understanding of God involves several fundamental contradictions to traditional understandings of logic, so much so that Islam and Judaism have considered Christians polytheistic for their belief in the Incarnation and the Trinity. Part of the problem arises from the confusion of the ontological model with other models of God. *Ontology* has to do with the essential being or nature of something. Christians share with Muslims and Jews the ontological understanding of God as "one," expressed by the shamai as "Hear O Israel, the LORD thy God, the LORD is one," or by the Islamic statement of faith, "Allah is one God." The Trinity is a relational model or way of talking about God. God relates to himself as Father, Son, and Spirit. None of the three exists as a being separate from the other; all three represent expressions of the one. This way of thinking involves a different form of logic than binary or dualistic thinking.

Different varieties of binary thinking occur in the world. Binary thinking forms the logic upon which computers operate. Something is on or off, black or white, up or down, right or left, true or false, hot or cold. The Incarnation and the Trinity suggest that something may operate in a singular way, such as one God. Some things may operate in a binary way, such as the Incarnation or the separation of light from darkness. Other things may operate in pluralistic ways, such as the Trinity.

The theological description of the sovereignty of God has typically occurred within a particular philosophical frame of reference which defined sovereignty. A classic definition of sovereignty from a Reformed perspective would state that God must ordain every event that transpires; to leave anything outside his control would mean he is not sovereign at all. The second part of this statement represents a philosophical value judgment on how God can legitimately exercise sovereignty. In other words, theologians have tended to impose upon Scripture a culturally derived understanding of what God must do in order for God to be considered sovereign in his reign over the universe. This tendency parallels the assumptions of science related to how electrons must behave. The sovereignty/free will debate also relates to the understanding of Incarnation and the Trinity. Before exploring sovereignty, however, it will be helpful to explore chaos theory as a reminder of what the Bible says about how God relates to his creation.

CHAPTER TWELVE

DIALOGUE ON CERTAINTY

WHEN ONE CONSIDERS THE SCIENCE OF THE QUANTUM WORLD, THERE are several issues that cause consonance and dissonance with religion. Before we examine the intersection of science and faith in regard to the quantum world, a word of caution. The quantum world is invisible. Quantum theory is a series of mathematical equations. The calculated results can be checked against experimental results. The predictions of these calculations can be experimentally investigated. By this process, scientists gain confidence that mathematical equations model the quantum world. Yet, one has not really gained "a picture" of the quantum world. The mathematical equations may tell us the energy levels that an electron is in, but the equations are not giving us a mental picture of an electron like we have a mental picture of a ball. Thus, a scientist has to interpret the calculated results. Since the only things we have ever seen are macroscopic objects, then our interpretations of the calculated results are in terms of macroscopic objects or contrasted to the behavior of macroscopic objects.

As one reads about quantum theory, one quickly realizes that it is sometimes difficult to separate in the narrative what is a calculated result and what is an interpretation. Thus, one is always trying to determine if an interpretation or an observation is being presented. For example, when one reads that a quantum jump is discontinuous or the electron disappears from one energy level and reappears at another energy level, is this an interpretation or a calculated result?

Since the quantum world is invisible and strange, it lends itself to mystic or spiritual speculation. Thus, probably more so than any other area of science, it is very important to know the philosophical viewpoint of the scientist writing on quantum mechanics. If the writings emphasize nonmaterialism or a holistic view of the sub-atomic world, do these statements come from the mathematics or the philosophy? As we shall see below, one can read two opposite "spins" on the same quantum event.

Some of the scientific-faith issues that come from quantum mechanics include: Can the same object express contradictory properties? Is the universe deterministic? Is the physical world really there? Each issue is discussed below.

Is the "Physical" World Really There?

Quantum theory has raised an intriguing question about the ontology (essential nature) of the universe. In observing the "quantum leap" of an electron from an inner orbit around a nucleus to an outer orbit or vice versa, the electron disappears. Its positional probability changes, but it does not travel. It ceases to exist in one orbit and begins to exist in another orbit without appearing to have a trajectory from one orbit to the other. This phenomenon raises the question: Is the "physical" world really there?

Scientific View

Heisenberg wrote, "[T]he idea of an objective real world whose smallest parts exist objectively in the same sense as atoms or trees exist, independently of whether or not we observe them . . . is impossible."[1] Why does Heisenberg say that there is no objective reality at the quantum level? A reason has to do with what is called the collapse of the wave function or the quantum jump. Let us consider a single atom in a sample of radioactive iodine. As we discussed previously, one-half of the sample will decay within eight days. Our atom under consideration has many possible states: it will not decay in the next eight days; it will decay after eight days; it will decay after seven days; it will decay in the next second; and so on. The wave function for this atom is a superposition of all these states with each state having a probability of being observed. Upon observation, the wave function collapses uncontrollably in a quantum jump to one of the possible states. There is no way to predict which state gets transformed from the possible states to an actual state. As Heisenberg further observed:

> The probability wave means a tendency for something. It is a quantitative version of the old concept of "potentia" in Aristotelian philosophy. It introduces something standing in the middle between the idea of an event and the actual event, a strange kind of physical reality just in the middle between possibility and reality.

The indivisible elementary particle of modern physics possesses the quality of taking up space in no higher measure than other properties, say color and strength of material. In its essence it is not a material particle in space and time but, in a way, only a symbol.[2]

So to Heisenberg, an electron is no more physical than color is. (Of course, this is a circular example since color in most cases is produced by the movement of electrons.) Schrödinger was not happy with Heisenberg's interpretation and said to Bohr, "If one has to stick to . . . quantum jumping, then I regret having ever been involved in this thing."[3] And to show how ridiculous this interpretation was to him, Schrödinger introduced in 1935 what is called Schrödinger's Cat Paradox.[4] Take the previous radioactive atom and place it in a box along with a detector, a bottle of poisonous gas, and a cat. Close the box. If the radioactive atom decays, the detector will cause the bottle to release the poison and kill the cat. When one opens the box after one day, will the cat be alive or dead? When the experiment begins, the wave function for the whole system (cat + atom) corresponds to a live cat. As time passes, the probability that the atom has decayed increases with the cat dying. The wave function becomes a mixture of cat-alive and cat-dead. Upon observation, the wave function uncontrollably collapses (quantum jump) to one of these outcomes. In this paradox, a macro-object, the cat, has been placed in quantum states of not-alive/not-dead until the observation is made. Schrödinger did not believe that this was reasonable and that quantum mechanics was an incomplete description of matter. (It is interesting that even though Schrödinger presented the Cat Paradox to show the incompleteness of quantum mechanics, some authors say that he presented the paradox to show the difficulty of interpreting quantum mechanics.)[5]

In conclusion, the views of the quantum world range from there is an objective reality independent of our observations (Einstein and Schrödinger) to there is a potential at the quantum level that our observation actualizes (Bohr and Heisenberg). Is the Bohr-Heisenberg view consonant with the Christian view that the order of the universe is contingent upon God?

Religious View

Different religions answer this question in different ways. The Zen Buddhist regards the physical world as an illusion.

Unhappiness and suffering come from the acceptance of the illusion. Christian Science in the West shares this same basic view, denying the reality of a physical world. The Christian Science emphasis on healing is based on the belief that the physical body does not really exist; therefore, it cannot be sick or injured. Within Buddhist thought *enlightenment* allows a soul to escape the illusion and reemerge with their concept of the divine or unconscious universal spiritual reality.

Hinduism in its diversity has some similarity with this perspective. Hinduism would affirm the existence of the physical world as an aspect of the divine but would tend to deny the differentiation of the physical world. In other words, everything is a part of the whole, which is actually spiritual rather than physical. This view is reflected in the statement from the *Vedas,* "That thou art." In pointing to any object (that), it can be said that each person is that object. A person is the flower they pass in the garden; they are the rain that falls on their face; they are the dust beneath their feet. Everyone is a part of everything else, and things only appear to be distinct from one another.

Christians, Jews, and Muslims believe the physical world really does exist. They believe that God created the physical world as a good thing. They believe that all of creation is separate and distinct from God. Furthermore, they believe that each aspect of creation has a clear distinction from every other aspect. Though the enormous number of aspects of creation may have an intricate interrelationship, like a family, still everything is unique and separate. Creation behaves in such a way that it can be known consistently over time. Because of the consistent behavior of creation, people can function within it on a day-to-day basis with certainty about how it will behave.

The doctrine of *creatio ex nihilo* (creation out of nothing) expresses the idea that God created the physical world out of nothing. Nothing existed, and then something existed. The findings of quantum mechanics suggest that "nothing" continues to play a role in the substructure of atoms. Between one orbit and another orbit, does the electron cease to exist? Is nothing there? As we saw in chapter 5, the activity of calling creation into existence described in the first chapter of Genesis is a continuing action. Is quantum existence an on-again, off-again existence of an electron that continually reappears from nothing? While quantum theory developed around the behavior of "large" pieces of the atom, we now know that the atom has a vast array of subatomic "particles" even smaller than the electron. The deeper we look, the more we find. The atom now looks more like a solar system that has the potential for being a galaxy. The atom now appears to be mostly empty space dotted with bits that sometimes are not there. In the face of quantum theory, the doctrine of *creatio ex nihilo* suggests that God continues to call the physical world into being from nothing.

Do We Live in a Deterministic Universe?

Quantum theory presents a challenge to the concept of the universe conceived by Sir Isaac Newton. Newton thought of the universe as a place that operated like a machine, but quantum mechanics suggests a much more subtle universe full of uncertainty at its core. If this uncertainty rests at its core, then does it "infect" the whole universe to the macro level?

Scientific View

Causality refers to the case where two events are in a cause-and-effect relationship. The first event causes the second to occur. If one knows the first event, then one can predict what will happen in the future. Philosophically, causality can be extended to *determinism*, which says that every event is the consequence of a preceding event. Determinism also says that every future event is predictable by a knowledge of scientific laws and current physical conditions. Quantum theory presents two challenges to causality and determinism: individual events cannot be predicted with certainty and the Heisenberg Uncertainty Principle.

Uncertainty in calculating individual events. When one thinks of causality, one thinks of Newton's Laws of Motion and universal gravitation of classical physics. To predict the future values for a physical variable of a system, one begins by specifying current values of the variables, usually position and momentum that are observable. These values are then entered into Newton's equations in order to calculate (predict) future values for position and momentum. In classical physics, one can calculate with certainty the behavior of an individual event. As this book is being written, Mark McGwire and Sammy Sosa are again battling to see who can hit the most home runs in a season. Knowing the position and momentum of the baseball as it leaves the bat, one can theoretically calculate its path under the influence of gravity and air resistance and thus predict whether the hit will be a home run.

In quantum mechanics, the important variables of the system are represented by the wave equation which is not observable. The Schrödinger wave equation performs the same function as Newton's equations; the Schrödinger wave equation allows the calculation of how the system changes with time. In classical physics, definite values are predicted for the future state. Quantum mechanical calculations result in only probabilities of allowed outcomes (the eigenvalues). The calculations result only in probabilities of which energy level is most likely, or probabilities of the region of space with the greatest probability of finding an electron. If hitting a baseball were a quantum event, one would receive a calculated probability for a home run, for an in-field fly, as well as all other possibilities. The standard or Copenhagen Interpretation says that these probabilities remove all information about causality or the trajectory of the electron or quantum baseball.

Another quantum event where one cannot obtain information about individual objects is radioactivity. Radioactive decay is a quantum event. One can determine the half-life of a radioactive substance. As an example, radioactive iodine, which is used to diagnose and treat thyroid diseases, has a half-life of eight days. If one has a pound of radioactive iodine, after eight days one knows that only one-half pound of radioactive iodine will be left. However, there is no way to predict whether or when an individual iodine atom will decay. It could decay in the next second, minute, day, month, and so on. All one can determine is that one-half of the iodine atoms will decay in eight days. One cannot make any accurate prediction about the individual atoms.

Heisenberg's Uncertainty Principle. This principle states that for all physical properties that come in pairs, one cannot know accurately and simultaneously both properties at the same time. Examples of these pairs are position/velocity and energy/time. For example, if one knows accurately the time that radioactive decay takes to produce an alpha particle, one cannot simultaneously determine accurately the energy of the alpha particle. In fact, the Heisenberg Uncertainty Principle further states that the more one knows about one property, the less one knows about the other. Since position and velocity are important in determining future behavior, one is left with an inherent uncertainty at the quantum level.

What have been the responses to these quantum challenges to causality? One response is represented by Einstein, Planck, and Schrödinger. They believed that the uncertainty of quantum mechanics was due to human ignorance. They thought the universe at all levels was causal and that ultimately a better theory would arise to reveal causality at the quantum level.

Heisenberg at first thought that the uncertainty arose from the limitations of experimental design. Electromagnetic radiation is used to probe the quantum world. As we discussed in chapter 10, electromagnetic radiation is about the same size as the subatomic particles. Thus, the probing of the quantum world by electromagnetic radiation should cause changes and thus uncertainties. This explanation of quantum uncertainty does not explain the inability to predict which individual atom will undergo radioactive decay. Heisenberg later said that this uncertainty is a fundamental property of nature; no experimental design modification will remove it. This is the critical realist view that scientific theories reflect how nature really is. The results of the EPR Paradox experiments seem to me to say that quantum mechanics is complete. Thus, the uncertainty reflects the ontology of nature.

Religious View

The idea of a deterministic world in which all of the courses of nature are determined in advance, including the course of human lives, has figured prominently in a variety of religious systems. Within the Hindu frame of reference, *karma* represents one of the central teachings. Every person has a karma that they live out. Ancient Greek and Roman religious perspectives included the idea of *fate*. Every person has a fate allocated. Even the gods are subject to fate. Among the Celtic peoples of Europe, the Druid religion included a view that the destiny of the gods and all people is woven into the great rope of life by a group of sisters. Often a deterministic religious view also includes a sense of progression, or "historical" movement, toward a goal or end. Within Hinduism this end will occur when Kali dances the final dance of destruction and Vishnu the Destroyer brings all things to an end. Within the Celtic religion, the end comes when the gods are consumed in flames along with their stronghold of Valhalla.

Within Christianity, Islam, and Judaism, the view of a deterministic world is overshadowed by belief in a personal God. God is not subject to fate, destiny, karma, or any exterior force, goal, or value. This God who created the universe, nonetheless, has power and authority over it. In classical Judaism, Christianity, and Islam, the God who created all things will also bring all things to completion at a final day of judgment, the end of the world.

Within the Christian community, the concept of determinism emerges from one's understanding of how God exercises authority to bring the world to a conclusion. If the end has been determined, then what events between the beginning and the end did God determine? Concerning revelation, is prophecy based on what God knows about the future or about what God has determined about the future? The classical formula of how God brings about his will may be stated that God has absolute sovereignty without violating human freedom.

The issue of human freedom has been increasingly important since the Reformation and the Enlightenment. The growth of humanism as a significant cultural perspective in the West led to a democratizing of theology and a tendency to exaggerate the polarities of divine sovereignty and human freedom. As has been common in so many areas of life and thought in the modern era, people tended to opt for either a sovereign God or a free human. This trend was accelerated by the spirit of revolution that challenged monarchy and the rights of kings in England (1642), the American colonies (1776), France (1789), and across Europe (1848).

Science contributed to the fragmentation of the understanding of sovereignty and freedom through the work of Isaac Newton. Newton conceived a totally deterministic cause-and-effect universe governed by laws that allowed one to know where the universe was going and where it had been. It was only a matter of time and experiment to understand what was determined by the laws of physics. This new determinism cut God out of the equation and led to the religious view call *Deism*. Deism conceives of a God who created the universe and established the laws of motion but is no longer involved. People could now have the security of scientific determinism without the burden of obligation to God.

The Western philosophical preference for either/or categories has led to a division in the Protestant community between Arminians (free will) and Calvinists (divine sovereignty). The breakthrough in quantum mechanics has sent shock waves through the scientific community. It had flourished for two centuries based on the security of the mechanical, deterministic universe of Newton. Science has now lost its certainty. For Christians the issues surrounding how God relates to the world include prayer, miracle, Incarnation, prophecy and fulfillment, salvation, and the final destiny of all things—to name but a few.

Quantum mechanics suggests that the modern preference for either/or needs to regain some of the ancient understanding of both/and. Quantum mechanics suggests that at the subatomic level, the universe is quite wide open. Whereas laws operate in a deterministic way at the macro level of everyday experience, the micro world operates in an indeterminate way. This permits God the freedom to interact without violating any of the macro laws.

The structure of quantum mechanics also demonstrates a dual feature of determinacy and indeterminacy. The position and velocity of an electron are indeterminate, and the "orbit" of the electron has a range within which it operates. The energy of the electron, however, has a fixed, determinate quality. It does not vary. Whereas the position, velocity, and orbit are indeterminate, the electron also has a determinate ontological dimension in terms of its relationship to the nucleus. It does not exist except in relationship to the nucleus.

The problem of quantum mechanics arose in part because of the model used to describe the relationship of the electron to the nucleus. The term *orbit* brought with it a huge collection of unspoken assumptions based upon what people know about the planets and other bodies that orbit the sun. These orbits have a deterministic character or regularity about them which is not present in the "orbit" of electrons. While the electron does change position all around the nucleus, it does not do it like a planet changes position around the sun.

The same problem arises when theologians apply a biblical model for God to the wrong attribute. The Bible describes God as both King and Shepherd. Both models are true, but they describe different activities of God. They do not describe the nature of God. Theologians have tended to use the model of the King to describe God's sovereignty while overlooking the model of the Shepherd. The King model describes God's right to rule and establish moral law, as well as his right to enforce the law and punish the offender.

In fact, the model of the King only describes the fact of sovereignty, not the manner of exercising sovereignty. The biblical model of the Shepherd describes how God exercises sovereignty. Like a shepherd, God allows a certain amount of freedom within bounds, but he keeps the flock together. As long as the sheep stay within the acceptable range, they are allowed great freedom of movement. If they wander outside that range, however, the Shepherd does what is necessary to bring them back. While the Shepherd model is neither Arminian nor Calvinistic, it is biblical and demonstrates how determinacy and indeterminacy, sovereignty and free will interrelate. This feature of quantum mechanics suggests the integral relationship of determinacy and indeterminacy, of divine sovereignty and human freedom.

Can Something Express Contradictory Properties?

One of the most prominent ideas in Western approaches to thought is known as the *Law of Noncontradiction*. According to this principle of logic, two contradictory ideas cannot be true at the same time. Both waves and particles may exist, even though they are contradictory ideas. From our macroworld perspective, their properties are mutually exclusive of one another. The problem arises, however, if a single thing is said to have mutually exclusive properties. An electron behaves like a wave and a particle. What does this scientific discovery do to the tradition of Western logic?

Scientific View

In certain experiments, electrons display the particle properties of mass (9.109×10^{-31} kilograms) and electric charge (1.602×10^{-19} coulombs). In other experiments, electrons display the wave property of wavelength. (A beam of electrons at an energy of 54 electron volts has a wavelength of 165 picometers.) Protons, neutrons, hydrogen atoms, helium atoms, hydrogen molecules, and fullerenes also show similar behavior. As we discussed in chapter 10, particles and waves are contradictory, with particles being discrete and waves being continuous. Thus, the same object can express contradictory properties.

Bohr developed the Complementarity Principle to explain these particle and wave phenomena. He stated that these properties are mutually exclusive and cannot be simultaneously observed. Bohr is saying that if the experiment detects waves, the experiment gives no information about particles. Many believe that Bohr was comfortable with combining these opposites because of his readings in Eastern religions. Bohr went as far as placing the yin and yang on his coat of arms.

Religious View

Eastern religion has a high tolerance for contradiction and paradox. Zen Buddhism is noted for its spirituality based on the contemplation of contradictory or irrational ideas, such as the question, "What is the sound of one hand clapping?" Hinduism is not a single religion and certainly not a systematic theology. It represents a vast religious heritage of many different peoples who have lived in the Indian subcontinent over the last four thousand years or more. Hinduism has a high tolerance for contradictory religious ideas which are then relativized as aspects of one greater whole that people experience through enlightenment. For this toleration of contradiction to work, Hinduism denies the substantial reality of the possible opposites, polarities, and extremes of existence as everything is regarded as part of a single whole. Thus, nothing can actually contradict something else, because everything is the One.

Even within the religions that appear to tolerate contradiction and paradox, however, the toleration veils a more subtle form of resolution. By reducing everything to the One, the modalism of Hinduism rejects the contradiction and says the polarities only appear to be mutually exclusive. The yin and yang of Tao collapses the "opposites" into a single unity so that the opposites are complimentary aspects of one another. The dualism of Zoroastrianism, on the other hand, allows no relationship between the opposites that war with each other. In both modalism and dualism, the paradox is not allowed.

Christianity in its classical formulation insists on retaining the paradox or contradiction as the most critical foundation of its faith. While it shares with Judaism and Islam the basic beliefs about a Creator God, its faith in the Incarnation of that God distinguishes Christianity from other religions. The Nicene Creed states the contradiction:

> I believe in one God the Father Almighty, Maker of heaven and earth, and of all things visible and invisible. And in the Lord Jesus Christ, the only-begotten son of God, Light of Light, very God of very God, begotten, not made; being of one substance with the Father, by whom all things were made: Who for us men and for our

salvation came down from heaven, and was incarnate by the Holy Ghost of the virgin Mary, and was made man; and was crucified also for us under Pontius Pilate.

The basic heresies of Christianity are judged on the basis of their refusal to cling to the contradiction. The tendency of people to reject the contradiction has resulted in a variety of heresies from the early Christian era that continue to reappear. The *Docetists* said that Christ was fully divine, but only *appeared* to be human. The *Arians* claimed Christ was fully human but not fully divine. The *Ebionites* claimed Christ was adopted by God and denied the genuineness of his deity. The *Apollinarians* believed Christ was half man and half God, denying the completeness of his humanity. The *Nestorians* believed a divine and a human person inhabited Christ, denying the intrinsic union of human and divine. The *Eutychians* believed Christ had only one nature after the Incarnation, denying the continuing presence of two natures. What all of these heresies have in common is their attempt to collapse the contradiction and explain it away.

Apparently the laws of physics and the laws of logic collapse as we approach infinity (physical world) and eternity (spiritual world). Rationality does not leave, but the traditional ways of understanding rationality operate with a different paradigm at the level of quantum mechanics and the Incarnation. Natural revelation (nature) and specific revelation (Bible) are as reliable as ever for knowledge, but the human philosophical systems used by scientists and theologians are fraught with dangers.

PART V

WHEN IS ORDER DISORDER?

THIS SECTION RELATES TO THE RECENT DEVELOPMENTS IN CHAOS theory which pose significant questions for the historic scientific worldview, and it relates to the Christian doctrines of eschatology and the sovereignty of God. How does the indeterminacy of quantum physics relate to chaos? What are the implications of chaos for the idea that history is moving toward a culmination point?

What is the relationship between predictability and chaos? A great value of science is its ability to predict, to relate cause and effect. For example, eclipse dates can be calculated thousands of years into the past or future. There are systems that obey the laws of physics, yet generate random behavior. The roll of dice, the flow of a mountain stream, and the weather are all such phenomena; all have unpredictable aspects. Scientists now realize that simple deterministic systems can generate random behavior. Such behavior is called chaotic.

Is the physical order moving toward a culmination (eschatology)? How is the present reign of Christ (exaltation) over the created order to be understood? How does "chaos" relate to the free will/predestination debate?

Does the presence of chaos make a case for a dynamically involved Creator, such that the world is constantly emerging from chaos (Gen. 1:2)?

CHAPTER THIRTEEN

CHAOS THEORY

IN PREVIOUS CHAPTERS WE HAVE DEALT WITH THE SCIENCE OF THE VERY large (chapter 4—cosmology) and the very small (chapter 10— quantum theory). In this chapter we will deal with the science of everyday objects that cause us headaches. Here we will examine questions such as: Why does the ketchup not flow regularly from the bottle? Why can the dripping of the kitchen faucet be so irregular? Why cannot the weathercaster get the weather forecast correct? Why did the character Malcolm keep talking about chaos in the book and movie, *Jurassic Park?* The science of chaos deals with these frustrating and seemingly unrelated areas. In this chapter we will see why chaos theory has allowed scientists to discover order in certain apparently random processes. We will also examine the effects of chaos theory on our philosophical view of our world.

The Weather

As we discussed in chapter 10, for years astronomers have used Newton's laws to predict the future positions of planets or comets. Although the atmosphere has more particles than the solar system has planets, the same laws govern the behavior of the particles in the atmosphere. Meteorologists believed all that was needed was enough data to specify today's weather and a computer large enough to calculate the weather forecast for tomorrow. By the 1950s and 1960s, meteorologists were optimistic that they could achieve their goal of long-term weather forecasting. More and more weather stations—to collect temperature, pressure, and wind speed/direction—were being built; and large, powerful computers were becoming available. No one intended to do a calculation involving every particle in the atmosphere. Rather, they would model the atmosphere by including only those factors that are important in forecasting. This type of modeling is common in science. For example, when an astronomer calculates the path of Halley's Comet, she does not include every heavenly body in the calculation. She would not include other galaxies. She would only include the planets that cause the greatest effect on the comet's path.

In 1960 one person attempting to model the weather was the American meteorologist Edward N. Lorenz at the Massachusetts Institute of Technology. Lorenz had created a model of the weather involving twelve equations that related factors such as the temperature, pressure, and wind speed. Every minute his computer printed out a row of numbers that represented a day of weather. A review of the printout, line by line, gave the impression that his model was following earthly weather patterns. Pressure rose and fell; air currents swung north and south. One day he decided to repeat a set of calculations. In order to save time, he decided to start the calculations at the midpoint of the run. He entered the appropriate numbers from his computer printout and began the calculations.

Because the computer in his office was noisy, Lorenz left to get a cup of coffee. When he returned an hour later, he discovered, to his surprise, the results obtained were different from his first run. After just a few "months," all resemblance with the previous run was gone. How could this be? The results of this recalculation should have been the same since he was using the same program. After examining how his program worked, Lorenz realized that the computer used six-digit numbers (.506127) in its calculations. To save paper the printout was only to three digits (.506). The difference of one part in a thousand had resulted in vastly different behaviors for his system. Lorenz's finding was amazing since a scientist would usually consider himself lucky to reproduce two measurements with this level of precision. Lorenz had discovered a system that was very *sensitive to initial conditions*. Today we would say that Lorenz had discovered chaos.

To further analyze the behavior of systems sensitive to initial conditions, Lorenz decided to simplify his system. He developed a three-equation/three-variable system that did not model the weather but did model convection, a part of the atmosphere. *Convection* is the bulk movement of heat through a fluid. In his 1963 paper[1] Lorenz listed the output of his calculations: (0,10,0); (4,12,0); (9,20,0); (16,32,2); (30,66,7); (54,115,24); (93,192,74).

Lorenz obtained hundreds of these triplets. He wished to determine how the variables changed with time; one way to analyze this output is to graph the data which Lorenz did. Lorenz used each set of three numbers to represent a point in a three-dimensional space. The result of this plot would be a series of points. Connecting these points yields a continuous path which is a record of the system's behavior.

Fig. 13.1. Lorenz Attractor.

Lorenz discovered that the resulting pattern looks like an owl's face or the wings of a butterfly (see Fig. 13.1). The path weaves back and forth between the "wings," never repeating itself. The behavior signalled *disorder* since no path ever recurred. At the same time the behavior signalled *order* since all the paths were confined in the overall pattern. Since each set of initial conditions will result in a different path within the overall pattern, Lorenz concluded "that prediction of the sufficiently distant future is impossible by any method, unless the present conditions are known exactly. In view of the inevitable inaccuracy and incompleteness of weather observations, precise very-long-range forecasting would seem to be non-existent."[2] Thus, Lorenz is saying that because of the complexity of the atmosphere we can never have enough information to perform accurate weather forecasts.

Chaos

What is this chaos that Lorenz discovered in his weather model? How does it vary from everyday use of the words *chaos* and *random?* Looking up these words in the *Oxford English Dictionary* reveals that the word *chaos* comes from the ancient Greek concept of the original state of the universe as a formless void out of which the *cosmos* or order came. Thus, a chaotic state is one of utter confusion or disorder. The word *randomness* comes from an old French word meaning "to run fast" or "to gallop." Thus, something is random when it follows a haphazard course or is without aim or direction. Both of these words imply confusion or disorder.

Science also uses the terms *chaos* and *disorder,* along with the term *nonrandom.* In science these terms are distinguished by their degree of predictability. A *nonrandom* process is one that in theory and in practice allows predictability. When one thinks of the triumph of the scientific method, one is thinking of this predictability. Using the law of gravitation, one can predict eclipses thousands of years into the future or past. A *random* process is totally unpredictable. What has happened previously gives no clue as to what will happen next. Raindrops hitting a surface represent a random process because the arrival of one raindrop gives no clue to the arrival time of the next raindrop. A *chaotic* process falls in between these two extremes of total predictability and total unpredictability. Because equations can be written to describe the behavior of chaotic systems, they are in theory predictable. Yet, in practice, they are only temporarily predictable and eventually become unpredictable.

Attractors

How different is the behavior of Lorenz's system from other dynamic systems? *Dynamic* systems have constantly changing conditions in contrast to *static* systems. To obtain a picture of the behavior of the dynamic system, scientists graph the changing values of the systems variables. The resulting graph is called a *phase space,* which is a plot of the system over time. The phase space plot provides an idea of what the behavior of the system is like. With time, the graph will settle into a geometric shape called the *attractor.* The dynamic behavior is "attracted" to this geometric shape.

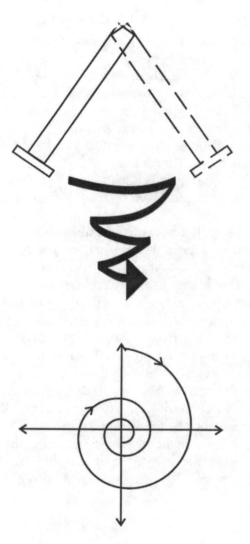

Fig. 13.2. Fixed-Point Attractor for a Playground Swing.

There are four kinds of attractors: fixed-point attractor, closed-curve attractor, torus attractor, and strange attractor. Figure 13.2 shows the behavior of a playground swing as it moves back and forth. Eventually, the swing comes to rest at a *fixed point*, its attractor. Start the swing again and it returns to this attractor.

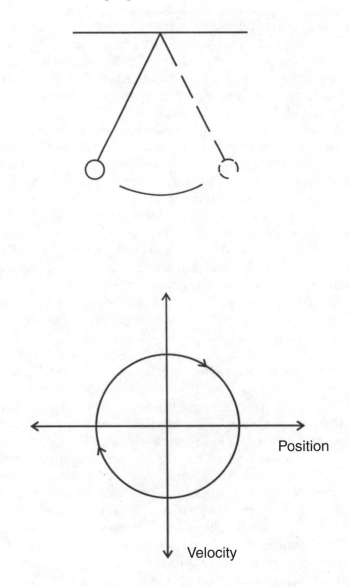

Fig. 13.3. Closed-Curve Attractor for a Pendulum Clock.

Drop a stone and it comes to rest at a fixed point on the earth, which is another example of a fixed-point attractor.

Not all attractors are fixed points. Some are cycles. A pendulum clock replaces its energy lost to friction by a spring or weight. Thus, the pendulum clock continuously repeats its swing. The attractor of the pendulum clock is a *closed curve* (see Fig. 13.3). The closed-curve attractor for the moon is its orbit around the earth. Systems can have more than one attractor, depending upon the initial conditions for the system. If the pendulum clock has only a small displacement of its pendulum, it will quickly come to rest—a fixed-point attractor. A large displacement sets the clock to ticking—a closed-curve attractor.

Another attractor is the *torus* (doughnut) which is seen in certain electrical oscillators. Imagine a torus attractor as walking on a large doughnut, going over, under, and around its surface. The paths taken by the fixed-point, closed-curve, and torus attractors are not sensitive to initial conditions.

The path taken in a *strange attractor* is sensitive to initial conditions. The strange attractor was named by the Belgian mathematical physicist David Ruelle and the Dutch mathematician Floris Takens in 1971. Strange attractors represent the behavior of a chaotic system. Strange attractors are complex, three-dimensional shapes that have detailed structure at all levels of magnification. If you magnify a section of a strange attractor, it never looks simpler; it looks complex on all levels. This behavior is like "a set of wooden Russian dolls, each containing a smaller replica of itself within."[3] Strange attractors are represented mathematically by fractals. A *fractal* is a complex geometric shape whose small-scale and large-scale structures resemble each other. Figure 13.4 shows a Koch snowflake, which is a fractal formed in just four steps by adding small triangles to the sides of larger triangles.

To understand why chaotic systems lose their predictability with time, we need to examine the attractor for a chaotic system. The attractor for a chaotic system is much more complicated than a predictable system attractor such as a fixed-point, closed curve, or torus. In a predictable system attractor, the paths that start near one another remain near one another. Or start a pendulum clock with a certain force and the system settles into the closed-curve attractor; change the starting force by a factor of one part in a thousand and the pendulum clock will settle into the "same"

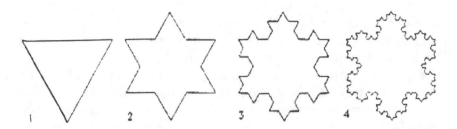

A fractal is a geometric shape whose large-scale and small-scale structures resemble each other. An example of a fractal is the Koch snowflake which can be made by adding small triangles to the sides of larger triangles.

Fig. 13.4. Example of a Fractal.

closed-curve attractor. Thus, the system is not very sensitive to initial conditions, and predictability is maintained.

Different or "strange" behavior is observed for a chaotic system. With a strange attractor, the paths that start near one another quickly diverge. It is as if the attractor space is being stretched; a model of this behavior could be the stretching of a lump of bread dough during kneading. This divergence of the paths is exponential. An attractor is finite and thus the paths cannot diverge forever. Thus, the attractor folds onto itself; again, this can be modeled by the folding of bread dough after it has been stretched. The paths of the attractor are shuffled by the folding. The stretching and folding of the paths makes the system very dependent upon initial conditions. Now one can imagine why a one-part-in-a-thousand change in initial conditions caused the system to follow a different path as Lorenz observed. The stretching and folding continues repeatedly, creating a fractal. Also the stretching and folding of the paths replaces the initial information with new information. Predictability is short-lived. Long-term, all causality is lost.

Just how sensitive are chaotic systems to initial conditions? Before the concept of chaotic systems, it was assumed that all systems are predictable and that the accuracy of the prediction depended on the accuracy of the measurements of the system variables. Chaotic systems changed this view. As an example, for a very simple mathematical model of a chaotic process, measuring the values of the variables to one part in a thousand allows one only to predict the sequence of events for twenty-four steps. Increasing the accuracy to one part in a million increases the predictability to forty-eight steps, with one part in a billion giving predictability to seventy-two steps. For nonchaotic systems there would be no limit to the number of steps for the predictions. For many variables, it is not practical to obtain an accuracy of one part in a million, let alone one part in a billion. In addition, most "real world" chaotic systems are more complex than this mathematical model, which would require even greater accuracy to maintain these levels of predictability. In all chaotic cases, one quickly comes to the point where predictability breaks down.

Transition to Chaos

Many dynamic systems begin as ordered, predictable systems and then change to a chaotic system. We remember a scene from a movie where a character puts a lit cigarette on an ashtray. The camera focuses on the smoke. Initially, the smoke rises in a smooth stream (order). Then, suddenly, the top of the smooth stream becomes wildly erratic and swirls in all directions. The behavior of the smoke has gone from *laminar* (order) to *turbulent* (chaos) flow. Other examples of the transition to turbulence from our everyday life occur when a regularly dripping faucet changes to a randomly dripping faucet, or when ketchup smoothly flowing from a bottle onto our fries suddenly acquires an erratic flow and lands on us as well as the fries.

Turbulence has always been lurking in scientific systems. In many cases it could be ignored, so the systems were studied as ordered. In others, turbulence could not be ignored, so the systems were ignored. Engineers hate turbulence. Turbulent airflow removes the lift from an aircraft's wing; turbulent oil flow in a pipeline causes drag. Until the advent of chaos theory, few thought that turbulence would ever be understood. A scientific myth says that the quantum physicist Werner Heisenberg said that he had two questions for God: why relativity, and why turbulence? Heisenberg is quoted as saying, "I really think He may have an answer to the first question."[4]

An important question is how flow can change from smooth to turbulent. Or more generally, how do ordered systems become chaotic? Is there a way to predict when this transition will occur? One clue to understanding this transition came from the American biologist Robert May, who was studying annual variations in insect populations. One might expect that a high growth rate would lead to a larger population while a low growth rate would lead to a smaller population, with extinction occurring if the growth rate is too small. Using a mathematical model which predicted next year's population based on this year's population, May studied the effect of an increasing growth rate on the population value. At low values for the growth rate, the population would settle down to a single value year after year.

At first increasing the growth rate increased the population to another stable value. Then a surprise happened. As soon as the growth rate passed a value of three in his model, the possible population value branched (*bifurcated*) into two solutions. The model was still being deterministic (predicting a solution); it was now predicting two solutions. At this new growth rate, the population would be at one value one year followed by the other value the next year; then the population values would repeat. Increasing the growth rate a little more caused the population value choices to jump from two to four; the model was still deterministic. Continuing to increase the growth rate would lead to four bifurcating to eight, eight into sixteen, and so on with the model still being deterministic. At a value of 3.57, chaos began in his model. At this point, it became impossible to predict future population values; all one could say is that the population value would be one among all the values in the strange attractor. Field biologists found that May's model did reflect the behavior of actual animal populations.

Is May's work applicable to other systems that make a transition from predictable to chaotic? An answer came from the American physicist Mitchell Feigenbaum,[5] who studied May's work and proposed that the transition to chaos involves what is called period doubling (the bifurcation that May observed). This is called the *period-doubling route to chaos*. It was also realized that the period doubling comes faster and faster until the sudden appearance of chaos. Feigenbaum determined a numerical constant (4.669) that governs the doubling process (*Feigenbaum number*). He also discovered that these results (period doubling and Feigenbaum number) were applicable to a wide variety of chaotic systems. At last science had a way to predict the onset of turbulence.

Applications

As scientists acquired an understanding of chaotic process, they realized some processes that they thought were random were actually chaotic. In some cases, the chaotic model allowed scientists to explain puzzling observations. In other cases, scientists now had a tool for predicting the beginning of chaos and thereby at last being able to prevent the beginning of chaos. A few examples of the application of chaos theory to problems in astronomy and medicine will be given.

Astronomy

In astronomy, scientists have mostly used chaos theory to explain observations. Certain regions of the asteroid belt between Mars and Jupiter are almost free of asteroids. Scientists assumed that the gravitational field of Jupiter had resulted in these gaps; but until the advent of chaos theory, scientists had no mathematical model for these gaps (called *Kirkwood gaps* in honor of their discoverer). Calculations, using chaos theory, show that the interactions between the motions of the asteroids and the motion and gravitation field of Jupiter create chaotic regions in the asteroid belt. Most of the asteroids are expelled from these chaotic regions, resulting in the Kirkwood gaps. The expelled asteroids are sent on a path that takes them toward the inner planets. Thus, some of the expelled asteroids cross the orbit of Earth; such asteroids have the potential for colliding with the Earth and causing great damage. Chaos theory gave scientists a framework to explain and tie together these two phenomena.

Most natural satellites (moons) in the solar system have an orbit period equal to its spin period. For example, the moon takes twenty-seven days to orbit the earth and twenty-seven days to rotate on its axis. This results in the same side of the moon always facing the earth. Hyperion is a potato-shaped satellite of Saturn. Hyperion has an erratic spin period and a constantly changing rotational period. Calculations, using chaos theory, indicate that the behavior of Hyperion is chaotic because of its interaction with Saturn and Saturn's large moon, Titan.

Medicine

In medicine, chaos theory has not only given scientists an understanding of why certain phenomena occur but in some cases a regimen for preventing the onset of certain conditions. The body's defense mechanism against disease has been analyzed as a chaotic process. When the body is invaded by a bacterium or virus, the body, apparently, tries defense strategies at random. A feedback loop is used to tell (indicate) when a correct strategy has been selected. Scientists are trying to mimic this process in drug development.

Analysis of historical data for the two childhood diseases, measles and chicken pox, revealed that their epidemics behaved differently. Chicken pox varied periodically, while measles varied chaotically. This means that at a certain number of measles cases, it is "impossible" to predict in which direction the epidemic will proceed. The strange attractor for the measles outbreaks helps epidemiologists see patterns in what had previously been "random and noisy" yearly data.

Several medical conditions, including heart fibrillation and attacks of epilepsy and manic depression, involve a transition from an orderly process to a chaotic process. Fibrillation is also called ventricular fibrillation. The *ventricles* are the two large pumping chambers of the heart that discharge blood to the lungs or body. The normal ventricular contractions of the heart are periodic, controlled, and coordinated. *Fibrillation* involves ventricular contractions that are rapid, uncontrolled, and uncoordinated. Under these conditions the ventricles cannot pump blood and death can occur unless the condition is corrected. Normal heartbeat can sometimes be restored by a massive electric shock to the chest using a *defibrillator*. Chaos theory has helped physicians in two ways. The period-doubling-to-chaos trend allows those monitoring a patient to detect the beginning of the transition to chaos and to intervene before fibrillation starts. Understanding of the strange attractor for fibrillation has allowed for the better design of defibrillators.

The Scientific Method and Chaos

As we saw in chapter 1, one approach to the scientific method is to verify a theory by testing predictions. We compare the flight of a ball predicted by a mathematical equation to the actual flight of the ball. For more complicated systems such as a collection of gas molecules, a scientist would use statistical techniques to examine the properties of the system rather than the properties of the individual gas molecules. The system properties are statistical averages of the properties of the individual molecules. Simple mathematical equations relating the system's temperature, pressure, and volume can be found. (Reducing the volume increases the temperature and pressure of the system.) No attempt is made to explain the variables for an individual gas molecule.

What about chaotic systems? Very short-term predictions are possible; in billiards, the agreement between the predicted and actual path of a cue ball is lost in a minute or less. Long-term predictions for chaotic systems are impossible. Long-term, the best one can hope for is agreement with the strange attractors. Even with this agreement, chaos is not explaining very much more than statistical techniques. Neither method is giving predictive information about the individual components.

Chaos challenges *reductionism*. Reductionism says that the whole can be understood by breaking it down and studying its parts; if one can determine the forces and components present, then one knows everything about the whole. This view has been very successful in physics and chemistry. Many scientists are now attempting to extend reductionism to biology; they believe if one can determine all the physical interactions and chemical reactions present in a living system, then one can totally explain that system. Chaos has shown that complex behavior arises from simple, nonlinear interactions of the system's components. This implies that the whole can be more complex than the sum of its parts.

Usually we emphasize the limitations of chaos, the loss of predictability. However, others have speculated about the positive effects of chaos in nature. It has been proposed that nature, by amplifying small fluctuations, creates novelty. Scientists wonder: Do prey use chaotic flight controls to evade predators? Does a chaotic process introduce genetic variability? Does creativity have an underlying chaotic process?

Summary

Chaos is not the same as randomness. Although chaotic systems are deterministic with mathematical equations that relate the behavior of their components, they lose long-term predictability. Chaotic systems have three characteristics: sensitivity to initial conditions, strange attractors, and period-doubling route to chaos. Chaos theory challenges the predictability that undergirds the scientific method; it also challenges reductionism. Although chaos may be seen as a limitation to our understanding of nature, chaos may be the mechanism by which novelty is introduced.

CHAPTER FOURTEEN

THE RETURN OF CHRIST

ACCORDING TO THE GOSPEL MESSAGE ABOUT JESUS CHRIST, AT SOME point in the future Christ will return to earth, time will end, and creation will be complete. In addition to the certainty of this affirmation of faith, Jesus Christ himself taught that it is impossible to know or predict when the end will come. The unpredictability of the future represents a subtle subtheme of the Christian faith which nevertheless affirms a certain outcome to time, space, and history.

People function on a day-to-day basis by relying on the patterns of previous experience, as Solomon wrote:

> Generations come and generations go,
> but the earth remains forever.
> The sun rises and the sun sets,
> and hurries back to where it rises
>
> (Eccles. 1:4–5).

Past experience, however, provides no assurance of the future. The expectation that tomorrow will come may have less to do with faith than with the numb assumption or taking for granted of past experience. James, the half brother of Jesus, warned against taking future prosperity for granted: "Now listen, you who say, 'Today or tomorrow we will go to this or that city, spend a year there, carry on business and make money.' Why, you do not even know what will happen tomorrow. What is your life? You are mist a that appears for a little while and then vanishes. Instead, you ought to say, 'If it is the Lord's will, we will live and do this or that'" (James 4:13–15).

The Bible assumes the uncertainty or unpredictability of life, despite the many patterns that we take for granted. Yet, the Bible also assumes that God has complete and effortless authority within the unpredictability to affect outcomes.

The Involvement of God

How is God involved in human affairs? God created the physical world in such a way that it is open and indeterminate while at the same time possessing qualities of regularity that give it a determinate character. God has the freedom to interact with the physical world while in no way disrupting the orderly regularity of his established processes. In the same way, God provided people with a spiritual dimension of sufficient complexity that it is described as the image of God. This spiritual dimension of human life provides people with freedom to act while at the same time providing God with the opening to interact. The fallen human spirit is itself a highly complex chaos system.

God's involvement with people occurs as interpersonal interaction. Communication which involves a degree of understanding occurs. The Bible does not present a static view of how this communication takes place nor of the degree of understanding that goes with it. The Book of Hebrews begins by alluding to the variety of ways revelation has occurred. The writing of the Ten Commandments on stone represented a far more precise communication of content with intellectual understanding than Peter's vision of a sheet full of unclean animals coming down from heaven (Acts 10:9–35). Peter's understanding of the vision came later in the course of life's circumstances. Even less graphic are the daily interactions of God with people in terms of basic decision making, assurance, and understanding.

All through the Bible, God works with people. Some respond, like Moses. Some do not, like Pharaoh. Some are molded over time, like Jacob, David, or Peter. God's manner of interacting with individuals over time, as with Abraham, or with groups of people over generations, as with Israel, illustrates a patience out of which God slowly weaves a fabric.

The Book of Revelation describes the culmination of God's plan. Yet, the culmination is unpredictable. No one will expect it when it comes. While Revelation devotes the greatest attention to the subject of the end of time found in the Bible, the theme occurs throughout the New Testament as well as in many of the prophets. The overall sense of the end appears to be distinct from a predictable natural phenomenon of the physical universe. It will not happen in the normal order of things. Of this unpredictability, Jesus said: "No one knows about that day or hour, not even the angels in heaven, nor the Son, but only the Father. As it was in the days of Noah, so it will be at the coming of the Son of Man. For in the days before the flood, people were eating and drinking, marrying and giving in marriage, up to the day Noah entered the ark; and they knew nothing about what would happen until the flood came and took them all away. That is how it will be at the coming of the Son of Man" (Matt. 24:36–39).

The beginning and the end represent singular happenings that have no basis for prediction. They represent nonrepeatable events. Nonrepeatable events do not offer the opportunity for observation that forms the basis for theory, experimentation, verification, and final grounds for prediction. The certainty of the assertion of the end of time at the second coming of Christ implies a determinate system, yet the unpredictability of the second coming and the end of time implies an indeterminate system. Can these two mutually exclusive ideas both be valid? It resembles the half-life of radioactive iodine. The scientist may know that something will suddenly disappear, but he or she has no idea precisely when it will happen.

In the beginning of creation, Genesis describes a situation of chaos. The description has a threefold emphasis: the earth was formless and void, darkness covered the deep, and this state was described as "the waters." The Hebrew phrase *tohu wavohu,* which is translated into English as "formless and void," represents the equivalent of the Greek *chaos*. The idea of darkness represents a spiritual concept throughout the Bible which stands at odds with God's will and purpose. Likewise, "the waters" represent the physical embodiment of chaos and darkness in the Hebrew worldview. Creation occurs when God moves upon the face of this chaotic situation (Gen. 1:2). In creation, God does something *to* and *with* the chaos. God takes the chaos and says, "Let there be light." Out of the chaos the light appears.

The swirling, churning currents of water, especially vast expanses of water, continue to represent the chaotic void throughout Scripture, and God continually exercises authority over the chaos. The flood marks a return to the beginning as God removes the separation of the waters above and the waters below, as God removes the separation between the seas and the dry land, as the deep swallows all of creation. The chaos responds as the Spirit of God moves it. Then God separates the waters below and the waters above once again, and once again God causes the dry land to appear. God has the freedom to act with certainty, predictability, and purpose in the chaos because the chaos has no certainty, predictability, or purpose of its own. It may go one way as well as another.

The flight of the Hebrew slaves from Egypt ended abruptly at the Red Sea. The ancient watery fear blocked the way of escape. All the ancient Hebrew dreads of the vast water as the place of death seemed fulfilled until God repeated once again the separation of the waters from the dry land. Like the chorus of a great hymn, the theme repeats itself again—God has authority over the chaos. God actually uses the chaos to accomplish his purpose.

The ancients worshiped the dreaded, fearful Deep in the form of Tiamet, Dagon, Poseidon, and Neptune. The ability of God to rescue Jonah from the deep, from the clutches of chaos, provides a basis for faith and hope in a God who can bring the most disastrous of situations to a satisfactory resolution. Ultimately, the faith in God to which the Bible bears witness is often a faith in spite of the unpredictable and disastrous situations of life. It is a faith in the ultimate certainty that God takes the chaos and moves it toward an end in keeping with his will. This final end will benefit people regardless of how the chaos along the way may have affected them. In reflecting on this idea, the apostle Paul observed: "And we know that in all things God works for the good of those who love him, who have been called according to his purpose" (Rom. 8:28). God does not keep people from the chaos, because the chaos itself is the stuff of life. Rather, God works in the midst of the chaos.

Recalling God's authority over the waters, Jesus Christ dramatically signified his identification with God by his authority over water. His first miracle involved changing water into wine. More reminiscent of the deep, however, Jesus calmed the stormy sea and walked upon the waters. Any one of these stories would be quite unbelievable, but they demonstrate the continuing authority that God exercises over the chaos. The episodes of authority over water provide a symbolic link with creation and the Hebrew dread of the sea. Other demonstrations of authority by Jesus illustrate this same utilization of chaos. Whether social systems or human body systems, Jesus acts to bring wholeness or healing.

A quantum universe made up of chaotic systems is wide open to the involvement of God. One might say that chaos suggests an openness to the intervention of God, but the notion of intervention suggests that God is not already intimately involved in the orderly processes at work in the midst of the chaos. Rather than intervention, a universe made up of chaotic systems seems tailor-made for continual involvement.

Moving Toward the Finale

While God has the freedom to act upon chaos without doing damage to the principles or the forces at work that were established to provide order to the universe, a sovereign God also has the freedom not to act. God has the freedom to let matters take their own course. Sovereignty means that God has as much freedom not to determine events as to determine them. Thus, the author of Hebrews observes, "Yet at present we do not see everything subject to him" (Heb. 2:8c).

If God is involved in the universe and has the power to determine events, then why does he allow bad things to happen? This question in theology is referred to as *theodicy*, or the problem of evil. The Bible suggests a variety of answers to the question, beginning with punishment. Bad things happen to people as a result of the judgment of God. Examples of this experience appear in Scripture from the flood and the destruction of Sodom and Gomorrah to the Babylonian Captivity. Yet, the Bible also provides examples of bad things happening to innocent people like Job. In some cases, bad things happen as the result of satanic attack. Bad things also happen for which the Bible gives no explanation; such as the Galileans whose blood Pilate mixed with their sacrifice or the eighteen people who died when the tower of Siloam fell on them (Luke 13:1–4).

In a deterministic universe, one would expect a single answer for all situations of suffering or evil. Suffering would be predictable and easily explained. In a chaotic universe, however, variable situations suggest multiple explanations for bad experiences. The presence of suffering in different situations may have different reasons or no reason. If God does not act, then reason and purpose vanish.

Both physical and social chaos systems lead to disaster. The physical order breeds earthquakes, volcanoes, hurricanes, tornadoes, floods, tidal waves, landslides, drought, fire, blizzards, pestilence, and supernovas. The social order fosters envy, jealousy, arrogance, theft, deceit, lies, violence, murder, bigotry, hatred, indifference, selfishness, and war. Suffering occurs in the context of the indeterminacy of chaotic systems for a variety of reasons. Jesus explained that the occurrence of earthquakes, wars, and rumors of wars would not constitute a sign of the end; rather, these situations are a feature of life.

God waited four hundred years to release the Hebrew slaves from their bondage in Egypt. Why the wait? They surely experienced suffering. The question of when God acts takes on as much importance as what God does in terms of suffering. Does it suggest a limited ability to act? Different theological traditions have staked out different positions on this spectrum of thought. Although the positions are quite different and frequently contradictory, the motive for the position is strikingly similar. Reformed theology holds that God determines every event that occurs, however small or large, in order to uphold God's sovereignty. The motive is to defend God from the assertion that he is less than all-powerful.

Some theological approaches today represented by such books as *When Bad Things Happen to Good People* by Harold Kushner (from a Jewish perspective) and *A Scandalous Providence* by Frank Tupper (from a Christian perspective) hold that many events lie outside God's control or power to act, in order to uphold God's love. The motive is to defend God from the charge that God is not good for allowing bad things to happen. Both are defensive theologies designed to protect God's reputation. Both are based on the idea that a standard exists for judging God such that if he does not determine each event he is not sovereign and if he does not prevent all suffering he is not a loving, compassionate God. This higher standard that undergirds the theology comes from the theologian's philosophical perspective. The philosophy, in turn, is developed against the backdrop of a number of unspoken and unrecognized emotional considerations. Thus, theology itself represents a chaos system capable of distorting revelation itself.

Theological traditions also differ on whether an end of time determined by God will occur at all. Some non-Christian theological traditions strongly emphasize an end of time and a divine reckoning. In Hinduism it will occur when Kali dances the final dance of destruction and Shiva the Destroyer appears to destroy all. In Islam the end will come when Moses, Jesus, and Mohammed appear to judge the world. In classical Judaism it will occur at the appearing of the Son of Man in glory. In classical Christianity it will occur at the second coming of Christ. Within Buddhism and some forms of Hinduism, however, the end is a personal matter along with judgment. Judgment is a process that occurs over and over through thousands of successive lives which are judged imperfect unless in one reincarnation a person finally attains the end of perfection—bliss, *nirvana*. In the nature religions, these questions do not play a central role. Instead, the focus is on the cycles of nature with the concern resting on how one can best prosper now. The moral/ethical, meaning/destiny questions give way to physical survival concerns.

In Christian theology, the study of the end of time is referred to as *eschatology*. Theologians will often speak of the end of time as the *eschaton*, which is the Greek word for "the end." Within the Christian tradition, several views of the second coming of Christ have appeared over and over again. The Book of Revelation refers to a one-thousand-year reign of Christ on earth which is known as the *millennium* or the *millennial reign*. The major views within classical Christian thought of the timing of the second coming relate to the millennium. Those who believe Christ will come before the millennium to establish his kingdom are referred to as *premillennialists*. Those who believe that Christ will come after Christians have established the godly society with Christ reigning through them are referred to as *postmillennialists*. Those who believe the millennium of Revelation is a metaphor for a spiritual reality, but that there will be no literal one-thousand-year kingdom on earth are referred to as *amillennialists*.

Philosophical Approaches

Apart from these approaches to interpretation of Scripture within classical Christianity, several attempts have developed in recent years to make God and progress compatible with naturalism. The most prominent of these approaches is *process theology*, which identifies God with the natural processes of nature which lead to complexity, especially as they relate to life. Process theology stands on the shoulders of *neoorthodox theology*, which accepted the presuppositions of naturalism but tried to make a case for classical Christianity without cognitive revelation (Barth) or miracle (Bultmann). Because naturalism has no place for the influence or involvement of God in the natural order, neoorthodoxy sought to make religion a matter of personal opinion rather than objective reality. The naturalist lost all grounds for objection to Christianity if Christians did not make truth claims. The Bible was not represented by neoorthodoxy to be revelation from God. Instead, it was a collection of testimonies of personal experiences of those who had revelatory experiences with God. Though Jesus Christ was held to be the highest revelation of God, knowledge of Christ came only through documents regarded as personal opinion. The Bible no longer held any higher authority than any other religious writings.

In the twentieth century, Christian theology has tended either to ignore science altogether or to use science as the basis for developing a theology. Karl Barth represents that camp of mainline Protestantism that believed general revelation or nature could tell us nothing about God. Another tradition, however, took the functional view that specific revelation does not occur as traditionally understood; therefore, an understanding of nature provides our only rational or reflective understanding of God. This tradition would generally include personal experience within the realm of nature.

Process theology builds a view of God and nature that no longer requires the same level of attention and reference to the Bible which neoorthodoxy followed. Process theology represents a philosophical approach to recognizing the existence of some kind of transcendent being within a naturalistic universe. Those process theologians who carry this line of thought to its natural conclusions identify God with the naturalistic process itself. God is mind, which actualizes itself in the process of nature. Nature has no fixed future. Thus, process theology allows for a deterministic process and an indeterminate mind behind the process. Process theology represents a departure from classical orthodox Christianity in that it is strongly influenced by evolutionary theory. Some of the major figures who have contributed to this stream of thought would not consider themselves Christian, though some have done their work within the structures of Christianity. A brief survey of several key process thinkers will serve to demonstrate how a philosophically based religion might develop from science.

Teilhard de Chardin

Teilhard de Chardin (1881–1955) was a French Jesuit priest as well as an accomplished paleontologist. In his most important book, *The Phenomenon of Man,* Teilhard propounded a theology of human evolution. His ideas are included in this chapter, however, because he based his theology on the point toward which people are evolving. He called this end point *Omega Point*. Thus, Teilhard used evolution to create a metaphysical system that explained the goal of the cosmos.

Teilhard argued that matter/energy is the ground of the universe. Man is a part of this matter/energy as a physical reality. As matter/energy becomes more complex, man appears. If at the end of this process of *complexification* there is mental energy as well as physical energy, then perhaps mental energy was there all along. Teilhard argued that at the beginning of the process of complexification, mental energy is already present as latent human spirit.

Teilhard described three major realms of complexification, or the upward drive of the organism. The basic physical realm he labeled the *cosmosphere*. A supersaturation of complexification at this level leads to a change of state, like hot water that suddenly becomes steam. This change of state in the purely physical leads to the next level that he called the *biosphere*. The biosphere is the realm of life. Supersaturation of complexification at this level leads to human life which belongs to the next level which Teilhard called the *noosphere*. Teilhard argued that complexification ended at the physical level with *cerebralisation* or the centralization of the nervous system. From the noosphere to Omega Point, complexification involves the development of the social dimension. Under the pressure of overpopulation, the noosphere will result in either totalitarianism or a society of mutual love. At Omega Point, energy takes the form of love. In this approach, *mind* is called physical energy at the lower level. This identification of mind and matter reverses the dichotomy that Descartes saw between these two.

William Temple

A theologian and later archbishop of Canterbury, William Temple (1881–1944) began his career as an advocate of *Hegelianism*. Hegel had regarded the universe as one mind thinking. The one mind moves itself through history, seeking self-realization. It begins in emptiness and moves dialectically. *Dialectic* involves a thesis which is countered by an antithesis which resolves into synthesis. The synthesis becomes the new thesis. All nature and history is God arguing with himself. As a dialectic process, God is a growing God. Temple never escaped the dialectic method. When confronted by communism which also utilized Hegel's dialectic method, Temple saw the need to develop a response that made room for God in the dialectic process. *Dialectical realism* represents Temple's response to the materialistic dialectic of Karl Marx.

Temple's dialectic begins with the process of evolution but operates in the area of *mind*. (1) The smallest organism is unaware and only moved by its environment. (2) The more complex life form has consciousness and self-motion. It has movement within nature and awareness of nature. It adjusts to its environment. (3) People have self-consciousness in addition to self-motion. People have the ability to adjust the environment to suit them. Temple argues that as mind becomes increasingly apparent and present in nature, nature becomes increasingly inexplicable, except with reference to mind. Behind the physical evolutionary process lies a mind that directs and guides the process toward a goal.

Alfred North Whitehead

Alfred North Whitehead (1861–1947) was a mathematician who took up philosophy after retirement. Though he was not a Christian, Whitehead had a significant influence on Christian philosophers and others interested in the relationship of science and religion.

Whitehead employed an organic model for the universe. The basis of response of an organism to environment is feeling, even at the unconscious level. Prehension is the lowest level of feeling, and it exists in a state of unconsciousness. An actual entity has a fleeting existence. An actual event is a dynamic series which takes time to realize itself or attain *satisfaction*. The physical pole of an entity can prehend another entity when it achieves satisfaction. An actual entity attains eternal objectivity when satisfaction occurs, but once satisfaction occurs, the entity perishes. The enduring object is a nexus of beads of actual occasions. Temporal and spatial nexuses are held together by prehension.

The mental pole prehends the subjective aims. Subjective aims do not come from within but from God. God is the principle that distributes subjective aims and gives direction. This does not imply that God created the process, because creativity is within the process and God is the first creation of the process. God is an enduring actual occasion which is inconsistent with the system. All actual entities are God's memories. Man's objective immortality involves enduring in the memory of God, who carries the memory of us to his satisfaction. This system allows no place for transcendence.

W. E. Hocking

W. E. Hocking (1873–1964) accepted all religions as equal. He was a realist because of his understanding of nature. The natural order made possible the encounter of finite minds with one another and with *Other Mind*. Nature is objective, not a creation of the mind. Minds come out of nature and are a part of the natural process. Despite their finitude, people are able to communicate and have fellowship. People encounter one another in nature on the physical periphery of their being. Hocking believed that people know one another by intuiting a pattern. Body and activity are outward manifestations of being, and revelation comes through the body.

Hocking was an ontologist who believed that in our own self-transcendence, people find God. When nature is investigated, it takes on an aspect of *Other Mind*. If something in nature is objective and parallel to my mind, then I am encountering *Other Mind*. God meets people in the world where they live and in the depths of their own self-awareness.

Charles Hartshorne

Charles Hartshorne (1897–) taught at Harvard with Whitehead. He believed that reality is bound together by feeling. The universe is made up of psychic entities characterized by feeling. He saw these *societies* at different levels: spatial, temporal, and temporal/spatial. Societies may be democratic (a heap of sand—inanimate) or monarchical (where one aspect orders the whole—animate). Upon moving beyond the plant level, the wholes of the monarchical level show themselves. A changing individual must have a persisting factor. A changing whole needs only one factor to change for the whole to be changed.

The accidence of becoming comes from God's involvement in the world. God's essence is love. Accidence enriches God's life as he fulfills his purpose, but this does not alter his essence of love. Because of God's involvement with his creatures, he can be said to suffer. God does not set down objective goals but constrains the world by his love. Applying the analogy of society, the universe must be monarchical; otherwise, there would be no order. In Hartshorne's universe, God does not know what will happen, but he knows the possibilities.

This progression away from classical Christian faith with all its rich diversity illustrates how one's philosophical presuppositions can result in a theological system that distorts revelation itself. These attitudes, which relate to basic presuppositions about knowledge and the superiority of scientific knowledge over revelation, are based largely on "old science." They emerge from a static, deterministic understanding of science, and they confuse the disciplined method of science with the philosophical presuppositions of naturalism.

Philosophical Views of History

The Bible presents a view of history with a beginning and an end. Philosophy would describe this kind of view as *linear history*. Among historians, a *historic period* would refer only to a period that left written records. Old Testament scholars will sometimes say that Abraham was not a historical figure. Within this technical definition used by scholars, the statement means that Abraham left no written records, nor did his contemporaries write about him. This does not mean that Abraham did not live or that the account of him in Genesis is not true. It means that the story of Abraham was preserved orally from generation to generation rather than in writing. God instructed the people of Israel to use this same method of transmission to keep the story of the Passover alive, and it continues to this day in Jewish families. Nonetheless, many historians will not accept as historical a figure who has no contemporary written record. This represents an area where history seeks to have a basis for certainty that corresponds to the scientific method.

Philosophers, on the other hand, view history in an entirely different way. Philosophers of history focus on the meaning or meaninglessness of history beyond the mere historical record. The historical record may be the least reliable source for understanding from the perspective of the philosopher. The old adage "The victor writes the history" suggests that people are not always objective in their accounts of themselves. The Bible—written over centuries, across many cultures, from the perspective of both victor and conquered peoples alike—presents a meaning to history. It presents this meaning not only in terms of what it says about events, but also in terms of the framework: a beginning and an end. History has a movement or direction to it, like a journey. It has an aspiration to it: a promised land, future generations, a coming kingdom, a time of peace. It has a sense of the contribution and foundation of the past and a future expectation of hope in which the present moment plays a vital role in what will come to pass. The end is certain, but what happens between the present and the end is not known; there-fore, present behavior, attitudes, and thoughts matter.

This *linear view* of history is not the only linear view of history. Karl Marx developed a linear view based on the economic struggle of the workers against their masters which would eventually lead to a perfect, materialistic workers' state. This linear view is the phi-losophy of history imbedded in communism.

Another philosophical view is *cyclical view*. The cyclical view of history regards history as an ever-repeating story. This view often appears in nature religions where life involves endless cycles of sea-sons, planets, births, and especially reincarnations. Philosophers of history, such as Oswald Spengler in *The Decline of the West* and Arnold Toynbee in *A Story of History* seek to detect patterns to explain the rise and decline of civilizations. The presence of pat-terns, however, does not require a cyclical view of history.

Within the linear view of history presented by the biblical writ-ers, one also finds patterns. The patterns, however, should not be understood as cycles. Cycles suggest a regular, inevitable rhythm, like the beating of the heart, the passage of the seasons, the phases of the moon. A cycle has a deterministic element to it. Solomon dis-cusses the patterns of life in Ecclesiastes. The sun rises and sets, but there is nothing new under the sun. Life is full of episodes: living, dying, laughing, crying (Eccles. 3:1–8). Solomon calls the patterns of life meaningless by themselves. They are all vanity. They are the patterns of chaos. The same elements may be seen over and over again, but in no particular order or duration.

Just as individual lives contain many of the same elements or patterns, the Bible explores the patterns for societies. Kingdoms may suffer the same fate, but these common experiences do not occur as an inevitable natural process or cycle. They occur because of human decision and divine judgment. The judgment, however, is not a detached judgment. The judgment provides a basis for mak-ing a fresh start, but the involvement of God in personal lives and social structures occurs to prevent the personal and social collapse that results from detachment from God. Spiritual renewal and the rejuvenation of societies represent unexpected features of history that stands at odds with the cyclical view.

In the midst of the chaos, new life emerges. At the personal level, regeneration occurs when God moves upon the chaos of a personal situation and something unexpected and unpredictable results. A person encounters God and is changed. He or she can never be the same person again. He may repeat old habits, but his perspective has changed. Once a person knows the world is round, it changes his or her perspective. God moves upon the chaos of entire societies as well. These periods of revival or awakening cannot be predicted. People like Charles Finney have attempted to classify the "laws" of revival to give such experiences the legitimacy of the scientific method, but they defy such regularity. People have also attempted to standardize the form that personal conversion takes, but conversion defies such a mechanical understanding. In revival, just as in conversion, people respond to the impulse of the movement of the Spirit of God. Not everyone responds. Perhaps very few respond.

Any consideration of the presence of suffering and evil in the world created by a good God must begin with a consideration of creation itself. The question does not begin with why there is suffering in the world but why there is any world in which to feel anything. What is the purpose of creation? If the image of God is essentially the spiritual aspect of people, then why would God begin by making people physical? Physical experience in its totality has something to contribute to life.

From the perspective of eternity, the period of human suffering is incalculably small. From the perspective of human suffering, however, eternity is a very long way away. Yet God does not seem to have physical prosperity and comfort as the goal of creation. For fallen humanity, comfort and luxury tend to make God more remote and less attractive. In the presence of suffering, however, when people lose their health, the people they love, their reputations, their possessions, or anything else dear to them, they become open to seeing God. The chaos provides the openness for discerning the presence of God.

The Bible never suggests that suffering, evil, pain, and distress are good. Instead, the Bible indicates that the sudden, unpredictable end is the means God has chosen to bring an end to suffering and pain, once and for all. In the meantime, death itself provides the door from this world to the next. That death will come is a certainty, barring the return of Christ; yet, it is an unpredictable event.

CHAPTER FIFTEEN

DIALOGUE ON CHAOS THEORY

CHAOS THEORY RAISES CONSONANCE AND DISSONANCE WITH RELIGION in regard to the purpose and direction of history. Is history under the direction of God? Is there a final outcome to history, and can we know the outcome beforehand? We will begin our discussion by reviewing the relationship between determinism and chaos.

What Is the Relationship Between Determinism and Chaos?

For nearly three hundred years, scientists thought that the deterministic laws of classical physics reflected nature. This view grew out of the triumph of Newtonian or classical physics. Classical physics began using the inductive method of Bacon (see chapter 1) to mathematically model observed phenomena. Galileo developed empirical laws (equations) to predict the behavior of falling bodies, while Kepler developed empirical laws (equations) to predict the behavior of planetary motion. Newton combined these two sets of motion into a single theoretical structure (his three Laws of Motion and the Law of Universal Gravitation). The predictive power of Newtonian laws became apparent with Newton's successful prediction of the return date of what is today called Halley's Comet. Newton's laws are deterministic; by knowing the position and momentum of an object, a scientist can use Newton's laws to predict (calculate) the position and momentum of that object in the future or the past. An almanac's listing of the dates of future eclipses of the sun or moon is an example of this type of calculation.

Since the laws of classical physics were deterministic, scientists began to assume that these equations reflected all of nature. They

229

assumed that nature was deterministic. Pierre Simon Marquis de Laplace (1749–1827) boldly stated this determinism as follows:

> All events, even those which on account of their insignificance do not seem to follow the great laws of nature, are the result of it just as necessarily as the revolutions of the sun. In ignorance of the ties which unite such events to the entire system of the universe, they have been made to depend upon final causes or upon hazard . . . but these imaginary causes have gradually receded with the widening bounds of knowledge and disappear entirely before sound philosophy, which sees in them only the expression of our ignorance of the true causes. . . . We ought then to regard the present state of the universe as the effect of its anterior state and as the cause of the one which is to follow.[1]

Scientists forgot how few and special were the systems that could be solved by classical physics. They ignored the fact that most systems could not be solved exactly. Even in astronomy, where Newton's laws had triumphed with the Halley's Comet prediction, approximations had to be used in dealing with three-body problems.[2] The behavior of gases was expressed in terms of statistics and probabilities; the behavior of the individual gas particle could not be predicted because so many gas particles were involved. Many phenomena were ignored or engineered out, with turbulence being an example. With hindsight, one sees that scientists of the classical physics period engaged in the fallacy of inducing from a too-small number of workable systems to the whole of nature. Also with hindsight, one sees that modern science would not have had such a success if there had not been systems that could be explained by deterministic mathematical equations. Without finding these patterns, there would not have been as much incentive to study nature.

Today scientists realize there are more chaotic systems than classical deterministic systems. They also realize that many of their classical systems can and do go chaotic. Some examples of systems that can exhibit chaotic behavior are three-body systems, chemical reactions, turbulence, heat flow, ecology, cardiac rhythms, population changes, the solar system, weather, and billiards. All of these systems have instances in which they become as irregular and unpredictable as a truly random system.

If one has a computer program that calculates random numbers and one wants to know the one-hundredth number generated by the program, one has to run the program one hundred times to obtain the one-hundredth random number. There is no rule that allows one to take a shortcut to predict that number. Likewise, for chaotic systems, the only way to find out how the system changes with time is to watch it change. Again, there is no rule that allows one to go directly from the beginning to the end. There is no shortcut. But there appears to be a shortcut because in many cases Newton's laws explain the behavior at each step. Yet, chaotic systems are so sensitive to initial conditions that one cannot specify the values of the variable with enough accuracy to gain predictive insight beyond only a few steps.

If I want to know the outcome of a billiard game, I have to watch the whole game. Once the game is over, I can review each step to receive an understanding of why it turned out the way it did. Even though Newton's laws allow calculation of motion involving collision of balls and walls, I am not able to predict the outcome of the game from, say, the half-way point. Why? The behavior of the ball is too sensitive to initial conditions (collisions with other balls and table walls, vibrations of the table, impacts from air molecules, and so on) to allow a deterministic prediction. Again, I have to let the game unfold to determine how it will end.

Human history may be an extremely complex chaotic system. Historians have not been very successful at predicting the fate of elections or nations. As in the case of the billiard game, historians have to watch history unfold to be sure of what will happen. Also, like the billiard game, by reviewing past events historians gain insight into why certain events actually occurred. What consonance and dissonance does this chaotic view of history have with religion and its prophecies, its view that history has a purpose?

Relationship of Law and Chaos

What is the relationship between law and chaos? Is there any relationship at all? Do the two concepts represent mutually exclusive ideas? Does the presence of chaos prove that the physical laws are only the illusions suggested by Eastern thought? The problem of the relationship between law and chaos applies as much to the spiritual as to the physical realm. Given the apparent chaos in society, can we legitimately speak of moral law?

From the opening verses of Genesis through almost the last chapter of Revelation, the Bible describes people and society as chaotic. For over a thousand years in a variety of social settings, the writers who were responsible for putting the words of Scripture in ink portrayed the human race in rebellion against the will of God. In spite of this chaotic situation, however, the Bible also describes a certain pattern or patterns to human behavior.

Not only Christianity but most religions of the world have within them some understanding of the consequences of bad moral behavior. In the present blip in cultural development in which moral values are viewed as relativistic and without objective meaning, we still know that bad behavior is behavior that hurts me. C. S. Lewis describes this universally understood concept in *Mere Christianity*. The universal experience that people do not like to have bad things done to them, however, does not prove that values have an eternal, objective quality about them.

Christianity holds that values derive from the existence of a Creator God. Universal values do not exist in and of themselves. Rather, they are the views, opinions, and judgments of the one who created all things. Because people are made in the image of God, they also have the ability to express views, opinions, and judgments that express their own essence as well. As a result, people inhabit a world filled with competing values. It is a world so filled with subjective and culturally contrived views, opinions, and judgments that people have a difficult time recognizing eternal values or distinguishing them from relative values.

Values exert a powerful force on people, depending on the source of the value. The expectations of individuals and groups represent forces that few individuals challenge on their own. Without a group consensus for the norms of behavior, on the other hand, society quickly descends into chaos. In the Bible, the Book of Judges comments on the absence of commonly held values in Israel before the anointing of Saul as king by saying, "In those days Israel had no king; everyone did as he saw fit" (Judg. 21:25).

Societies establish laws to exert force on the tendency of people to do as they see fit. The expectation of others is sufficient force to cause most people to obey the law. The fear of punishment will cause others to obey the law. Still, there will always be some who disregard the law. In that sense, human law is like Plato's Ideal. It describes the ideal society, but the way people behave may be quite different.

Science establishes laws to describe the forces at work in nature which have been observed. The expectation of science is that nature will always behave according to the laws. In society, if people violate the law, they are punished. In science, if nature violates the law, the law is punished. In that sense, scientific law is like Aristotle's Form. It describes perfect order expressed in its substance. If perfection is violated, then the law must be wrong. Over the centuries, scientific law and human law have changed a great deal.

What about divine law? What is its purpose and how does it operate? God gave the law specifically to the nation of Israel, yet Israel became a corrupt society that oppressed the poor. God gave commandments related to worship within the law, yet the religion of Israel grew polluted and idolatrous. The law did not preserve Israel as a nation or keep it holy. The law of God was not intended to control the behavior of people the way gravity controls the orbit of planets around the sun. The law of God exerted a force upon people, but it was a personal force.

Even more than fear of punishment or concern for the expectation of the crowd, obedience to the law depended upon how highly people regarded the God who gave the law. We might call this regard *the fear of the Lord* or faith, but it is a highly personal, relational matter. In this regard, the law itself was never the point. Like Plato's Image, it is but a faint shadow of God's perfect will. Yet, like Aristotle's Substance, it points toward that which is perfect. In this sense, Paul described the law as functioning like a custodial schoolmaster in the ancient tradition: "But before faith came, we were kept under the law, shut up unto the faith which should afterwards be revealed. Wherefore the law was our schoolmaster to bring us unto Christ, that we might be justified by faith" (Gal. 3:23–24 KJV). The law teaches about the perfect will of God, but it is not the perfect expression of that will.

The greatest conflict Jesus had with the religious leaders of his day dealt with the distinction between the law and the will of God. Jesus explored this issue in the Sermon on the Mount in which he explored the laws on murder, adultery, divorce, oaths, and vengeance as well as the piety related to alms, prayer, and fasting (Matt. 5:21–6:18). Continually he taught that something higher lay behind the law, and he stressed the *fulfillment* of the Law (Matt. 5:17). He also taught that the law contained things which God allowed, but which were not God's perfect will, such as divorce (Matt. 19:3–9).

Is the Universe Determined or Open?

Is chaos theory, like quantum theory, another nail driven into the heart of determinism? Does the fact that chaotic systems lose their long-term predictability mean that the universe is open? As we saw previously, Laplace was convinced that there was no openness in the universe. His previous quote says that events in the universe attributed to religion (final causes) or randomness (hazard) are really determined. To Laplace, the "ignorance" of the observer causes the observer not to see the underlying determinism. As Laplace also said in the 1814 edition of *Analytic Theory of Probability:*

> If an intelligence, for one given instant, recognizes all the forces which animate Nature, and the respective positions of the things which compose it, and if that intelligence is also sufficiently vast to subject these data to analysis, it will comprehend in one formula the movements of the largest bodies of the universe as well as those of the minutest atom; nothing will be uncertain to it, and the future as well as the past will be present to its vision. The human mind offers in the perfection which it has been able to give to astronomy, a modest example of such an intelligence.[3]

This "intelligence" is not God, since Laplace replied to Emperor Napoleon Bonaparte that he had no need for that hypothesis. For generations, some theologians struggled to explain how God could act in such a determined universe.

In one regard, Laplace was wrong. Quantum mechanics has shown that one cannot simultaneously determine the position and momentum of atomic and subatomic particles. The accuracy of a prediction is limited by Heisenberg's Uncertainty Principle. Many see chaos theory as weakening Laplacian determinism even further. However, on the one hand, determinism is extended by chaos theory. Before chaos theory, processes, such as arrhythmic heartbeats or turbulence, were thought to be random. Now using the chaos theory's concept of "period-doubling to chaos," scientists can predict when these chaotic systems are going to occur and in many cases prevent their occurrence. In addition, the chaos theory's concept of "strange attractors" allows scientists to analyze these systems deterministically. Does Laplace have a last laugh?

On the other hand, chaos theory does set a limit to determinism. Although one can predict when chaos will begin, once chaos begins, predictability is short-lived. After only a few steps, cause and effect are lost. At this point, one can only present probability values for the behavior of the system. Long-term chaotic systems are as unpredictable as a truly random system. Thus, there is a causal limit in dynamic systems. Although chaos theory gives insight into the behavior of a chaotic system, we are limited in that we do not know the outcome until after the fact.

Putting together the insights of quantum mechanics and chaos theory, what can one say about the openness of the universe? From quantum mechanics, one discovers that each measurement has a limit on its accuracy. This limit is much more important at the quantum level but is present in all measurements. From chaos theory, one sees that for complex systems there is a limit to predictability. One can gain an insight into the broad picture of what is going to happen (strange attractor), but one cannot know the actual outcome until after the fact. Thus, the universe is not the deterministic box that Laplace envisioned. It is more open than scientists since Newton have thought it was. The model of the universe has gone from the predictability of a rigid clock to the predictability and unpredictability of a complex organism.

Is the Fate of the Universe Determined or Open?

The Bible paints a picture of the outcome of the universe that has an inseparable link with the human race. The end of the cosmos and human history both emerge from chaos. The chaotic systems of the physical order may be observed and described by the scientific method. The social sciences, sometimes called "soft sciences," observe and describe people. These disciplines include psychology, sociology, anthropology, and history. The hard sciences have not extended the hand of fellowship and membership in the guild to the soft sciences because of the difficulty of legitimate observation and the unpredictability of human behavior. Oddly enough, these two features form the basis for quantum theory and chaos theory in modern science. By definition, science does not address the question of God because God as a nonphysical being cannot be observed by the senses.

The soft sciences, on the other hand, have had a great deal to say about God and religion. Because people are religious and the social sciences are concerned with the study of people, the social sciences must comment on God and religion. In an effort to gain a sense of legitimacy still denied by the hard sciences, the social sciences have attempted to adapt the scientific method as practiced by physical science to the study of people. This adaptation of the methodology of one discipline to the study of another discipline has brought with it some philosophical baggage. While the social sciences must deal with religion, they do so only as an observable phenomenon. They search for some explanation for the practice of religion among people that comes from some source other than the existence of God.

For decades, the various social sciences followed a *reductionist* approach to religion as well as other facets of human behavior. They reduced the explanation for human behavior to one essential cause. Sigmund Freud reduced human behavior to sex and elaborated his explanation with discussions of guilt and suppression. God represented only a projected wish on the universe. Karl Marx reduced human history to economics and the materialistic dialectic that would eventually lead to the perfect state. Marx described religion as "the opiate of the people," a narcotic to prevent the masses from rising up against their masters. People who follow such a reductionist approach might attempt to isolate the cause of the American Civil War the way an epidemiologist might attempt to isolate a virus.

In examining the chaos of human history and behavior, one soon realizes that simple explanations will not do. How could a well-educated, technologically and artistically advanced society like that of Germany have embraced Adolf Hitler? The question defies a simple, reductionist answer. A complex system of undercurrents converged to make the time ripe for Adolf Hitler. One might also ask how Hitler could have possibly lost his war against Britain. A series of "ifs" might be posed to change the equation. If an isolationist Republican had defeated Franklin Roosevelt, could Britain have ever negotiated the Lend-Lease Treaty or would Japan have felt the need to attack Pearl Harbor? Human behavior and history are a swirl of unpredictable events that may be influenced by emotions, intellect, character, talent, or survival.

The Bible provides a narrative of selected episodes of human history that suggest that any number of motives and underlying causes may lie behind the behavior of people. Rather than a single cause driving human behavior, the Bible portrays a variety of people and groups driven by different causes at different times and places. One might expect the Bible to portray God as the driving motive, yet the Bible shows very few people for whom God is the great passion. One might even expect the Bible to portray God as determining, decreeing, and causing every event and circumstance of all human life. While the Bible makes clear without qualification that God has absolute power and authority over time and eternity, the description of the exercise of sovereignty appears more artistic than totalitarian.

God did not cause Adam and Eve to sin, but he interacted with them to move beyond the great disaster. God consistently interacts with people in their own circumstances, in the chaos of human events. The Bible describes God as effortlessly interacting with all manner of human situations to move humanity toward his ultimate goal. Like a master chess player, it does not matter what move his novice opponent makes. He has the final victory in sight from the first move. It is all a matter of patiently taking time for all the moves. One of the most familiar passages in the Old Testament speaks of this interaction of God. After being sold into slavery by his brothers and eventually rising in rank to become prime minister to the pharaoh, Joseph said to his brothers: "You intended to harm me, but God intended it for good to accomplish what is now being done, the saving of many lives" (Gen. 50:20).

The central event of the faith of Israel occurred in the Exodus, when Moses led the Hebrew slaves out of Egypt. Behind this grand spectacle, however, lies another story that the Bible relates. It is the story of the collapse of Canaanite civilization. As it turns out, God had not chosen Israel because of the goodness of the Hebrew people but in order to bring an end to Canaanite civilization. The central feature of Canaanite religion involved child sacrifice. With the call of Abraham and the substitution of a sheep for the child whom Abraham intended to sacrifice to God, events were set in motion to show God's disgust for the Canaanite practice of child sacrifice. From the descendants of Abraham's son Isaac, who was spared from the altar, God would produce an army to destroy the Canaanite culture.

Centuries later, the Bible describes God as bringing the Assyrians to destroy the northern kingdom of Israel and the Babylonians to destroy the southern kingdom of Judah. Neither the Assyrians nor the Babylonians considered themselves to be the servants of the God of Israel. On the other hand, they did not give any evidence in the Scriptures that they felt in any way coerced, forced, bullied, or manipulated by God into invading Israel and Judah. The armies of these pagan nations set about satisfying their own ambitions, yet in doing so they accomplished the purposes of God. At the same time, the ambitious motives of people stand in contrast to the righteous purposes of God: What people intend for evil, God uses for good.

CHAPTER SIXTEEN

CONCLUSION

THIS DIALOGUE BETWEEN SCIENCE AND CHRISTIAN FAITH HAS suggested a continuing problem related to human understanding of the kind of world in which we live. Both science and faith deal with data that requires interpretation. Unfortunately, both science and faith can mistake an interpretation of the data for the reality behind the data.

Issues in Dialogue

When a person observes the sun rising in the east, making its way across the sky, and setting in the west day after day, year after year, the self-evident truth of the movement of the sun is obvious to all. This commonly held worldview did not require elaboration, because everyone knew it. People accept the worldview, living their lives based on this elaborate view of how the world works, until some great catastrophe shakes confidence in all the assumptions of the society. People rarely recognize the difference between the data and their interpretation of the data.

Five hundred years ago, Western society was beginning to go through a change in worldview. It involved more than a single catastrophe. New ways of understanding the world had been emerging with greater rapidity since the thirteenth century. In the fifteenth century, however, the eastern Roman Empire and its glorious capital of Constantinople fell to the Turks, and a series of adventurers sailed to a new world, eventually circumnavigating the globe. By the early sixteenth century the authority of the pope and the holy Roman emperor had been challenged in such a way that neither would ever recover their old position within society. The assumptions of the average person were changing. The old feudal system with a top-down series of relationships was giving way at all levels of society. Local princes wanted autonomy from the emperor. Clergy challenged the authority of the pope. Peasants wanted a life of their own.

Ideology and Philosophy

During the modern age, the commonly agreed upon worldview in the West gradually broke down. Despite a nominal acknowledgement of the God of the Bible, a Western worldview with a pantheon of players began to emerge. The West became a place of ideology. Ideologies come in many forms. Ideologies may be political like fascism, democracy, or communism. They may also be economic like capitalism or Marxism. They may be social like utopianism, populism, or Social Darwinism. They may be scientific like naturalism or religious like fundamentalism and liberalism. These ideologies provide only the briefest example of the extent to which Western culture fragmented and lost a common integrating basis for worldview. Many more examples could be cited within these categories, and many more categories could be named.

When a person adopts an ideology, he or she then interprets life experience through the assumptions and affirmations of that ideology. The ideology becomes "the truth." Government bodies interpret the actions of their adversaries or of other nations through their ideology. Scientists interpret the meaning of their data through their ideology. Christians interpret the Bible and base their actions on their ideology. The ideology represents the highest value because it becomes the standard for declaring the laws of nature or the will of God. Ideology can be extremely dangerous. Ideology is a philosophical term.

Since science deals with the natural world, it is very easy for a scientist to assume that only a naturalistic interpretation of the data is valid. Dialogue is nearly impossible if the scientist says only natural processes can be used to interpret data from the natural world. An advocate of naturalism forgets that the scientific method has no mechanism for validating nonphysical phenomena. The advocates of naturalism make the logical leap that what the scientific method cannot prove must not exist.

The Problem of Interpretation

The conflict between science and faith in the late modern age, from Darwin to the present, has not been a conflict between the data of science and faith. It has been a conflict of the interpretation of the data. This statement should not seem surprising when we consider the differences of interpretation that arise within the scientific community and within the faith community over matters that relate primarily to internal debate.

Luther and Calvin disagreed within the Protestant community over the nature of communion, while both disagreed with the Roman Church, which disagreed with the Eastern Orthodox Church. Yet all agreed about the basic data: "That the Lord Jesus the same night in which he was betrayed took bread: And when he had given thanks, he broke it, and said, Take, eat: this is my body, which is broken for you: this do in remembrance of me. After the same manner also he took the cup, when he had supped, saying, This cup is the new testament in my blood: this do ye, as oft as ye drink it, in remembrance of me" (1 Cor. 11:23–25 KJV).

In coming to the data of Scripture, everyone brought a different set of assumptions and patterns of thinking about "what everyone knows" which affected how they interpreted the data.

Within the scientific community, Einstein and Bohr disagreed with each other over the nature of the subatomic realm. Einstein saw a universe that was determined. He consistently interpreted events in the macroworld and quantum world in such a way as to reinforce this deterministic view. In contrast, Bohr, with his studies in Eastern religion, was comfortable with an indeterminate, discontinuous quantum world. Although Einstein and Bohr never agreed upon the interpretation of the quantum mechanical observations, both did agree upon the quantum mechanical experimental data. While both agreed that quantum theory was very successful, Einstein philosophically saw quantum theory as incomplete, while Bohr philosophically saw quantum theory as complete.

The history of the relationship between science and religion contains numerous examples of the clash between ideologies. The clash was not so much between the Bible and observations of the physical world. The experience of Galileo is often cited to demonstrate the ignorant superstitions of religion and the bigotry of religious people. Galileo's experience actually represents a clash of ideology within the academy of scholars. Galileo's methodology and observations clashed with the Aristotelian ideology of the academic power structure.

The Scopes Monkey Trial is perhaps the most famous example of a science-and-religion clash in the twentieth century. Again, the term has become synonymous with ignorance and bigotry, although few people realize the ideological nature of the struggle. On the surface, it was between evolution and a one-step creation of man. For William Jennings Bryan, however, it was a fight between populism and social Darwinism. Bryan opposed Darwinism because the data of the fossil record had been interpreted to mean that the white race was the superior race. This interpretation gave great encouragement to the imperialism of the Western powers from the mid-nineteenth century through the world wars. Bryan did not oppose evolution because of the six days of Genesis 1; he believed that an old earth was consistent with the Bible.

Because of the mixture of ideology with interpretation of the data, people grew confused over what the scientific theories actually suggest and what the biblical accounts actually say. Distinctions in terminology between evolution and natural selection escape most people. Natural selection represents an ideological position that goes beyond the data to assert that life developed and proceeds entirely on its own. It excludes the possibility of God. Evolution represents a description of the data of the fossil record that indicates simple forms of life appeared first, followed by more complex forms of life over a great period of time. Evolution does not exclude God's intentional creation of life because it is only a description of the data.

At this point the conflict between science and religion rests on the meaning of time in Genesis 1. We have suggested that the text of Genesis 1 as delivered by God in Hebrew has a much wider understanding of time than the English text traditionally gives. We have suggested that the English translation tradition developed during a period in which fascination with scientific certainty influenced the interpretation of the text by the translators. This issue also affects the conflict between a Big Bang origin of the universe and an act of creation by God. The conflict centers on the discrepancy between a universe that has taken fifteen billion years to arrive at its present state and a universe which God created in one day. We have suggested that a fifteen-billion-year-old universe created in one day is not inconsistent with the biblical text.

Which Science?

We have suggested that the intense conflict between science and Christian faith over the last one hundred and fifty years arose because Christianity had developed the habit of identifying itself too closely with science. After all, modern science is the child of Christian theology. She was born in the monastic schools that grew into the great universities. The great rationalistic tradition that produced proof for the existence of God and the philosophical tradition of systematic theology never quite let go of the desire for certainty which scientific inquiry promised. Over and over, theologians have accommodated themselves to the latest understandings of science. Accommodating to Newton produced Deism, a remote God in a mechanical universe. Accommodation to naturalism produced existentialism, neoorthodoxy, and process theology, attempts to make a case for religious experience without cognitive meaning. But what happens when the science changes?

If we were writing this book in 1900 instead of 2000, the issues would be quite different. First of all, it would have been easier to write since we would not have had to muddle our brains with quantum mechanics and chaos theory. We would be living in a static Newtonian universe, uninfected by theories of relativity and the Big Bang! It would be like living on a flat earth again before Copernicus and Columbus inflated it. If we accommodated our faith to that science, just how progressive, informed, intellectual and reliable would we be?

We have not endorsed the Big Bang cosmogony, evolutionary biology, quantum mechanics, or chaos theory. Neither have we endorsed Calvinism, Arminianism, Dispensationalism, or the social gospel. Scientific theories and Christian theologies share the fallacies of the makers. God is the maker of neither theology nor theory. God may have spoken the world and the Bible into being, but these are different from theories about the world and theologies based on the Bible.

Rather than an antiintellectual stance, we mean to advocate a more rigorous intellectual approach that recognizes our limitations as well as our possibilities. We do not disparage Sir Isaac Newton because he seems to have gotten it wrong about the universe. His Laws of Motion are helpful enough to save countless lives through the modern use of seat belts. Neither do we disparage Thomas Goodwin because he seems to have gotten it wrong about the return of the Lord Jesus Christ in 1666. He still had a fruitful ministry that brought great comfort and consolation to thousands during a time of great social turmoil.

Whatever the science is today, new discoveries made possible by the accelerating technological capacity to conduct experiments will inevitably change our understanding of major aspects of science that we take for granted. It is highly appropriate for science and faith to dialogue in such a way that Christians interact with current science and its theological implications. It is quite another thing, however, for current science to provide the basic resource for theology. For Christians, the Bible provides the basic resource. Likewise, theology cannot form the basic resource for science. The physical world provides that basic resource.

Future Dialogue

We have suggested that just as the Bible is the Word of God written, the physical world is the word of God demonstrated. As it takes faith to read the Bible with understanding and the expectation that God will make something known, it takes faith for the scientist to read the physical world. The scientist must believe the world actually exists.

The question of the objective existence of the world is probably the greatest philosophical question faced by modern science. Christians have largely missed this current crisis while focusing on old issues. Who would have ever thought that the inability to locate one tiny electron would throw the scientific community into disarray? That tiny electron has caused the kind of catastrophe that destroys an entire culture. It destroyed the ideological myth of scientific certainty. Some scientists have arrived at the logical fallacy that if you cannot know everything, then you cannot know anything.

As we have seen, alternative theories are emerging about whether the physical world actually exists. Is the world a construction of the mind? Is it an illusion? It is not necessary for a scientist to believe in God in order to do good research. Belief in God will affect other significant areas of the lives of scientists, but it is quite possible to do good research without a knowledge of God. It is possible to be a successful banker without believing in God. To be successful, however, the banker must believe in the existence of money. Likewise, does a scientist, to be successful, have to believe in the existence of the physical world? Up to now, science has never flourished in cultures that do not believe in the existence of the physical world.

Eastern religions offer a view of reality that provides for an insubstantial universe. This view has great appeal to some who are struggling to understand the nature of reality in light of quantum mechanics. This quest to understand the nature of reality is a conversation to which Christians can contribute.

The science-and-faith debate has suffered from a conception that the Bible contains the details of creation, and it is either right or wrong. However, the Bible does not contain details about a lot of things. The Bible does not explain how quantum mechanics works. It does not describe the substructure of the atom or the relationship of DNA to heredity. But the Bible has a great deal to say about the ultimate nature of reality and the basis of the physical world. The Bible does not provide a plan for national monetary policy and the regulation of interest rates. It does not provide a plan for foreign aid to underdeveloped countries. It does not give details on how to revitalize a deteriorating inner-city slum and provide a future for its children. Most of the issues faced by modern society have no detailed strategy mapped out in the Bible. Nonetheless, the Bible contains broad transcultural principles that address these and countless other issues.

The Bible deals with broad issues that science cannot address: What is the nature of reality? What is the nature of life? Is there meaning? The Bible makes clear that God is the answer to these and other similar questions. Instead of a static universe of Bishop Ussher and Sir Isaac Newton in the sixteenth century, the grammar of the Hebrew text suggests that God is calling the universe into existence every moment from quantum chaos. This may not be what God is doing at all, but the fact of a physical universe has tremendous implications for the future of science.

The choices of science also have implications for the dialogue of faith and science. Normally referred to as ethics, science faces some enormous questions related to what it has the capacity to do. Scientific discovery inevitably leads to technological application. Did Charles Townes have any idea where his research would eventually lead when he did the groundbreaking work that resulted in the laser? Everything from speeding up checkout time at the supermarket to eye surgery have come from it. We never know where research will lead.

Did Madame Curie envision that her work would result in a nuclear arms race that almost brought the world to extinction and may yet result in nuclear terrorism? In the interplay between science and technology, the realm of faith offers a counterbalance for thinking through the implications of the use of technology. The scientific method does not contain within it a basis for moral decision making, yet at some point someone must make moral decisions related to the application of scientific knowledge. Even the decision to make no decision represents a moral decision.

One school of thought would advocate the pursuit of knowledge wherever it leads. A thought that can be pursued should be pursued. We could apply the same view to other realms of human endeavor, whether it be commerce, philanthropy, crime, art, agriculture, gambling, religion, or sports promotion. One may say that a qualitative difference exists between human endeavors. We would agree. People approve some endeavors and disapprove others. The difference, however, suggests values—and the scientific method has no inherent value. Value comes from some other source. Value may arise solely from individual and collective human experience, or it may come from outside the human realm—from God.

If value is merely a personal opinion or a community opinion, then no essential difference exists between science and sports promotion, or faith for that matter. The nature of reality raises enormous questions about the source of values that people take for granted.

We have suggested that ideology and cultural worldview (both expressions of community opinion) represent a major source of value in the world. We have also suggested, however, that science and faith share a commitment to a value source that lies beyond the human realm. Both are driven by a desire to know what is not seen or evident, yet both proceed with the assurance that what they seek will be found.

When theology accommodates itself to science so that the theology depends upon a particular interpretation of the data, it becomes as obsolete as the old science when a new scientific understanding arises. Likewise, science can easily drift into theology when its philosophical assumptions lead it to make statements about reality that go beyond the scientific method. These issues will probably never go away. Realizing these dynamics, however, will help in pursuing constructive conversation about the nature of physical reality and ethics.

ENDNOTES

Chapter 1

1. Howard J. Van Till, Davis A. Young, and Clarence Menninga, *Science Held Hostage* (Downers Grove, Ill.: InterVarsity Press, 1988), 16.
2. Ibid., 12.
3. Ibid., 16.
4. Del Ratzsch, *Philosophy of Science* (Downers Grove, Ill.: InterVarsity Press, 1986), 104.
5. Ian G. Barbour, *Religion and Science* (San Francisco: Harper San Francisco, 1997), 107.
6. Ibid., 106–36.

Chapter 3

1. Jacques Monod, *Chance and Necessity* (New York: Alfred A. Knopf, 1971), 169.
2. Thomas M. Ross, "The Implicit Theology of Carl Sagan," *Pacific Theological Review* 18 (1985), 3:24–32.
3. Stephen Jay Gould, *Rocks of Ages: Science and Religion in the Fullness of Life* (New York: The Ballantine Publishing Group, 1999), 4.
4. Arthur D. Peacocke, *Theology for a Scientific Age,* enlarged edition (London: SCM Press, 1993), ix.
5. Ian G. Barbour, *Religion and Science: Historical and Contemporary Issues* (New York: HarperCollins, 1997), 77–106.
6. Quoted in Dietrich Schroeer, *Physics and Its Fifth Dimension: Society* (Reading, Mass.: Addison-Wesley Publishing Company, 1972), 103.
7. "The Tables Turned,"in *William Wordsworth: Selected Poetry,* ed. Mark van Doren (New York: The Modern Library, 1950), 83.
8. J. W. von Goethe, *Faust,* translated by Carlyle F. MacIntyre (Norfolk, Conn.: New Directions Publishing Corp., 1949), 29–33.
9. Quoted by David S. Dockery, "The Grandeur of God and Real Education: A Strategy of Integrating Faith in a Post-Christian Culture," in *The Future of Christian Higher Education,* ed. David S. Dockery and David P. Gushee (Nashville, Tenn.: Broadman & Holman Publishers, 1999), 175–76.
10. "Ode on a Grecian Urn," in *John Keats: Poems,* ed. Gerald Bullett (London: J. M. Dent and Sons, 1974), 192.
11. Gwyn MacFarlane, *Howard Florey* (Oxford: Oxford University Press, 1979). Chapter 8 discusses the discoveries of Fleming.
12. John Paul II, "Evolution and the Living God,"in *Science and Theology: The New Consonance,* ed. Ted Peters (Boulder, Colo.: Westview Press, 1998), 149.
13. Ted Peters, "Science and Theology: Toward Consonance," in *Science and Theology: The New Consonance,* ed. Ted Peters (Boulder, Colo.: Westview Press, 1998), 12.
14. Albert Einstein, *Nature* 146 (1941): 605.

15. John Paul II, "Message," in *Physics, Philosophy, and Theology, a Common Quest for Understanding*, ed. Robert John Russell, William R. Stoeger, and George V. Coyne (Vatican Observatory: Vatican City State and Notre Dame: University of Notre Dame, 1988), M13.
16. Ernan McMullin, "How Should Cosmology Relate to Theology?" in *Science and Theology in the Twentieth Century*, ed. Arthur Peacocke (Notre Dame: University of Notre Dame Press, 1981), 39.
17. Ted Peters, ed., *Cosmos as Creation* (Nashville: Abingdon Press, 1989).
18. Ian Barbour, *Religion in an Age of Science*, vol. 1, The Gifford Lectures 1989–91 (San Francisco: Harper and Row, 1990).
19. Willem Bernard Drees, *Beyond the Big Bang: Quantum Cosmologies and God* (La Salle, Ill.: Open Court, 1990).
20. Robert John Russell, "Cosmology: Evidence for God or Partner for Theology?" in *Evidence of Purpose: Scientists Discover the Creator*, ed. John Marks Templeton (New York: Continuum, 1994), 80.

Chapter 5

1. John Joseph Owens has emphasized that the *waw* consecutive construction does not convert the imperfect verb to a perfect state. See Kyle M. Yates and John Joseph Owens, *The Essentials of Biblical Hebrew*, rev. ed. (New York: Harper & Row, 1954), 41, 103–104. I am indebted to Professor Owens with whom I studied the Hebrew text of the Book of Genesis (HLP).
2. Note that the figure used to portray the monistic understanding of God looks exactly like the figure used to portray the ontological model of God of classical monotheism (see Fig. 3.3). Yet the Hindu concept of God differs dramatically from the Jewish, Islamic, and Christian concept of God. This discrepancy illustrates again the failure of models to convey adequately the reality of God. For purposes of comparing Figure 3.3 and Figure 5.3, everything inside the circle in Figure 3.3 is God, while everything outside the circle represents God's creation. In Figure 5.3, everything inside the circle represents everything, while nothing remains outside the circle.

Chapter 6

1. Jacques Barzun, *Darwin, Marx, Wagner: Critique of a Heritage*, 2nd ed. (Chicago: University of Chicago Press, 1941, 1958, 1981), 36.
2. Fred Hoyle, "The Universe: Past and Present Reflection," *Annual Reviews of Astronomy and Astrophysics* 20 (1982): 16.
3. Hugh Ross, *The Creator and the Cosmos*, 2nd expanded edition (Colorado Springs: NAVPRESS, 1995), 118–121.

Chapter 7

1. Roger Lewin, "A Lopsided Look at Evolution," *Science* 241 (1988): 291–293.
2. Peter H. Raven and George B Johnson, *Biology*, 5th. ed. (Boston: McGraw Hill, 1999), 409.
3. An early example is: Alfred M. Elliott, *Zoology*, 3rd. ed. (New York: Appleton-Century-Crofts, 1963), 758–59.
4. Michael N. Mauerus, *Melanism: Evolution in Action* (Oxford: Oxford University Press, 1998).
5. Charles Darwin, *Origin of Species,* 6th. ed. (New York: New York University Press, 1988), 154.
6. Ernst Mayr, *Populations, Species, and Evolution* (Cambridge, Mass.: Harvard University Press, 1970), 1.

Chapter 8

1. All Hebrew terms in Genesis and their use in context may be reviewed in John Joseph Owens, *Analytical Key to the Old Testament,* vol. 1 (Grand Rapids: Baker Book House, 1990), 4–5, 7.
2. See the article on *nephesh* by H. Seebass in *Theological Dictionary of the Old Testament,* ed. by G. Johannes Butterweck, et al, trans. by David E. Green, vol. 9 (Grand Rapids: Eerdmanns, 1998), 497–519.
3. *Oxford English Dictionary,* vol. 10, Sola-Sz (Oxford: Clarendon Press, 1933), 460.

Chapter 9

1. Quoted in Michael H. Brown, *The Search for Eve* (New York: Harper and Row, 1990), 241.
2. Rebecca L. Cann, Mark Stoneking, and Allan C. Wilson, "Mitochondrial DNA and human evolution," *Nature* 325 (1987): 31–36.
3. Robert L. Dorif, Hiroshi Akashi, and Walter Gilbert, "Absence of Polymorphism at the AFY Locus on the Human Y Chromosome," *Science* 268 (1995): 1183–85.
4. Ian Barbour, *Religion and Science* (New York: Harper San Francisco, 1997), 55.
5. George Gaylord Simpson, *The Meaning of Evolution* (New York: Mentor Edition, 1951), 143.
6. Jacques Barzun, *Darwin, Marx, Wagner: Critique of a Heritage,* 2nd ed. (Chicago: University of Chicago Press, 1941, 1958, 1981), 11, 36.
7. Bertrand Russell, quoted in Nancy R. Pearcey and Charles B. Thaxton, *The Soul of Science* (Wheaton, Ill.: Crossway Books, 1994), 117.

Chapter 10

1. Quoted in David Halliday and Robert Resnick, *Physics* (New York: John Wiley & Sons, 1962), 1178.
2. Markus Arndt, Olaf Nalrz, Julian Vos-Andreae, Claudia Keller, Gerbrand van der Zouw, and Anton Zeilinger, "Wave-particle duality of C_{60} molecules," *Nature* 401 (1999): 680–82.
3. Albert Einstein, Boris Podolsky, and Nathan Rosen, "Can Quantum-Mechanical Description of Physical Reality Be Considered Complete?" *Physical Review* 47 (1935): 777–80.
4. Arthur Robinson, "Loophole Closed in Quantum Mechanics Test," *Science* 219 (1983): 40–41.
5. Paul Davies, *Other Worlds* (London: Abacus, 1982), 125.
6. Louis de Broglie, "Forward" in David Bohm, *Causality and Change in Modern Physics* (New York: D. van Nostrand, 1957).
7. Quoted in Abraham Pais, *"Subtle Is the Lord . . .": The Science and Life of Albert Einstein* (New York: Oxford University Press, 1982), 443.
8. Neils Bohr, *Atomic Theory and the Description of Nature* (New York: Cambridge University Press, 1934), 18.
9. Quoted in Nancy R. Pearcey and Charles B. Thaxton, *The Soul of Science* (Wheaton, Ill., Crossway Books, 1994), 202.
10. Quoted in Nick Herber, *Quantum Reality: Beyond the New Physics* (New York: Doubleday Anchor Books, 1985), 18.
11. For example, Fritzof Capra, *The Tao of Physics* (London: Fontana Paperbacks, Flamingo edition, 1975, 1983) and Gary Zuka, *The Dancing Wu Li Masters* (New York: Bantam Books, 1979).
12. Frederik Pohl, *The Coming of the Quantum Cats* (New York: Bantam Books, 1986).
13. Quoted in James Gleick, *Genius: The Life and Science of Richard Feynman* (New York: Pantheon Books, 1992), 436.

Chapter 12

1. Werner Heisenberg, *Physics and Philosophy* (New York: Harper & Row, 1958).
2. Werner Heisenberg, *Philosophical Problems of Quantum Physics* (Woodbridge, Conn.: Ox Bow Press, 1979).
3. Quoted in M. Jammer, *The Conceptual Development of Quantum Mechanics,* 2nd. ed. (New York: Tomash Publishing Co., 1989), 344.
4. Erwin Schrödinger, "The Present Situation in Quantum Mechanics" in J. A. Wheeler and W. H. Zurek, eds., *Quantum Theory and Measurement* (Cambridge: Cambridge University Press, 1983), 157.
5. As an example, see *Larousse Dictionary of Science and Technology,* gen. ed. Peter M. B. Walker (New York: Larousse, 1995), 967.

Chapter 13

1. Edward N. Lorenz, "Deterministic Nonperiodic Flow," *Journal of the Atmospheric Sciences* 20 (March 1963): 130–41.
2. Ibid., 141.
3. Uri Merry, *Coping with Uncertainty: Insights from the New Science of Chaos, Self-Organization and Complexity* (Westport, Conn.: Praeger Publishers, 1995), 40.
4. Told in James Gleick, *Chaos: Making a New Science* (New York: Viking, 1987), 121.
5. M. J. Feigenbaum, "Quantitative universality for a class of nonlinear transformations," *Journal of Statistical Physics* 19 (1978): 25–52.

Chapter 15

1. Pierre Simon Marquis de Laplace, *A Philosophical Essay on Probabilities,* 6th ed., trans. F. W. Truscott and F. L. Emory (New York: John Wiley & Sons, 1961), 3–4.
2. The real roots of chaos theory are found in the work of Henri Poincaré (1854–1912), a French mathematician, and his work on the three-body problem. In response to a mathematical competition to honor the king of Sweden, Poincaré discovered that the equations for the three-body problem exhibited chaos. His various papers on this subject were published in the 1890s.
3. Quoted in James T. Cushing, *Philosophical Concepts in Physics* (Cambridge: Cambridge University Press, 1998), 169.

INDEX

251